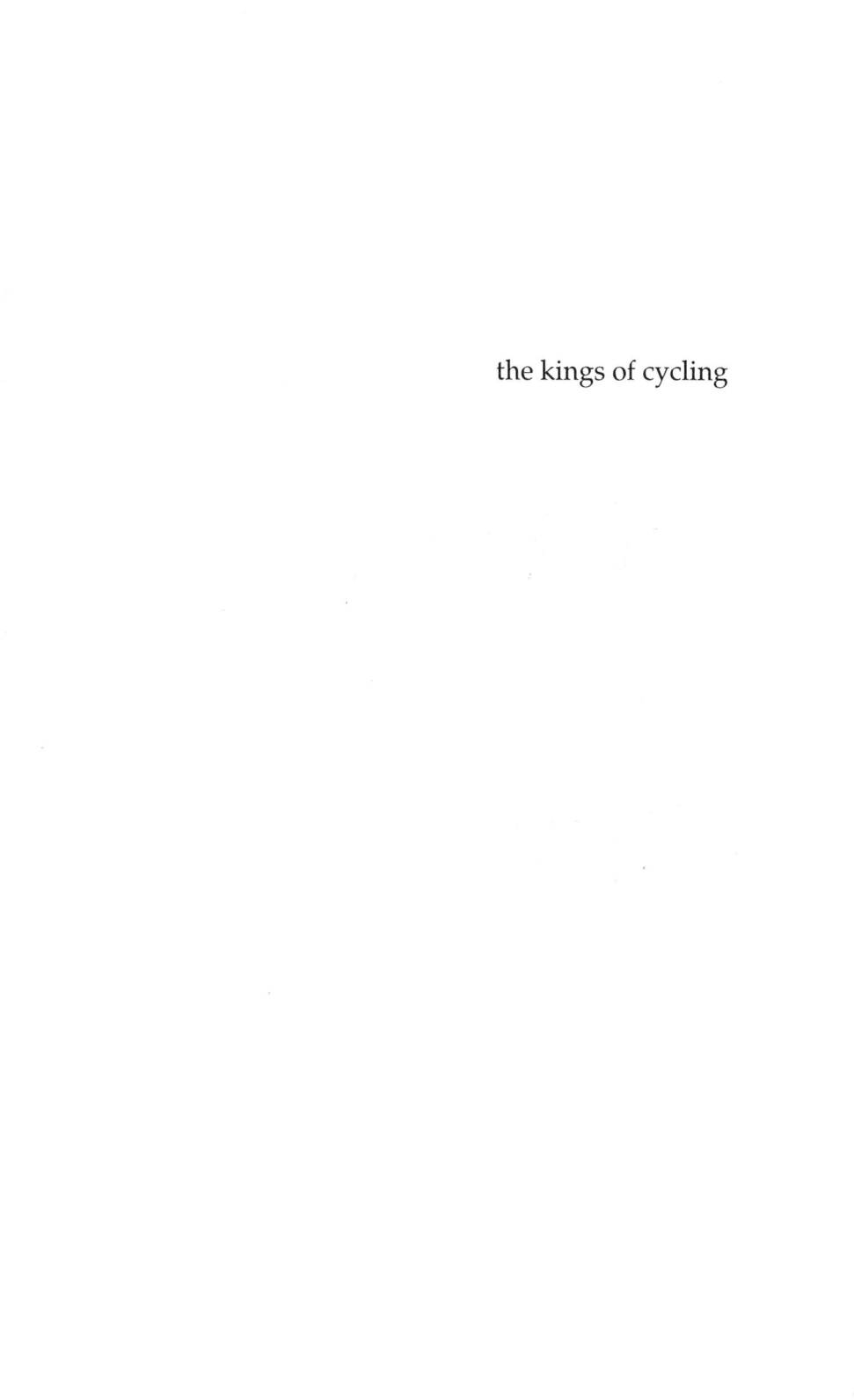

the kings of cycling

Noël Truyers

THE KINGS OF CYCLING

CODA, Antwerp

Dedicated to Solange, Anneleen and Tineke

Colophon

Truyers, Noël
THE KINGS OF CYCLING

Photos: Archives 'Het Belang van Limburg' -
Mons, Kiefel - Iris, Brussels
Graham Watson
Archives of the riders
Lay-out: GRAPA, Louvain
Translation: Steve Hawkins

ISBN 90-5232-082-9

© CODA, Antwerp
All rights reserved.

CONTENTS

Foreword	7
Djamolidin Abdusjaparov	9
Moreno Argentin	19
Eric Breukink	28
Gianni Bugno	39
Claudio Chiappucci	51
Mario Cipollini	60
Pedro Delgado	69
Dirk De Wolf	78
Gilbert Duclos-Lassalle	86
Laurent Fignon	94
Maurizio Fondriest	104
Miguel Indurain	115
Laurent Jalabert	128
Sean Kelly	137
Greg LeMond	146
Frans Maassen	162
Charly Mottet	173
Johan Museeuw	183
Stephen Roche	193
Tony Rominger	202
Eric Vanderaerden	211
Edwig Van Hooydonck	225
Erik Van Lancker	235
Alex Zülle	244

FOREWORD

The cycling peloton is a collection of widely differing characters. Behind every rider is a personal story, and ultimately it is a unique tale he tells about his background and his upbringing, his personality and his ambition, his triumphs and his disappointments, all of them factors which help shape and colour his career.

"All top riders have appalling characters," you may hear it said. And if that were the case it would hardly be surprising, because 'racing' is much more than riding a bike. It is all about battling and suffering, crashing to the ground and getting back up again, domination and submission, bending and breaking. Racing demands sustained training and enforced medical and physical attention. The need to perform, envy, pressure and stress are also part and parcel of the sport. Each rider has his own personal way of handling feelings and situations, and of coping with the glory and the pain. And they all laugh and cry in their own way.

This has all combined to keep cycling, after more than a hundred years, an intriguing world of contrasting personalities, lifetime friends and enemies, clashes and conflicts, celebrated performances and painful disenchantments. Nobody who has had any association with the sport can ever really divorce themselves from it completely.

In the portraits contained in this book, my intention has not only been to draw a sketch of the star and his career, but also of the sort of person he is and of his life. I hope that both expert and newcomer to the sport - the supporter and the layman - alike will get to know a little more about these captivating figures and the fascinating world of cycling in general.

Noël Truyers

DJAMOLIDINE ABDUJAPAROV

CRAZY TARTAR

Djamolidine Abdujaparov - 'Abdu' to cycling followers and 'Djafier' to his Russian fans - is an unusual sort of chap. He wears an ordinary training suit and shuffles round in dated khaki gym shoes with laces far too long. Nevertheless, since he went crashing into the road on the Champs Elysées in Paris in July 1991, Abdu has become the new star of the peloton. He is extremely popular, he earns a tidy sum and besides that he has everything else going for him: an oriental, sallow face, deep eyes and prominent cheekbones. "Manga Bambini," the Italians cry - "The baby eater." "Poor thing," sigh his supporters.

Abdu is a daredevil too. He doesn't shy away from danger in the sprint and that goes down well with the crowds. What is more, he is a typical underdog and, when all is said and done, he is obstinate. "He is half Mongolian and half Tartar," is how they describe him in the peloton. "When people like that dig their heels in, they don't give up."

Cotton

Born on 28th February 1964, Abdu is an Uzbeki. He comes from Tashkent in the Asiatic part of the old Soviet Union, between the Aral Sea and central Asia. The people of Tashkent are Islamic, and Abdu is no exception, even though, according to his team-mates, he doesn't fanatically follow the laws of his religion. In any event, he certainly did not let it stop him becoming a cyclist. "He eats meat, the same as anyone else," say his team-mates. But it is no use asking him anything more about his religion, because he will not tell you a thing.

Abdu used to be a corporal in the Soviet army. "For nine years," he says, "but all I ever had to do was ride my bike." But he would rather not say any more about those days, nor about the political situation in his native country.

He is, however, quite happy to talk about his own family. He has two older brothers: Siervier 32 and Kamaldine 30.

"I also have two younger sisters: Szerfe 26 and Gulnare 22. They all work for a living. My mother is now a pensioner and my father owns his own lorry on which he transports building materials. My two brothers do the same work. It is unusual, but not a single member of my family works in the cotton industry even though it is still by far the most important industry in our region. It has an ideal climate for growing cotton: mild and dry.

When I am in Europe I live in an apartment in Manerba del Garda. Although it looks out over water, I'd still like to move, as northern Italy is too cold and damp for me. It really gets to me and I prefer it much warmer. It's also a little too cramped here, with only two rooms. I'd like to have a bigger place because I'd eventually like to have my mother come over and live with me. She makes a lovely cup of tea. I miss it feeling like home. One of my sisters lived here for a while and my brothers have been to visit me too. I don't have a telephone; the landlord won't let me have one installed."

Alone

Abdu therefore has to look after himself most of the time. He cooks, washes and goes to the bathroom. "And it's not the ideal situation," he grumbles. "Not that being on my own really bothers me, but it could be better. I train with two Polish lads, Marek Szerszynski and Zenon Jaskula who live a couple of kilometres away. Another five kilometres beyond that is where my team-mate and compatriot Poulnikov lives. At first he lived nearer to me but his wife wanted to live in the bustle of the city and they moved to Salo. Racing keeps me here, but it won't for very much longer. If things stay the

Abdu after his heavy fall on the Champs Elysées at the end of the 1991 Tour de France

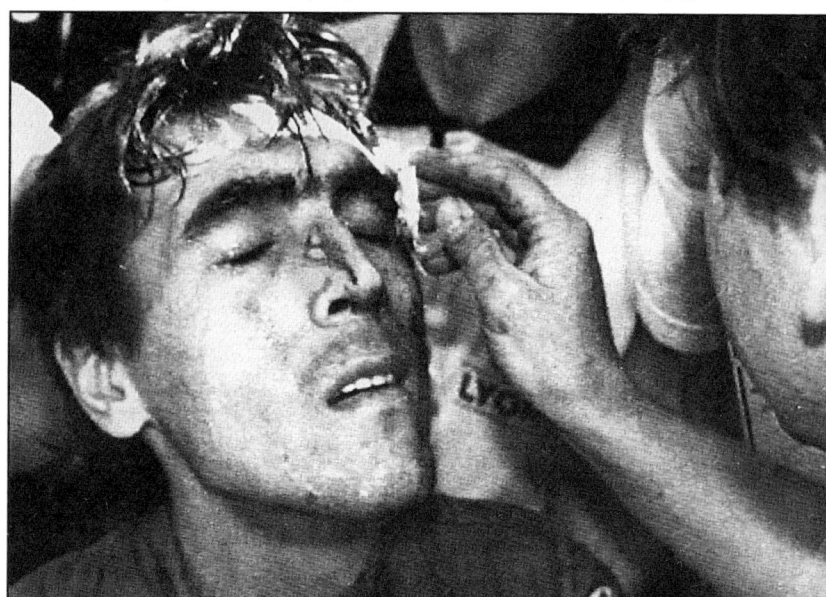

way they are now, I'm planning to retire at the end of the 1994 season and go back home to Tashkent. What I'll do after that, I don't know. Maybe I'll resume my sporting studies. I started a course some time ago, but when I turned professional I had to give it up. And if there is any cycle racing going on in our region, I'll become a trainer. I would love to organise an event along the lines of the Tour de France in my homeland. Obviously it wouldn't be at the same level but that type of thing. The Tour of Uzbekistan or a race counting to the World Cup. Particularly to show people how things are done in the world of professional cycling. It would help raise the standard of riders. At the moment there are between 100 and 150, but only 30 at the most reach any sort of decent level. That needs to change."

Dangerous

Experts say Abdu is the fastest sprinter around. "Only Cipollini can get anywhere near him," it has been said, but in Ghent-Wevelgem in '91 the Italian really copped for it. "Abdu hindered me!" roared Cipollini at the time. "First he shoved Vanderaerden out of the way, then me." Ghent-Wevelgem the following year was even more dangerous. Cipollini wavered from his line in the sprint, Abdu grabbed hold of his shorts and caught him right at the finish, before being disqualified. Unjustly according to some eye witnesses, correctly according to others. Abdu, the scapegoat, had victory taken away from him.

When there is mention of the name Cipollini, Abdu's eyes start to flicker. "Cipollini has turned it into a big joke," the Uzbekistani protests, and you can see by looking at him that he is not happy with it. "In Ghent-Wevelgem in 1992, either we both should have been disqualified, or neither of us, and certainly not me alone. Cipollini forced me out of the way and I had to grab hold of his shorts to stop myself falling. Davide Boifava, my directeur sportif, told me to lodge a protest. But how on earth was I supposed to do that? Nobody could understand what I was saying. I couldn't defend myself. I'm aware that because of my silence, I'm becoming more and more the scapegoat for the whole peloton.

Cipollini has turned it into a spectacle, even when nothing happens. I still remember a stage in the Tour: the sprint began, I went into top speed and suddenly he was there next to me. "What are you doing here?" he cursed, and it goes without saying that he put in his protest. I had no idea what had happened. Cipollini plays it all for laughs, let him get on with it, that's what I say. I don't have to use my mouth to prove anything, I let my legs do my talking for me."

Abdu took his revenge for the events of Ghent-Wevelgem. By the time the next event - the Tour of Spain - was a week old, Abdu had pocketed £35,000. He won four stages and was second on two occasions to Jean-Paul Van Poppel. It didn't go as well in the Giro. Abdu was suffering with hay fever and had to abandon. In the Tour de France he finished outside the time limit on the tough stage to Sestriere. It was all over, and Abdu's reputation suffered quite a blow.

Strong as an Ox

Abdu has a bad name in the peloton: he's known as a 'dirty' sprinter, a crazy Tartar. His sprinting technique is simple: he pushes, pulls and kicks his way to the finishing line. "He doesn't look at anything or anyone," says Johan Museeuw, cursing him. And yet he still respects the Uzbeki rider. "No one can flash through like Abdu can. A real cannonball."

Olaf Ludwig was Abdu's big rival during his amateur days: "When he was an amateur he was rather more quick than strong. Abdu was the man you had to watch out for in the final hundred metres. To beat him you had to start from a long way out and get him into the wind. Since then, though, he's made a lot of progress and I've been left treading water. Now he knows how to take on long sprints as well. If it came down to a man-to-man fight, I reckon there is nobody who could touch him."

Whichever way Abdu chooses to tackle the sprint, his technique does not let him down at all. He had several offers for the 1993 season. Carrera wanted to hang on to him but the Italian Lampre team, managed by Algeri, were prepared to fork out the most cash for him. They are clearly happy at having secured his services.

"On 31st December, Djamolidine arrived back in Italy," adds his new directeur sportif. "To illustrate what a friendly sort of lad he is: who was the first person to ring me on 1st January to wish me a happy new year? Abdu. I believe in him and I think he has a good chance of becoming world champion in Norway. What Abdujaparov wants most is just a good season.

"I wasn't happy with the way 1992 went," he says. "I wanted to reach my peak during the Vuelta and I did, winning four stages. Then the sponsor came along and spoiled it all. He insisted I started in the Giro. But that takes place at exactly the time that I'm most badly affected by the pollen, and I need my rest most then. But no, I was made to ride it and I paid the price for it in the Tour. My condition wasn't there and I abandoned. In 1993 I will only be riding the Vuelta and the Tour, as well as the classics. I want to get my revenge in Het Volk."

School

Abdu reacts impassively to the comments of his rivals. "I'm no more dangerous than anyone else. All sprinters push and pull. If you want to win there is only one way to do it: find the shortest route to the finish, otherwise you've had it. I'm one of those riders who doesn't need any team-mates around during the final metres. I look after myself, I make my own decisions and I make sure that I'm in the right place. It makes no difference to me how the sprint develops. I've won races from 400 metres out and from 300 metres and I'm a strong jumper.

I couldn't actually tell you whether that's something I've always been able to do. I know that I had the talent within me, but it only slowly

came to the surface. My first love used to be swimming, but when they closed down the baths at Tashkent that was the end of that. After that I tried athletics and was very good at the 100 metres - telling me something even then - but I never raced in serious competition. Then I moved to another school where they expected you to take an active part in sports. The master, Alexander Pietrovitch - a former rider - asked if anyone wanted to race bikes, and I put my hand up. There was no history of cycling in my family, nobody else did it, only me. September 1975 was when I started. At first it didn't go too well, and it took me no less than seven years before I won my first race, in 1982."

Back Wheel

Interestingly, Abdu's first victory was not won in a sprint finish but in a time trial. "At the time I didn't know what I was capable of, and there was no one around to tell me how to train until another, older rider came to live nearby. I saw him go training and started to go with him, and we would do some sprinting on the way. On the first occasion I finished two lengths behind him, later on I got up to his back wheel, and finally I beat him by two clear lengths. That was the last time he let me go training with him. From then on I won a lot of local races. It was only in 1983 that it began to go better at an international level. That year I came third in the Soviet championship and was picked for the national team. I was allowed to ride abroad so that I could develop further as a racer. During that time I rode the Peace Race on many occasions. It was often a battle against Olaf Ludwig. In those days the German was quicker than me, but fortunately, now we are professionals it is the other way round. Don't ask me who is the fastest man of all because I couldn't tell you. Museeuw is quick too. Cipollini took me down a peg or two in the 1991 Giro but you shouldn't read too much into that. During May and June I am always bothered by pollen, I'm allergic to it, and I'm never in peak condition. That also explains why I abandoned halfway through the 1992 Giro. Once June is out of the way, my suffering is over."

Ghent-Wevelgem 1992: after a lot of pushing and pulling, Abdu squeezes past Mario Cipollini. After a complaint from the Italian, however, he is disqualified.

Doping

Abdu's first year as a professional was 1990 and it was spent with Alfa Lum, an Italian aluminium producer who could see that Soviet riders had something to offer. The company came up with a deal with the Soviet cycling federation, in which any rider considered too old to go to the Barcelona Olympics in 1992 was allowed to go abroad.

"I was almost 26 then, and at that age you are indeed too old. As a sportsman you are as good as finished and you're more trouble than you are worth. For many riders that's the time to quit. Fortunately for me, that's when I got the chance to turn professional with Alfa Lum. I didn't hesitate for one minute because it suddenly presented me with a fresh challenge. Within the team, however, things didn't go well. Everyone rode for themselves, they all thought about their own results and no one worked for anyone else. I didn't win a single race during that season, although I did come second no less than nine times. They were not ideal circumstances. Firstly, it was only after a great deal of difficulty that I got my visa enabling me to ride in Italy. At the time I spent a lot of time worrying about it, and that is no good for you at all. I was also ill-prepared. During the previous season I was forced to sit out six months through suspension, and that meant I lacked competition practice. The suspension was as a result of being found positive during the Peace Race, but I still insist that I was knifed in the back. In one particular stage I was sprinting against Olaf Ludwig for the umpteenth time. Olaf hindered me, I couldn't get past him and I lodged a complaint. Afterwards I was told to withdraw it but I refused. I felt that I had every right to do so. The organisers were furious. The next day I was thrown out of the race. Efedrine had been found in my urine."

Boifava

At the end of the 1990 season Alfa Lum withdrew their sponsorship. Several first-year Soviet professionals were in a state of panic. "It was not a happy time. Suddenly one day we were out on the streets. Luckily I didn't have to worry myself, as I had already had an offer from the Spanish Seur team. I was all ready to accept it too, but after some thought I realised that Italy suited me and I didn't really want to leave. I rang Davide Boifava to ask him if he could squeeze me into a place in his Carrera team. "No problem," he said, and he drew up a good contract for me. Preparations went just the way I wanted. There was nothing to worry about and I was able to do the required amount of training. That is what set me up for the season. By the end of it I had won ten races. The victory which gave me the most pleasure was

Ghent-Wevelgem. I knew nothing about the race but had spotted Eddy Merckx's name on the list of previous winners. That signalled to me that it must have been an important race. I also won two stages in the Tour de France and took the green jersey. That drew a great deal of attention because I was the first Soviet rider to ever achieve it.

What bothers me at the moment is that I am constantly being held back in sprint finishes. I sprint because speed is my greatest weapon, but I know I have even more to offer than that. I'm a good time triallist too. I came seventh in the time trial finishing in Alençon during the 1991 Tour. I can also ride well in the mountains, but the team management get furious if I latch on to leading groups. They want me to save my energy. In my opinion, though, you have to be somewhere near the front in the Tour because it is good for your morale. You have to keep an eye on the top riders. I reckon I could finish quite high on the final classification in the Tour.

There is one race that I would really love to win: Paris-Roubaix. That is my dream. I had heard so much about it; the terrible roads with their pot-holes. I'm glad I was allowed to ride in it in 1991. I have the right posture for it. My morale was high too, and really that is the most important thing. I rode over the cobbles very smoothly and really wanted to win, but I punctured twice - both at bad times - and as a result I had to wave goodbye to my chance. I fared no better in the '92 race, but I'll be back and I'll keep coming back until I win it."

Cobbles

The Champs Elysées, Paris 1991. There is huge interest in the final stage of the Tour de France. The crowd is looking forward to a big bunch sprint, although on this occasion it takes a little longer to take shape. The Belgian Johan Museeuw is an absentee, having long since packed his bags and returned home. Abdu sprints blindly towards the finish, head bowed. He doesn't look up or around, rides into a huge Coca Cola advertising bottle and goes catapulting into the air. It was a miracle that in the end only his collar bone was broken. Abdu cannot remember much about it. "I have no idea what exactly happened. I have seen television pictures and photographs of it since then, but I'm still not conscious of having made a mistake. I'm just happy that I was able to cross the finishing line so that I hung on to my green jersey. I couldn't even stand up on my own. They have told me that I was in a state of shock. I'm sorry that I had to miss the presentation; I would have liked to have stood alongside Indurain, Bugno and Chiappucci on the podium. That was put right, however, at the presentation for the 1992 Tour when I officially received my green jersey. A marvellous moment.

I no longer have the green jersey I was wearing on the Champs Elysées stage. The doctors cut it up in the hospital and kept the pieces as souvenirs. As for the other jerseys, they have all been given away to friends and acquaintances. No, it was not a very nice time. On the first night people from Carrera came to visit me in hospital, but after that I never saw another soul. No one even came from the embassy. I was just left to lay there. When I was able to leave I took the first flight I could back to my parents. That is where I eventually calmed down. I never showed them the photographs of my fall. I don't want my parents to worry when I'm away in Europe.

The fall obviously meant that I missed out on the chance of making a great deal of money. I had already signed many contracts for criteriums in Belgium. What did it really matter, though? What was I supposed to do with the money? In Tashkent there is nothing to buy; the shops are empty. All there is are vegetables and fruit. My parents did a wonderful job of taking care of me, and within ten days I was able to climb back on to my bike. I slowly began building myself up again without pushing myself too hard, to stop me suffering any reaction. Later in the season I even won the Tour of Piedmont. My fitness was soon back to normal. The crash has certainly not left me feeling frightened. Fear is something you should never have as a sprinter."

Guimard

Abdu rarely laughs, but he does have a sense of humour. While we are interviewing him, Cyrille Guimard comes past and Abdu gives him a hefty pat on the backside. The two of them know each other. "Last year Abdu was riding for Carrera and now he is riding for Lampre, but I was interested in signing him five years ago," Guimard informs us while Abdu nods enthusiastically. "The Russian federation botched the whole thing. I remember us sitting round the table. I had travelled to Russia especially. Abdu was sitting there, his head shyly bowed, his hands on his lap. "Do you want to turn professional," I asked. I saw him nod in the affirmative. "You only have to pay him the minimum wage and everything will be alright," said the federation spokesman. I was rubbing my hands at the prospect, but he hadn't finished yet. "We want a decent sum for ourselves so that we can run our clubs and pay for the cost of our trips abroad. In cash, please." I couldn't believe what I was hearing and, needless to say, I returned home without Abdu."

Fishing

We only saw Abdu smile once, and that was when we asked him what his hobbies were. "I regularly go fishing with Marek Szerszynski. When we do we get up at five o'clock and arrive home with at least five kilos of fish. Besides that I don't do a great deal. I enjoy living in Italy but I still prefer my homeland, Uzbekistan. At home I keep racing pigeons. I breed them, train them and race them and I miss that here. Now my brothers and my father have to look after them. My birds are a good reason for why I return home regularly. I don't have girlfriend, at home or in Italy. When I stop racing I'll have plenty of time to find myself a wife. I don't have a car either; in the old Soviet Union it is difficult to get hold of one, while in Italy I drive a Citroën belonging to the team."

At home

"I usually go home in the sponsor's aeroplane. In 1990 Carrera opened four jeans shops in Uzbekistan and stocks have to be replenished on a regular basis. I'm allowed to go then, for nothing. Another advantage of that is that I get home much quicker. Scheduled services are always via Moscow or St Petersburg, and that makes the journey take far too long.

Although I'm now an established professional cyclist, it doesn't mean I have become well-known in my own land. The neighbours know me, but that's where my fame ends. They have still never heard of the Tour de France. Nevertheless, cycling is quite popular. Three years ago, when I was still taking part in local races, it was more so. But now that I am no longer around the popularity has fallen away quickly. Football and athletics have become much more popular. There is no coverage of cycling on television, and in the papers there is little in the way of reporting. Any publicity the sport gets arrives on the grapevine with predictable consequences. After my fall, for example, it was reported that I spent days in a coma when, in fact, I had never lost consciousness."

MORENO ARGENTIN

COMPUTER

Rolf Sörensen, former team-mate of Moreno Argentin in the Italian Ariostea team, said of him last year: "I prefer him being on my side to him being against me. I dread to think what it would be like competing against him, as he is very difficult to beat. I have already learned a great deal from him. He understands like no other the art of staying cool. The way he works on his bike, the way he looks after himself, such as the way he prepares himself. If he says that he wants to win a particular race, 9 times out of 10 he'll win it. Actually, he only has one fault: he is too soft. If I fall I get up straightaway, at the same time crying out for a new bike. Moreno is different, for him when that happens it means the race is over. I suspect that it is because he is such a perfectionist that he simply cannot tolerate setbacks. It goes against his nature. If anything happens to spoil that he lets his head drop."

Demanding
Valerio Piva, son-in-law of Yvo Molenaers, the former Belgian rider, and for years a domestique of Argentin adds: "Moreno is super-professional. He gives himself to his profession completely and thinks everyone else should do the same. In that sense he is very demanding, hard to live with even. Apart from that he is a real gentleman. He is extremely fair in his dealings with others. He never gets involved in gossip about his rivals; it doesn't interest him. He is straightforward. He handles his riders in a proper way and expects them to be proper in their dealings with him. He is a good boss. I know few riders who can lead a team so well. He also respects what his domestiques do. He is always giving them a pat on the back or a complimentary word or two. He's a diplomat too. He fits in well with the peloton; he's everybody's friend. Bugno is his best pal. I remember that when he won the Flèche Wallonne in 1990, Bugno was on the telephone that evening to congratulate him. They have similar characters, they are both quiet and rather reserved. Moreno has a great deal of self confidence. When he sets his heart on something he does everything he can to get it, he doesn't let anyone stand in his way and feels that he can't be beaten. That's where his weak spot is, however. If the slightest thing goes wrong his morale drops. That's

why he is not cut out for long stage races. He has the legs for them but not the head. In a stage race there are likely to be some days when things do not go the way you would like. Argentin is the sort of rider who finds that difficult to put up with. For him it is all or nothing."

Barber

He's an unusual chap is Moreno Argentin. When he is standing on the podium it looks as if he doesn't enjoy cycling. He rarely laughs, he doesn't look

Moreno Argentin after winning the World Championship Road Race at Colorado Springs in 1986

enthusiastic, and you hardly ever see him throwing his arms into the air with joy. He is sober and cool at all times. The Italians also regard him as a hothead, and since he refused to give the winner's bouquet to the wife of his team-mate Cassani during Tirreno-Adriatico in 1992, he has also been called a big-head. Argentin is an individualist, as are most champions for that matter. In contrast to many of his compatriots he is always clean shaven, he has a neat haircut and is polite. Criticism does not bother him at all.

Invalid

Moreno Argentin is an intelligent young man. In actual fact, it is amazing that he ever took up cycling in the first place. "Dad was fascinated by the sport. He was an ardent Coppi fan. I was ten when I rode my first race. I also really liked football, and I still do for that matter. I regularly go to watch Inter Milan. My father was very strict with me. He didn't think I had enough spirit. My first victory was when I was 15. I usually tried to get in a group of two or three riders and then go on to win the sprint. Our domestic financial situation was not that good. Dad, now 77, was on a war pension. My mother did the housework. I have three sisters too. My family is very important to me. I still live with my parents in fact. That is to say, I have totally renovated the family home in Passarella - not far from Venice. Mum and Dad live on the ground floor and we live on the first floor."

Honours List

It is apparent how talented a rider Argentin is from his honours list. It makes impressive reading: winner of the World Championship at Colorado Springs in 1986, Liège-Bastogne-Liège four times, the Tour of Flanders, the Tour of Lombardy, Flèche Wallonne, Italian champion, several stages in the Giro and the Tour. The style Argentin has used to win these races has always been the same. He has an explosive burst of speed and uses the biggest gears, but he does it so smoothly and fluently that you can set your watch by it. "When youngsters ask me how they should train, I always say that they should start their careers on the track. That's the way I did it and I felt it was ideal for me. Most importantly it meant I had the chance to complete my studies at secondary school. At the same time it meant I didn't ride myself into the ground like many youngsters do nowadays. I worked to a very limited road programme and I always used small gears. I had a very flexible training schedule and occasionally rode short stage races abroad. I even rode in the Tour of Belgium for amateurs once; Etienne De Wilde won it."

Steam

Learning on the track the way you could in the past is no longer possible, and Argentin finds that a real pity. "It's almost dead and that's a disaster. Experts say that my greatest strength is that I am able to peak perfectly. That's another thing I learned on the track. Because a track racer doesn't ride many events he gears himself exclusively towards championships. So it comes down to having to do it on the day or the chance is gone. What that teaches you above all else, is to be able to handle stress. Once one event is out of the way, you start building yourself up for the next one. In that way you learn how to plan things. But you have to watch out, however, because there are pitfalls to this system. For instance, I never learned how to stay in top form for months on end, and that means unless I regularly let off steam I would go mad. At the start of my professional career I did things too casually too often. I probably could have done more back then but I didn't know how far I could go. Since then I have become aware of my limits, and I've also found out how to use distribute the effort over races."

World Champion

At the end of the 1980 season, Moreno Argentin turned professional with the San Giacomo team. He then moved to Sammontana and won the G.P. Prato and two stages in the Giro and finished second in the Tour of Lombardy. In 1982 he once again won a stage in the Giro and one in the Tour of Switzerland. By that time he had well and truly arrived. From then on, he gathered big victories every year. Yet it was strange that in the weeks before and after these wins he did nothing.

In 1983 he won the Italian championship, the following year he won two stages in the Giro and the year after that saw his first Liège-Bastogne-Liège triumph. In 1986 he won this Walloon classic for the second time and he also won the World Championship. His results were so impressive that Felice Gimondi was able to persuade him to sign for Gewiss-Bianchi. In 1987 they saw Moreno take Liège-Bastogne-Liège for the third consecutive year, as well as three stages of the Giro and the Tour of Lombardy.

Challenge

1988 was a less successful year. Argentin was a mere shadow of the winner he had been. Although he won three minor races, he failed in the big ones. That season he once again won the Italian championship, but that was about it. "Moreno stayed with Bianchi for too long," says Valerio Piva, one of his domestiques at that time. "He was the unchallenged number one in the team.

Argentin winning a stage in the Tour de France

You could compare his role with that of Laurent Fignon with Castorama. There was no one to tell him what he should do. When he switched to Ariostea in 1989, he had to start all over again - at the bottom. He suddenly found himself in a team with several good riders and with a tough directeur sportif. That's what motivated him again. Argentin needs new challenges."

Argentin himself sees it somewhat differently: "At Bianchi nothing was ever organised. I'm the sort of person who likes to set out my own programme, but it wasn't possible to. I want people around me who I can trust, a doctor who is 100% behind me, and a directeur sportif who lets me make my own decisions but who also has confidence in me. At Bianchi I couldn't count on any of that and I protested, because after all it was my career that was being messed up. That's why I went to Ariostea and I was very happy there. Over the years, of course I have made mistakes myself. During the period that Moser and Saronni dominated cycling in Italy I would have been better keeping my mouth shut. I was yet to prove myself, but I was already demanding to be up there with them. I acted as if I wanted to change the world and that was the wrong thing to do. It isn't that I've lost my nerve since then, it's just that I've learned to look at everything a little more realistically."

Peaks

After his move to Ariostea, Argentin was suddenly firing on all cylinders again. He even succeeded in peaking on several occasions. In 1990 he won the Tour of Flanders, the Flèche Wallonne and a stage in the Tour de France. He even took the brave step, as an Italian, of not riding that year's Giro. In 1991 he won Liège-Bastogne-Liège for the fourth time, the Flèche Wallonne again and yet another stage in the Tour.

"The reason I was suddenly doing well wherever I rode was to do with my health. At the beginning of 1992 I was again riding really strongly and that was because I had been lucky enough not to fall sick in the weeks leading up to the season. In the early part of the year it was often a different story. I'm rather prone to catching colds and flu. I always seemed to have to interrupt my pre-season training. For once, though, at the start of 1992 I was spared. When I joined Ariostea I changed the way I trained. I wanted to avoid stress, and each year I was there, I went to an exotic country to train. The first year it was La Réunion, in '91 it was South Africa and last year it was the Canary Islands with my wife Antonietta, our two small children, my team-mate Lelli and the team doctor. It went brilliantly. The course was testing, there was a lot of wind and there were climbs of 10 to 15 kilometres. Perfect.

In January 1993 I went even further; to San Diego, California. Once again my wife and two children came with me, and this time my new team-mates Imboden and Pierobon came too, as did Tony Rominger and they all took their families. We all rented individual apartments. When we went out working and training, our wives went out shopping. The whole family thought it was great. If we had done enough work on the previous day we would go to Hollywood or to Disneyland which was close by. We even went on a trip round the Universal studios. It was very interesting and everything was very good value for money. I will probably go back again some time."

Downhill

Looking back on the 1992 season, the punishing pre-season training was not enough to help Argentin win Milan-San Remo early on. Yet at the start he was the firm favourite, as he had dominated proceedings in Tirreno-Adriatico and was the strongest contender for this event. By the Poggio climb he had seen off all his rivals, but on the descent the Italian rode so shakily that Sean Kelly was able to get back to him and beat him in the sprint. "I can't descend," Argentin says apologetically. "I lose ground at every bend."

The Walloon classics shortly after also saw no repeats of earlier victories, and in the Tour de France he even abandoned. "I had nothing left. It simply wasn't there. As soon as I abandoned I went straight to hospital for an examination. Everything was alright and, with a view to the World Championship in Benidorm, I went off for altitude training in St Moritz."

Money

Moreno Argentin is comfortably off. Like Rolf Gölz he has a house in Monaco. "For tax reasons, obviously; but it is not just a postal address, I stay there quite often. My wife also goes there a lot with the children when I am racing abroad. I also think it is a lovely place to train.

I do not have a blinkered outlook. There are plenty of other things going on in the world besides cycling. I look after myself well. Health is the most valuable thing a person can have. I spend ten or eleven hours in bed. I need at least nine hours sleep or I can't function. I love music and I always carry several CDs with me. I read a lot, too. In one of the Italian newspapers there is a cartoon character called Diabolic who is a little like Batman, and I'm a big fan of him. I'm not someone who likes to talk a lot about cycling. When they start on about it at the dinner table I make my protests. I always put 100% into my profession, but I think you can go too far.

I talk about fast cars quite a lot - I love speed in general. A dream of mine is to one day own a Ferrari. The problem there is that you have to wait a full year after ordering one before you get it. I also have six horses, the first of which I bought after winning the world title in Colorado Springs. The stables are only 200 metres from my house. My father looks after them. I have a jockey working for me and he rides them in races. He has already won once. I love riding horses myself. I often go on long walks too."

Blah-Blah-Blah

Argentin is a close friend of Gianni Bugno, but he wants nothing to do with Claudio Chiappucci. Just mention his name you get a stinging reaction. "Chiappucci is a showman, pure and simple," says Moreno, and he thinks he takes it too far. "Chiappucci has finished 2nd in the Tour and 2nd in the Giro, and all credit to him, but that still isn't enough to warrant acting like a star. To do that you need to have won them. Indurain would be entitled to make a song and dance about it, but he just stays quiet. Bugno is the same. They both let their legs do the talking. All that blah-blah-blah is nonsense. I even think he's already started to show off this season. Look at the way he's acting here, in the Tour of the Mediterranean. He has even organised a press conference for himself!"

Blame

Moreno Argentin was a member of the very strong Ariostea team, but that chapter of his career is now closed. He has now moved to the modest Mecair team.

"Small it might be, but it is big enough to enter all the races that I want to win," says Argentin. "We don't have enough points to qualify for the Tour, but I'm not worried about that. This year I'll be riding the Giro with the specific aim of winning stages. I will also be there in the classics, so what have I to complain about? My other target for this year is the world championship, and I can ride that without the help of the team. The most important thing is that my new directeur sportif is Emanuele Bombini. We were team-mates at Bianchi for four years.

Why did I leave Ariostea? I didn't have any problems with Ferretti, even though he pinned a lot of blame on me during last year's Tour. I didn't ride well and he said that I hadn't trained hard enough for it or looked after myself enough beforehand, but that was a lie. If you suffer a heavy fall in the Flèche Wallonne and are injured on your knee, then you can hardly be expected to catch up on your fitness just like that. I was inactive for 25 days.

When I resumed training I worked really hard at getting back, but I never really reached the same level. The big boss wasn't satisfied with my explanation. I've a feeling there was more to it than that. When you think Sörensen and Gölz have left too. The company was bought up by a big international group at the end of last year and that changed things quite a bit. I have the impression that by the end of 1994 they will stop sponsoring a cycling team.

In contrast with that, my new employer, Mecair, have far-reaching plans. I'm well acquainted with Signor Castaldi, the director of a major Italian insurance company. His hobby is cycling and he went out looking for sponsors. He managed to persuade the management of Mecair to go into professional cycling sponsorship. Last year they sponsored an amateur team. It was their intention to start small, but within four years they intend to be big. For next season they will be signing more top riders, as it is their intention to put the team in for the Tour de France. And that's fine by me, because I would like to ride it one more time and then call it a day. 1994 is going to be my last season."

Punctual

When he is riding the Walloon classics, Argentin always stays at the 'Hove Malpertuus' hotel in Herderen, belonging to Yvo Molenaers. "Moreno never says much," Molenaers tells me. "He is never boisterous, always friendly and polite to everyone he meets, but he is certainly an extremely punctual man. If you have a three-o'clock appointment with him, never turn up at ten past, because by then he'll probably refuse to see you."

Business

Moreno Argentin reckons he will continue to race until the end of the 1993 season.

"If I feel like it, I'll carry on for longer. I want to get as much out of my career as I can. I would never retire feeling that there is still something I want to achieve. Providing my enthusiasm is still there that is, if not I might as well pack it in and start something afresh. There are several possibilities. I have invested some money in a wood company. Wood is one of my passions. Two winters ago I went with my brother-in-law - who runs the business - to Poland and (the former) Yugoslavia to buy trees. I really enjoyed it. We mainly work with walnut. Our company prepares the wood for furniture makers. Besides that I also deal in real estate. I buy, build and sell, and that's doing nicely too. We shall see how it develops."

ERIC BREUKINK
ANTITHESIS

At first sight, Eric Breukink looks too respectable to be a really top cyclist. Champions are supposed to have rather egocentric characters, they are supposed to swear and shout at their domestiques, they are supposed to curse themselves. Breukink is different. He too is a team leader, the Dutch stage racer of the last decade even, but he is the antithesis of the authoritarian commander. He gives the impression that it would take a lot to make him lose his cool. He is no boaster, no hell-raiser, no show-off, but a silent force, an intelligent, friendly, forthcoming young man. You are aware that he is from a good family. He knows the rules of the game and is very approachable.

It was often said of Breukink very early in his career - and fervently hoped - that he was 'the new Zoetemelk.' Somebody was needed to fill the void left by the departure of Joop. That hope was consciously stirred up as Breukink was only 22 when he won a stage and the mountain classification in the Tour of Switzerland. That was back in 1986. Breukink was on his way up, kept battling and became stronger for it. A year later, after riding a superb prologue, he won the first stage of the Giro and three weeks later was standing on the podium having finished third. Peter Post, who was his directeur sportif at that time, was more than satisfied.

In the meantime Breukink was diligently continuing his work. 1988 was an even better year. He won the memorable and terrifying 'snow' stage during the Giro and ended second in the final classification. A little later on in that season he finished 12th in the Tour de France, winning the best young rider competition. Post had still more reason to celebrate.

Morale

1989 may have been expected to have been the year when that progress would reach its climax, but it turned out somewhat differently. Breukink won the prologue and the time trial in the Tour of Romandy and the prologue in the Tour de France but disappeared from the latter race during the 13th stage with legs like lead and deeply disenchanted. This time Peter Post was far from happy, and over the next few months let himself be convinced by Steven Rooks that Gert-Jan Theunisse was the man he needed in his team.

Breukink drew his own conclusions from this and departed, despite there being some time left to run on his contract. Post did not stand in his way. The split between the two became irreparable when Post declared doubts about his protégé's Tour potential. "Breukink will never win the Tour de France," he said. "I don't think he is able to control a race, and he always has one bad day. Merckx and Hinault used to have bad days too, but they knew how to

disguise them. They knew how to call other riders' bluff. Eric doesn't. If he is dead that's it, he grinds to a halt. With Breukink days like that don't just come without warning, when they occur they always follow extremely demanding days. Eric doesn't recuperate quickly enough. That's his weakness and in the Tour it's fatal."

At the end of July 1992 it looked as though Post's doubts were well-founded. Once again Breukink didn't have the best of Tours. Although he was the father of a baby daughter by the end of it, the race itself had been a great disappointment to him. The leader of the PDM team had finished 7th, 18'51" behind winner Indurain. It was the best he could do. "I didn't ride well during the first week. It was the same two years ago but then I started to come into form for the second week, but not this time. It was in the time trials particularly, which are so important, that I just couldn't find my normal form. I never got into a rhythm, my legs weren't turning like they should and Indurain was just incredible. I take my hat off to the Spaniard. I'm conscious of the fact that I hadn't been able to put the year before's disastrous Intralipide affair from behind me. I had worked hard to get my revenge in a fair way. In the Vuelta it had gone well in the time trials. I thought that was a foundation on which I could build. But it seems that it was not the case."

Incubator
The Dutch cycling world quickly realised Eric Breukink was a major talent. "Bear in mind, however, that he is a spoilt young man. His father is a retired director of the Gazelle company. There's no lack of money behind him. Eric has everything he wants, he has never had to learn to fight for things. In a tough world like this, he'll never last the pace." Eric laughs when we confront him with this statement. "Maybe I am pampered. I'm the youngest of four children, I have two sisters who are well into their thirties. My brother is ten years older than me, too. Really we come from different generations. It was hardly surprising that they treated me gently. I was also an 'incubator' baby, born too soon. "That's why you're a year behind the others," my father always used to say, and still does. "You're 28 now, but I reckon your body's only 27. You'll have to keep going for a year longer."

Own Course
When Eric Breukink turned professional at the age of 21, he was described in the press as a "the rich man's son who got a contract thanks to his father's intervention." This is because Gazelle had been supplying teams such as Willem II, Frisol and Skala and as the director Willem Breukink called the shots,

it was naturally assumed he had put in a word. Eric says, however, that he never felt any push from his father.

"My father didn't pull any strings. Although he has been involved in the cycle industry for a long time, I have always followed my own course. I remember breaking a frame during my first year of racing and having to work at the Gazelle factory over the Easter holidays to earn a new one. I raced because I enjoyed it, because I wanted to do it myself, and not because I was under pressure from my parents. That's why I put so much into it. My family is a very sporting one, my father was once the captain of the Dutch Davis Cup tennis team. He also plays golf and often goes cycling. I think he was pleased that I took up cycling although he never let it show. I played football first of all: I was centre half for Dierense Boys,

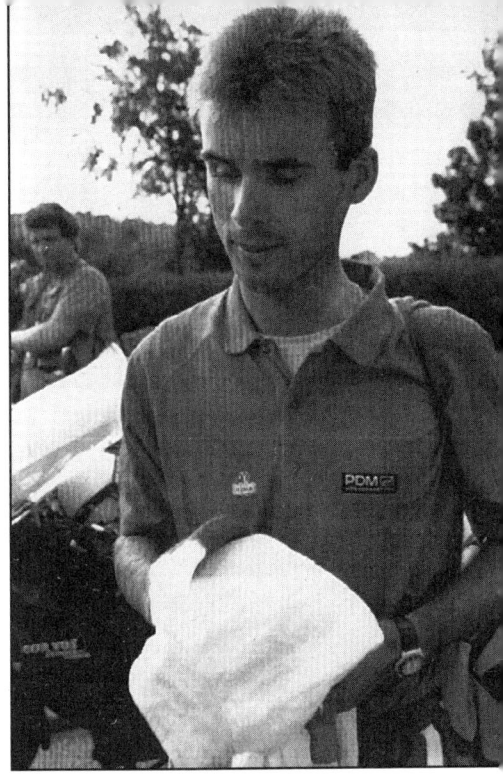

Eric Breukink after being forced to abandon during the 1991 Tour, to his huge disappointment

closing gaps in the defence. By the time I was 16 I'd had enough of it. I wanted to do something where the responsibility for success or failure was more down to yourself. By coincidence we were on holiday in France at the time. I went out on my bike quite often and I enjoyed it so much that I wanted to carry on doing it. I had a friend, Ronald Gerritsen, who was a racer. I went training with him and I was bitten by the bug. I joined the Zwaluwen club in Doetinchem and in the third race I rode in, I won."

Studying

From the start, Eric Breukink was good at disciplines in which he is still one of the best: time trialling and climbing. "I like working on my own; I'm happy to concentrate on my own performance. I like battling against myself. That explains my aptitude for time trialling. It was like that from day one, actually. When I was a second year junior I was the Dutch pursuit champion and during my amateur days I was chosen for the 110 kilometre team for the Olympic Games in Los Angeles. It was in America that the ambition to turn professional grew in me. At the time I was studying economics at college but I packed them in. It was impossible to study and compete in top-class sport. In spite of that, I passed my first year, but I eventually had to choose. I know that my father would have been happier at the time if I had completed my studies. He had some strong words for me but I wanted to carry my plan through. I promised that I would go back to my studies if after three years it looked as if I was not going to make it as a professional. At first the plan was to fit in studying economics during the winter but nothing came of that. A rider is so wrapped up in the sport that it is impossible for him to concentrate on other things."

Step Up

In those days Eric Breukink was a member of the Gazelle-Vredestein amateur team, managed by Ben Van Erp. Once again Breukink senior had grounds to protest.

Breukink in the leader's pink jersey during the Tour of Italy

"He would have preferred it if I had ridden other makes of bike, just to stop the gossip, but I got my own way again. When the team was revamped into the professional Skala-Gazelle outfit a year later, in 1985, I made the step up to the professionals at the same time. Under normal circumstances I would have stayed with them for the 1986 season but one or two things happened that made me want to leave. With new sponsors, Skil, a lot more new riders were signed. Besides that, Ben Van Erp, with whom I had enjoyed working greatly, was rather unceremoniously shown the door. For me that was that."

Tough

Eric Breukink signed for Peter Post's Panasonic team. "I had other offers but I had reached an agreement with Peter months earlier. Your word is your word, as far as I'm concerned. My time with Post made me harder, especially during the first two seasons. He wanted to know what sort of rider he had got himself and he put me to the test. Peter doesn't do things like that cautiously, he sometimes really laid into me, the way he did with any newcomer. If he thinks you're lacking in a particular area, he will let you know in no uncertain terms. Perhaps that might have been too much for some riders to take, but not me. It merely made me want to show him in the next race what I could do. At that time I didn't have the same toughness that other riders had by nature. It was only as a pro that I learned to really put myself through it. And there was certainly no shortage of suffering. In that first year I could ride 160 or 170 kilometres comfortably but anything longer than that and I was burned out. I didn't want to abandon so I would simply bite back the pain. I knew what my problem was: I was particularly lacking power. On the climbs I rode on two teeth less than the older pros. "If you have the strength of character to train harder and to push yourself beyond your limits during races, you'll get there," Post said.

I had another problem too: it was clear that I lacked the authority a team leader is supposed to have. I even made jokes about it at the time. I had a labrador, Dandy, and I couldn't even make him obey me. Since then I have learned to assert myself. I don't rant and swear but I do stand up for my rights. I also realise that a good, loyal helper knows exactly what is expected of him. You do not have to tell him."

Bernard Hinault

At the end of 1992 Eric Breukink was 28, but he was once a lad of 15 and a supporter of Bernard Hinault and Johan Van Der Velde. "I was always full of admiration for Van Der Velde, for what he could do on his bike I raise my hat! Joop Zoetemelk, on the other hand, didn't really appeal to me. I don't know why. I am a little too young to know much about the Eddy Merckx era. I just know that he always wore a jersey with the number 1 on his back. Merckx was number 1, that fact is ingrained in me. Someone whose career I followed with great interest was Bernard Hinault. I even rode in the same peloton as him for a year. At that time Bernard's career was almost at an end, while mine was just beginning. It was unbelievable the way he could push those pedals. On several occasions I deliberately rode close to him and that gave me a great feeling. It was marvellous the way the Frenchman dominated the peloton. He was also a distinctive figure. He wasn't afraid to try anything and his personality radiated all around. I would have liked to have been an Hinault-type of rider."

Cinema

Dutch riders who earn a decent living from the sport tend to go to live in Belgium. Adri Van Der Poel and Eric Breukink fall into that category. Breukink has moved into a villa in Kalmthout in the north Kempen. "Some of them do it for tax reasons, but I didn't. I did it because I like living somewhere quiet and closer to races. I also like the countryside. I'm no boozer, going out does not interest me. I like staying at home, lounging on the sofa. My wife Gea is the same. We listen to music when we are in the house. I like U2, particularly the quieter numbers. When I hear hard rock I switch it off. I also go to the cinema quite often, and we watch videos, although I miss the atmosphere. I prefer a nice, artistic picture house. I follow the news closely; I keep an eye out for what is going on around me. In the winter I play tennis, I go skating and I take my dogs out walking. I have two labradors. Recently my wife had our first baby and it's great playing with the little toddler. I don't really have any other hobbies."

Black

17th July 1991 is a day Eric Breukink will never forget. On the day before he had lost five of his team-mates on the Tour stage to Quimper in Brittany: Van Poppel, Earley, Boden, Raab and Verhoeven. They were all terribly ill. Breukink complained of muscular pains and headache and felt awful. The next morning the whole team pulled out. "Food poisoning," was the initial reaction. "Doping," was how the French newspaper L'Equipe put it. For several weeks an incredible spectacle was played out in public, until Breukink put an end to it on Dutch television. "Intralipide, a harmless pick-me-up is the culprit," he said, immediately prompting a huge row. "I wasn't aware that I was letting the cat out of the bag when I said that. I certainly didn't go to the studio with the intention of telling them everything. I thought that everybody already knew what I and all other riders knew. I had been told that a telex had been sent to a press agency earlier with the same information. The message had been wrongly translated, however, but I didn't know. Afterwards I understood why it caused such an upheaval. I've never regretted that events turned out the way they did, though. In the corridors there were whispers that I had played it in such a way to spruce up my image, but that had absolutely nothing to do with it. When all is said and done, I think there are far worse things to worry about. It is not the end of the world. I slept badly for several nights but I'm generally calm, something I take from my father who remains unruffled whatever the circumstances. I do blow my top on occasions, I did over the next few days after we withdrew from the Tour. That's a trait I get from my mother who is much more explosive. But it soon blows over.

Breukink wins the stage to Pau during the 1987 Tour.

Of course the incident made a big impression on me, as it did to everyone else, but I can put things into perspective more easily. I just thought it would blow over quickly, but that's not what happened. The aftermath was the worst thing. When you have to leave the Tour the first few days are really difficult, but after that it's alright. But on that occasion it was just the beginning. I really had to be on my guard.

The team doctor resigned afterwards, and that was to be expected. During that time some unbelievable stories were circulating. But I never had the feeling that anyone was messing around with my body. Why should I? If you were to ask questions about everything that goes on within a team. You cannot check everything. You have to trust everyone, and that's what we did. Anyway, at the exact time all of that was going on, it was also pretty unclear to us. All we knew is that we were sick. The press made a meal of the whole situation. It immediately became sensational news. That's how the press works. The side issues become more important than the race itself. As far as the rest is concerned, I have no more questions to ask about it. Neither has my wife. Why should we?"

Martyr

Dutch cycling fans did not feel very strongly about it at first. In fact, if anything they felt that the riders were martyrs. "I did get a lot of mail at the time, letters and cards from people expressing their sympathy. Everyone thought it was a terrible shame. None of them reprimanded or blamed me. I never thought of myself as a martyr though. In that year's Tour de France I had a good chance of finishing near the top but it fell apart, and for me that's the central issue. As a sportsman, it was that which upset me terribly. I was 27 that year, and it is said that a rider is at his strongest between the ages of 26 and 28. So I missed a serious chance, but life goes on. In 1992 I had another opportunity but I missed out.

Later, I read in certain places that the whole affair was good publicity for the sponsor, PDM, because everyone remembered their name afterwards. That may be so, but it's not how I see it, and neither does the company. We all wanted to ride a good Tour, we had been working really hard for it for months beforehand. In the end it all went wrong and we were very disappointed. I don't know whether I would have been able to win the Tour. All I do know is that I was at my strongest and that I would have been at the top of my form during the final week. I have learned many lessons from the experience. The main one is that a sportsman is very vulnerable and that we live in a very tough world in which you have to adopt a tough attitude. And we do. Later, when a new team doctor was chosen, we all had our say in that decision."

Bugno

In 1993 Eric Breukink is riding for the Spanish ONCE team and as a result becomes team leader to the Belgian Johan Bruyneel. Before he moved, the rumours doing the rounds were that he would be joining Gianni Bugno's Gatorade team. That is because as far back as the end of the 1991 season they were angling after Breukink. And Breukink was prepared to move even then. "Indeed, I wasn't very happy at the time, nobody in the team was in fact. They were all angry and unhappy and that's not right. The press wrote about it and that started the ball rolling. Gatorade did indeed make an offer, but I didn't really want to leave. It never reached the stage of sitting round the negotiating table. I spoke to PDM first, but the transfer fee would have been so high that I couldn't have moved. From then on I never pursued the matter further, and I think the way I acted was proper. So I stayed in the end, I was paid compensation and I battled on. I even rode in two of the major stage races even though I had sworn never to do that again. I hit my peak rather early, however. In the Vuelta I won a few time trials and then I geared everything towards the Tour de France, but it didn't work out. The Tour remains my number one target, I would really love to win it, more so than the world championship, even."

Calm

Breukink signed for ONCE and will definitely be riding for them until the end of the 1994 season, but there were other possibilities. "Ariostea, Motorola and even Peter Post approached me, but I had already made my mind up," says Breukink.

"Saiz had already showed an interest in me back in 1991, and continued to do so and that made me feel I could trust him. At the end of last year Manolo came to my house and I gave him my word then. I had a good feeling about it. During my time with Post, he was the perfect organiser, but he found it difficult to assess what was good for each individual rider. The way he saw things did not suit certain riders. Gisbers stayed calm whatever the situation. He could motivate you in a quiet, relaxed way, without pressure. His only fault was that he sometimes let go of the reins a little too much. Manolo Saiz combines the best elements of both of them. Apart from the fact that he is young anyway, he is close to his riders through the intense way he supervises them. Discipline within the team is very strict. Manolo draws up the plans and no one grumbles. In Holland, that wasn't always the case. I am pleased with my choice."

Winning

ONCE have a strong feeling that in Eric Breukink they have the man to win the Vuelta and the Tour for them. The reason Peter Post once let him go was precisely that he no longer believed he could. "There will always be that one bad day," said Post. Saiz laughingly dismisses that remark. "Eric will use a different method of training and that will help get rid of his poor days. He

now has the best team in the sport backing him up. It is a question of having total belief in himself. Last year he was the best time trial rider up until June. So why shouldn't he be the best in July, too? We shall be working on that."
Breukink is happy with the faith they are showing in him. "Things like that come across to you. We are going at it from the point of view that I'm going to do it," he says. "As for the bad days, actually it's only the winner who doesn't have them. I am now 28 and the opposition is probably now the strongest it has ever been. And I am indeed training differently. Saiz can see that there are problems, and he is busy working on them and giving me advice. I'm now working on power. Over the last few months I have been going running 2 or 3 times a week, I've been swimming, I trained on the road 3 times a week, something I only very rarely did at one time. During the winter I only ever used to do cyclo-cross. In terms of condition I'm in a much better state than I've been in previous years. Saiz says that that's the basic condition coming to the surface."

Gianni Bugno

BEETHOVEN

1992 was yet another year that was going to be Gianni Bugno's. The world champion staked everything to win his first Tour de France. To that end he decided not to ride the Giro, a move which did not go down well in his homeland. All the more so because his hopes of taking an early-season classic had been dashed. The Tour de France was going to put it all right. However, Miguel Indurain dominated throughout and Bugno was able to do little about it. He was lacking speed in the time trials, he lacked rhythm, suppleness and endurance in the mountains and had to settle for third place. Even his great rival Chiappucci did better. But in the World Championship at Benidorm, Bugno once again showed just how strong he can be. Although he was not the pre-race favourite, he beat Laurent Jalabert, Dimitri Konychev and 14 others in the sprint, and in so doing, he saved his season to a large extent. Bugno followed the Belgians Georges Ronsse, Rik Van Steenbergen and Rik Van Looy to become the fourth rider in cycling history to win two successive world titles.

Friend
Gianni Bugno is rather an enigma: a friendly but introverted man with an inscrutable face. He rarely makes statements that may cause surprise or shock. "He is a friend of the whole peloton," say his rivals. "When Rudy Dhaenens became world champion in the professional road race at Utsunomiya in Japan, and Bugno stepped on to the podium having finished third, he was happier with Dhaenens' victory than the Belgian was himself. And it wasn't pretence, it's the way Bugno is. He wouldn't harm a fly, he's quiet and he keeps his mouth shut. He does not have the capacity to be a natural leader, as he lacks a little self confidence. He has the strongest legs around, but he doubts himself a little too much."

Computer
Bugno's secret weapon is his professionalism. The Belgian rider Dirk De Wolf became Bugno's team-mate in the Gatorade team at the start of the 1992 season: "I chat about the carnival season," says De Wolf, "but Gianni only ever

talks about racing. He eats, sleeps and drinks it. He goes into the finest detail. If Gianni gets to the top of a climb and feels something hurting his little toe, he abandons, dashes into the nearest café and rings his trusted confidant Claudio Corti to ask him what he should do.

The rest of the time Bugno is like a computer: he does everything according to schedules; he even rides many of his races according to a working schedule drawn up in advance. Suppose that at around the 40 kilometre mark it says he should be riding at 45 kph, he moves through to the front of the group and starts forcing the pace. Up to the point that his schedule allows him to ease off.

But Gianni is a lovely chap. Actually he is too nice to be a team leader. I've never heard him swear, he lets everyone do what they want. He does lay down the law in certain situations, such as in hotels; there should never be more than five teams staying there and the courses of a meal must be served quickly after another. He doesn't like waiting. He always checks what he eats because he doesn't want to run the risk of anyone doing the dirty on him. A bottle of mineral water must be opened on the table or it is sent back. Bugno also has another fixed habit: in the evening he likes drinking a glass of beer."

Gianni Bugno (right) with Laurent Fignon: team-mates at Gatorade

Switzerland

Gianni Bugno lives in Robecco, a hamlet close to Carpenzago, a small town 40 kilometres from Milan, in fact just a settlement comprising four houses. There is no village pub. It is a place in which he doesn't have to protect himself from the outside world.

Bugno is very sensitive, very much a family man, totally committed to his wife and small son Alessio. He is, however, a doubter. He is very unsure and lacks self confidence. It has been said that it has something to do with his upbringing. Part of his childhood was spent being brought up by his grandparents. "You are the way you are, no matter what," Gianni counters. "Being brought up by my grandparents has nothing to do with it. My father was a carpenter. In the north of Italy there was little work, so he and my mother went to live in Switzerland, in Brugg. That's actually where I was born. It was a pretty hard life for immigrant workers and my father felt it would be better for me if I grew up at my grandmother's house in Venice. Twenty days later I was taken there and that's where I stayed until they returned to Italy. I was six by then. With the money they had set aside, they were able to open a launderette in Monza.

I like peace and quiet, that's true. I hate bustle. I live close to Milan, but you won't find me there any more than is necessary. I need quiet, and so does my wife Vincenzina, although she is used to it being different. She used to work with her mother in a road-side restaurant with many regular customers and lorry drivers. She is very good at being able to put up with the hustle and bustle you get in a place like that; much better than me. She is very important to me. She also knows a lot about racing, as she used to be the race commissioner for small races in our area."

Hinault

Bugno himself began racing when he was almost 15. "The thing I remember most about my youth is that I actually wanted to be a pilot, because I wanted to see the world. I know I used to play football because everybody else did, but I didn't really enjoy it. Like nearly all youngsters of my age I went once or twice to watch motor racing at Monza. But there was so much noise that I preferred staying at home. I found it hard to sit still, I wanted to have something to do. I tried out many sports but I wasn't outstanding at any of them. I wasn't strong enough, and I never put everything into them. I wanted to become a bike racer even though there was no family tradition in it. My father never raced, and although my grandfather used to tell me about Coppi, it all seemed to be from another age. I never had any heroes. I can't remember

Merckx racing because I was too young. I did, however, always have a great deal of admiration for Bernard Hinault. The things he could do on a bike... I was fascinated by his exploits. I will never forget the stage over the Stelvio in the 1980 Giro. I was at home watching it on television. Hinault had sent his domestique Bernaudeau out to the front and then went himself. Incredible. That man had something about him. He was the boss. I have even ridden against him. At the time his career was drawing to an end, but he was still the undisputed leader, there was no doubt about it. I'm not that sort of figure, I never will be. I lack that charisma."

Small Coin

Gianni Bugno chose cycling back then because the individual nature of the sport appealed to him: "You are responsible for your own results, that's what did it for me. I was brought up to be rather self-sufficient. And anyway I was very interested in bikes. Anyone living in northern Italy knows about cycling. When I was a small boy I often saw the Giro or the Tour of Lombardy come past. And Beppe Saronni didn't live far away - in those days he was a real star.

The first important race I won was the Coppa d'Oro held near Trentino. Although it is no longer run, when I made my debut it was the one you wanted most to win. Everybody entered for it. There were guaranteed to be 500 starters. We didn't receive the prize money in our hands, it was paid afterwards by the race organisers into the accounts of our cycling clubs. So really you were entering purely for the honour of taking part and for the old small coin worth one lira that everyone was given at the start.

I have always been able to win many races. As a junior I was chosen twice for the world championships, and as an amateur once. It was very quickly a foregone conclusion that one day I would turn professional. I never thought of doing anything else, although it didn't cross my mind that I might not succeed. I was prepared to sacrifice all else. Dad, however, wanted me to study, and although I was not bad academically, I stuck to my guns. He thought that I was just being carried along in the excitement but I replied that I didn't think there was any point in studying. "If I can't become a cyclist, then I'll go and become a lorry driver." And that's how I quit my studies."

Balance

Gianni Bugno was an outstanding amateur and his name was one of those mentioned as a potential world champion. Things took a different turn, however, and in September 1985 he turned professional with Atala, under directeur sportif Cribiori. "I even rode Paris-Brussels and Créteil-Chaville that year. It was a good platform for the following season. And I did ride well in 1986, even winning the Tour of the Apennines against Moser. I now wish I hadn't, though, as it messed things up a lot for me. That was the day the press singled me out as being the new hero. I had beaten Moser and in those days that was saying a lot.

The victory came too early and I was caught in a trap. The journalists started writing that I was the new top man, and I believed them. It made me more determined to win, and although I did all I could, it didn't really work out that way. I won races that suited me, but in the big races circumstances dictated that I lost many of the opportunities I was getting. To perform at your best, there needs to be the right balance between your physical and mental strength, and for me that wasn't the case. The problems were so bad that I panicked. I consulted Dr Ferrari and he gave me a thorough examination. "Physically and psychologically you are not yet mature enough to be at the top," he told me. "You will have to be patient." That reassured me. It was then I realised, however, that my directeur sportif was not the type who would give me the chance. Cribiori pulled the strings. I wanted to learn my trade, but Cribiori wanted me to win everything. He was a good man but he handled me the wrong way. He was an emotional man, and so was I. The more he screamed at me, the worse I rode. The way to deal with me is by keeping quiet. I'm aware of myself, I do what I must, and more besides; but you must leave me to do it my way. At the end of 1986 I signed a contract with Chateau d'Ax. They understood me at once. "You're getting a contract for four years," they said. "Take your time, but at the end of that time you must have reached the top." I thought that was very reasonable of them.

Gianni Bugno, the 1992 world champion

Beethoven

Bugno makes it sound as if everything was rosy, but it so nearly turned out wrong. His third year with Chateau d'Ax, an Italian furniture maker, was an out-and-out fiasco. Bugno won one stage in the Tour of Italy and that was all. "I was tearing my hair out at the time. There was something wrong with my health, that much was clear, but I didn't know what. My main problem was pain in my stomach, but on descents I also had trouble with dizziness, and when that happened I lost the wheel in front. That's what happened on several occasions in the Tour of Italy. The Milan-Turin stage was the ultimate catastrophe. I had gone on the attack on the final climb and Rolf Gölz had jumped onto my wheel. The two of us climbed to the top, but as soon as we were over I had to let him go. I was getting nowhere, and even a wheelchair would have overtaken me that day. There was definitely something wrong. After that the team insisted that I went for tests.

My stomach problem was soon put right. I had developed an allergy to dairy and flour products. When I ate a biscuit I was sick. That was no good to me, I wanted to eat what everyone else ate. I didn't want the soigneurs to have to make me something different every time. I don't like needing special attention. Taking medicine finally helped get rid of the ailment, although I still have to be careful what I eat. For the most part, though, the problem has gone.

My descending problem was a different question entirely. After Milan-Turin, when there was such an extreme example of it, Moser had a real go at me. He said on television that it was scandalous that I descended so badly. I wanted to put it all right and get my revenge. I had an examination and that's when it was discovered that what was wrong was my ear, and it was giving me problems with my balance. I followed a unique course of therapy: in order to relax I had to listen to music by Mozart. Don't laugh, but as a result of Mozart I have become a fan of Beethoven. The Ninth Symphony in particular is wonderful. I spent months working with that therapy, but I eventually recovered. Fate decreed that it was the self same Rolf Gölz, who had ridden me off his wheel in that infamous Milan-Turin descent, who reacted to my escape on the Poggio during Milan-San Remo in 1990. But on this occasion I shot down the descent like a kamikaze pilot with Gölz behind me, and he never got back up to me. That was 1990's godsend to my morale. In fact, I regard it as my finest victory, my first major win, the beginning of my career. A nice touch is that my son Alessio was born a few days later. So I will always be reminded of it for the rest of my life."

Room

Bugno's victories for the remainder of that season were too numerous to count on the fingers of one hand. He won the Giro, on top of three stage wins, he won two stages in the Tour and finished seventh, he won the Wincanton Classic, he was the overall victor in the World Cup, he came third in the World Championship, fifth in the Championship of Zurich, seventh in Liège-Bastogne-Liège and eighth in the Amstel Gold Race. 1991 was different but no worse. Bugno won 13 races including three stages and third place overall in the Giro, he was champion of Italy, he won a stage in the Tour de France and took second place overall. He won the World Cup event held at San Sebastian, and in Stuttgart he became the road-race world champion.

"I'm happy that it turned out this way. The take-off happened just in time, as I had already decided to play it by the book. Chateau d'Ax had given me four years to reach the top and at the end of 1990 they would have been up. In

Italy a team leader is a team leader, the domestiques do everything for him, without question. I was finding the situation difficult to deal with, I was feeling guilty about it. When the 1990 season started I made a clear pledge to myself: you've only got one chance left, you either succeed or you become a domestique. Wanting to be a team leader but failing to live up to expectations is not being fair to your team-mates.

My directeur sportif Claudio Corti has played a very important part in my rise. He knows me like no one else does. He was a professional rider himself and we roomed together for three years. Claudio felt that I was racing for 360 days a year. "You can't always go at it 100%," he said. "You even race when you're training." He felt that I trained too much and that I should work to a more efficient schedule. "You must ride with smaller gears," he said, "otherwise you'll use up all your reserves of energy." I listened to what he said and it has taught me a lot. People may see it as a sign that I lack self confidence, but I don't, I see it as good supervision. They also say that I ought to lay my cards on the table more and organise races from within. But I can't do that, it's not the way I am. Corti is really the perfect man for taking care of that, he delegates."

Legacy

Riders who win many races and who are constantly impressive, carry a heavy burden: they need to do better each year. Bugno, however, has no problem keeping up with that.

"I thought you might mention that. Let me say, then, that I never let it get to me. When you've had a good season, there is one great advantage to it: bettering it would be difficult, and that is reassuring. I cannot win everything. So I don't even try to, because it won't work. I don't want to be lumbered with an obsession. I'm not the best rider in the world and I'm still convinced that luck has played its part in helping me to win the races I have up to now.

I have always impressed on myself that I don't just want to win in Italy. We have three major races: Milan-San Remo, the Giro and the Tour of Lombardy. The others take second place to the important races abroad. I really like Liège-Bastogne-Liège. Paris-Roubaix, on the other hand, doesn't interest me; I'd rather not race it really, I hate cobbles.

The Tour of Italy is very important to an Italian. It's the event where you achieve your fame. But unless I win the Tour de France, I'll never be a great champion. I have now ridden the Giro and Tour double four times, and on each occasion my legs have always been less strong in France than I wanted them to be. That's why I decided to do things differently in 1992. I didn't let

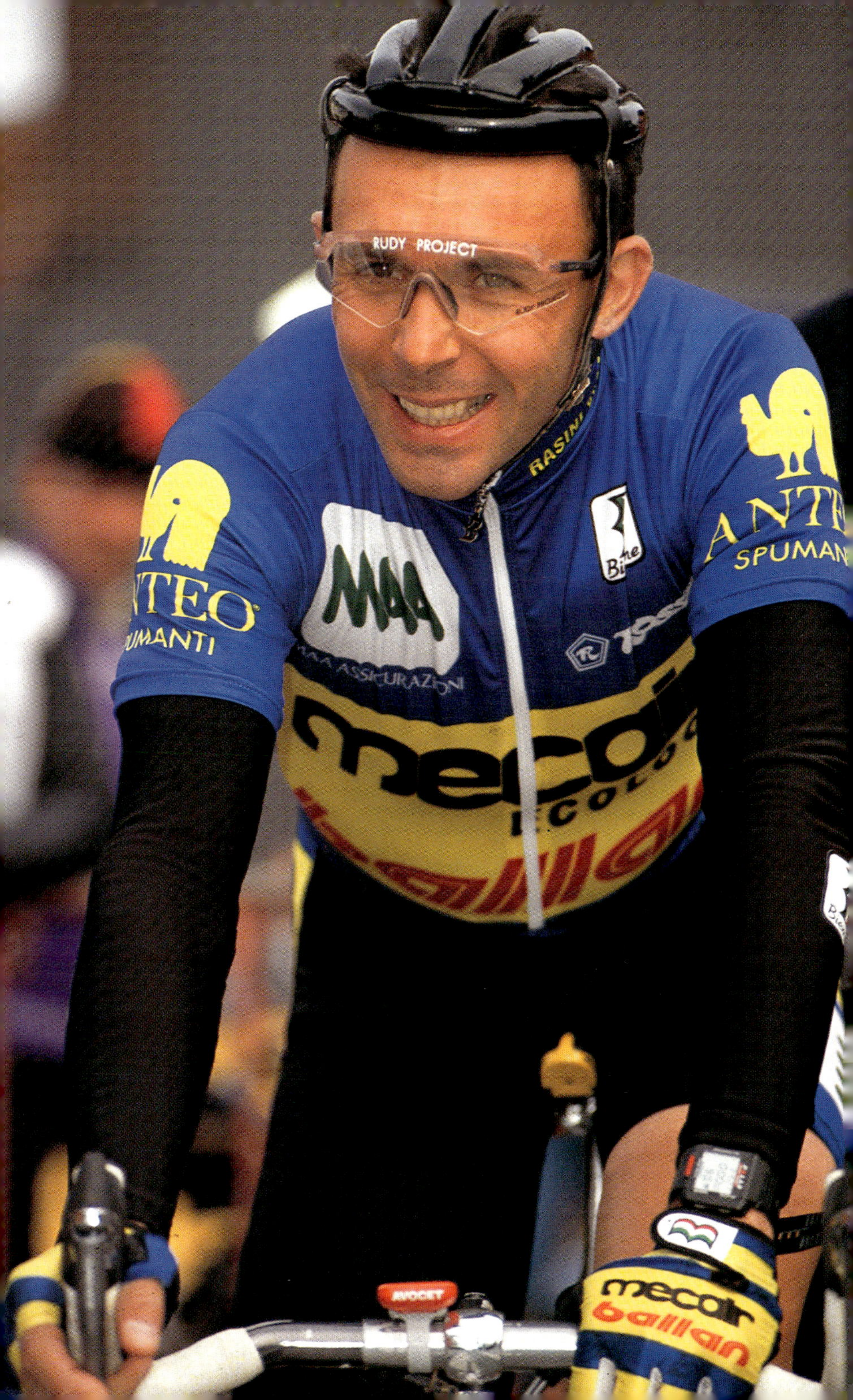
RUDY PROJECT
MAA
MAA ASSICURAZIONI
AVOCET
mecair
ballan

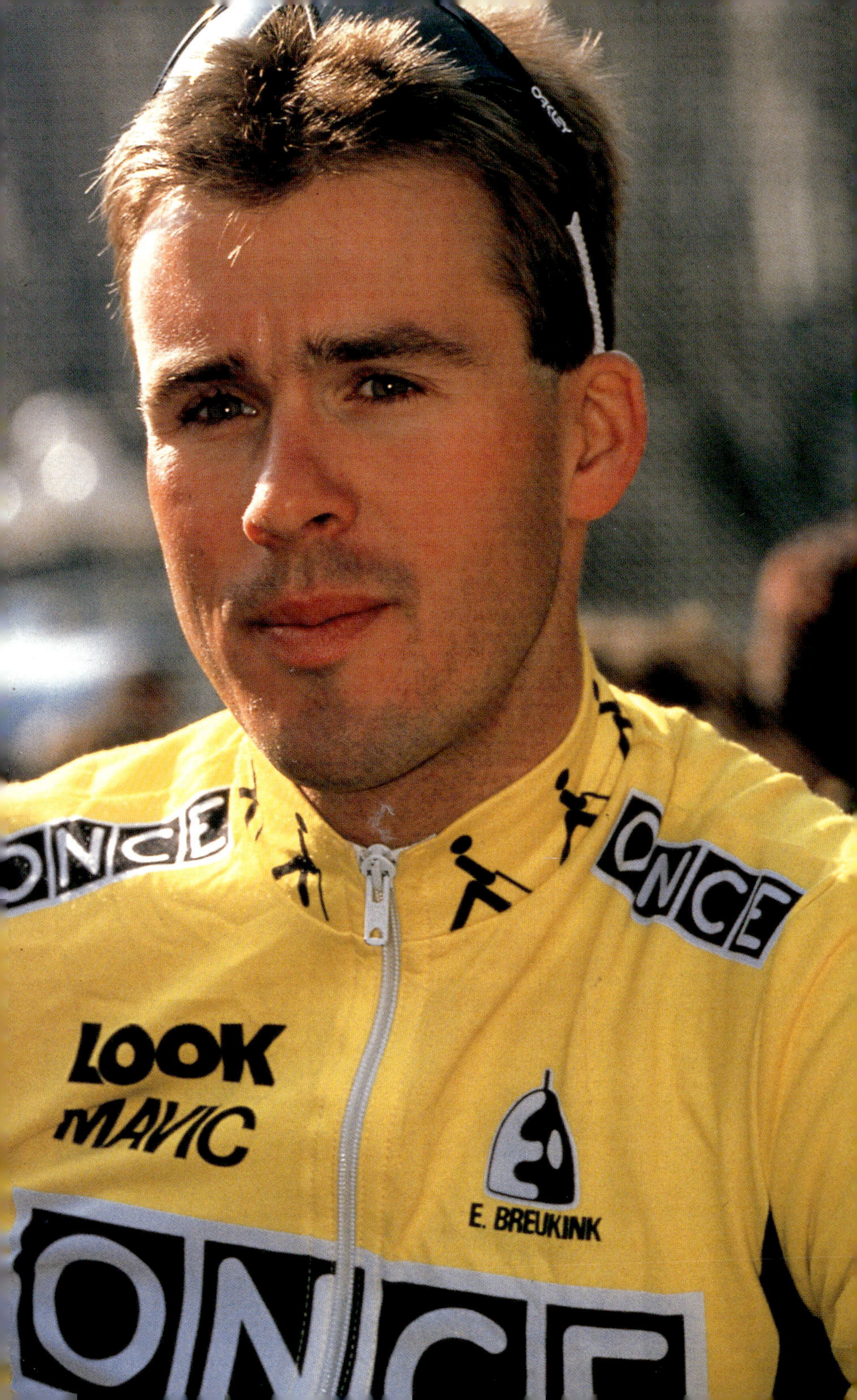
ONCE
ONCE
LOOK
MAVIC
E. BREUKINK
ONCE

anyone put me under pressure to race in the Tour of Italy; neither the press - who sometimes still give me a difficult time - nor the sponsor, nor the supporters. Looking back on it, it would seem I did the wrong thing. During the Tour it became clear to me that I would have been better riding the Giro, and in 1993 I will be combining the two again."

Swimming Bath

Italian cycling thrives on conflict and rivalry. Over the years there have been cold wars between Coppi and Bartali and Moser and Saronni. Although Bugno does not want to lock horns with anyone, it does not seem to get in the way of his popularity.

"What good is controversy? In his day, Gimondi wanted nothing to do with it and he reached the top. Deeds rather than words, that's the way I see it. After Coppi there was a transitional period in which things went quieter with Gimondi, Bitossi, Motta and Adorni. I suppose that after Moser and Saronni, we are also part of a transitional generation. But as far as I'm concerned: you can shout as much as you like, it's your results that do the talking.

I don't want to fall flat on my face. LeMond can predict when he is going to perform well. I can't. I do my best and I get as much out of myself as I can. Cycling is not the kind of sport where you win a race and that's that! After to-

Gianni Bugno with his wife, Vincenzina, and his pet dog

day's race you immediately have to be preparing yourself for tomorrow's, because the supporters and sponsors are always demanding more. It's hard work. I promise nothing, only that I do my best and give 100% in trying to win. That doesn't mean I lack ambition. After all, the way I perform is not down to me alone. My team-mates work themselves into the ground for me. Actually I don't want to be any trouble to anyone. Sometimes I feel a little guilty. After the finish of the World Championship in Stuttgart was one such occasion. I thought it was outrageous that all the honour was bestowed on me and that I wore the rainbow jersey, when really my jersey was the result of the entire Italian team's hard work. On that occasion I gave up my share of the win bonus, and as a result everyone made good money. I even let them throw me into the hotel swimming pool, but really I think they all deserve a little rainbow on their jerseys, or at least a sticker, because I didn't win the race on my own."

Humble

Opnions on Gianni Bugno are remarkably unanimous: not only is he the best Italian rider, he is also the nicest chap. Dr Yvan Van Mol, team doctor for Chioccioli, Cipollini and Ballerini, and a man who for years worked with Beppe Saronni, knows a lot about the Italians: "As a person, Gianni is the best. The Bugno who finished the 1992 season is no different to the Bugno of four years ago. He has no pretensions, not even to his rivals. He is appreciated by them all, and that has helped his career. Divide and rule, if you know what I mean. His previous bosses had little faith in him, but since his friend Claudio Corti became his directeur sportif, things have been different. He has got rid of his uncertainty, and that was his biggest problem. He is a thoroughly complete rider, he has everything. The only thing he is lacking is charisma. He is humble yet popular, he attracts support. Bugno appeals to losers. In contrast to someone like Eric Vanderaerden, he is a rider for the masses, the not so adventurous types."

CLAUDIO CHIAPPUCCI

INDIANO MONZON

Claudio Chiappucci is without any doubt the must colourful figure in the present-day professional peloton. We regret that there are not more riders of his calibre. The organisers of the Tour de France must have gone down on bended knees to thank the Lord that he was around in 1992. Without his input it would have been a dreary affair. That's because the word lazy does not exist in Claudio's dictionary, and he attacked every day head on with new heart. After the first time trial in Luxembourg it was already clear that Indurain was on his way to winning his second successive tour, but Chiappucci was determined not to lie down and die. He had put in some serious training in and around St Moritz in Switzerland. He went on a special training camp there and trained constantly in the mountains, and all of this was to bear fruit. He won the stage to Sestriere - 40 years after Fausto Coppi - in a style that will still be talked about in ten years time. Chiappucci rode almost 200 kilometres on his own at the front. In the closing stages he beat off a counter attack from a visibly wilting Miguel Indurain. Chiappucci was superb throughout the Tour, and he thoroughly deserved his second place. "What I think is most important about it is that I finished in the first three for the third year in succession. That was what I was aiming for. I wanted to show everyone once and for all that I was no hanger-on, and they would have to look out for me in the future. Last year I wasn't considered to be among the favourites. Well, it will have shown them. Besides, I never strike bargains with anyone. I'm a partizan who fights for what he can get."

Domestique

Five years ago Claudio Chiappucci was a domestique serving no one specifically, earning a living riding for Stephen Roche, Urs Zimmermann and Roberto Visentini. In the 1990 Tour de France, he undermined the established order. In the first half-stage, he was the very first rider to attack, and he was joined by Steve Bauer, Frans Maassen and Ronan Pensec, and the four of them turned the Tour on its head. Chiappucci gave that year's Tour some colour. He was the first Italian since Moser in 1975 to wear the yellow jersey, and it was only taken from him on the penultimate day.

Chiappucci was not like other champions. Within a week he had argued with Argentin and LeMond, and Bugno had ridden past him without a word of greeting. Claudio continued attacking and shaking things up, and in no time had become extremely popular with the fans.

Fire

Two years later and Claudio Chiappucci is still a law unto himself. He comes over as a friendly chatterbox, an amiable character who says what he thinks and who is determined not to let anyone get in his way. He never turns down an interview. It makes no difference where they are held: at his mother's around the fire, in his hotel room, at the bar, before or after a race, it is all the same to him. Chiappucci is also a telephone maniac. Wherever you come across him, he always has his mobile phone with him. "So that he can ring mama," say his team mates.

Much information is known about Claudio Chiappucci: his weight is 67 kilos, his height is 5'8", his shoe size is 7, and we even know he puts 3 teaspoons of sugar on his muesli at breakfast. It is also no secret that he kept his girlfriend Rita hanging on for seven years, and kept putting off their wedding day.

Claudio Chiappucci with manager, Firmin Verhelst

"I'm not yet mature enough to get married," he would claim. Nevertheless, Rita was always around, at the hotel before the start, on the podium afterwards. "She knows what she's doing," grin his colleagues. "Claudio is not averse to living it up a little."

Nicknames

At the present time, the popular Italian has more nicknames than you would think imaginable. Some people call him 'Calimero' - "I don't know myself why." LeMond calls him 'Chiappuccino' - "I think it's a disgrace the way he couldn't even remember my name after that infamous Tour, but he certainly knows it now." The Italian journalists call him 'Andreotti', after the former Italian president, because of his broad shoulders. Others say 'Monzon' because he has a real boxer's nose, others are 'Chiappi,' 'Motopertuto,' or 'Indiano.' "Because I look like an indian with my black hair." Calimero admits that it is something he appreciates and finds pleasing. His own name for himself is 'the bionic man.' "You have to go along with things like that. I let anyone pat me on the back, I give the fans a friendly smile and an autograph. The effects are clear to see. I realise I'm popular. I get a great many letters, most of which come from Belgium, the Netherlands and France. Italians don't write to me."

Miserly

People who have done business with Claudio speak less flatteringly of him: "Nothing is ever right with Chiappucci. He always wants to have his cake and eat it, but even then he grumbles. He looks to see how far he can go and how much you will let him get away with. At the moment everyone is knocking him about his stinginess. He is stinking rich, but he hoards everything away."

There are one or two tall stories going the rounds on this point. "Never take him with you to a café. When the waiter comes, he says he is not thirsty. He doesn't order anything, but when they put your glass on the table, he drinks half of it. But it's you that pays the bill, and to him nothing unusual has taken place." At the time of the G.P. Eddy Merckx in 1991, he walked into a record store in Aalst and bought £50 worth of CDs. At the counter he said to his companion: "Get them to knock something off that, it's much too expensive; it can't cost that much."

But is he really so stingy? He has been asked that question a hundred times before? " Me stingy? Come on! The fact is, I don't squander my money. Riders need to be careful. I allow myself a good car, a BMW 521, I have a motorbike which I use for riding through the countryside, and every year I go on holiday. That is all the luxury I need. I must provide for my future; the years that lie ahead. Anyway, I try to keep away from all that financial worry. I employ a financial adviser to look after my money."

Flannel
Chiappucci's earnings now flow in like water. After his first eye-catching performance in the Tour in 1990, he increased his monthly earnings ten-fold. After finishing third in 1991, he demanded £650 a day to ride the Grenoble Six Days. Yet the millionaire still lives at home with his mother, still keeping

his sideline going: selling vests. His parents have been travelling the markets of northern Italy their whole lives, selling woollen underwear and linen. In 1985 his father died and his mother wanted to stop all the travelling. She then opened a small textile shop in Uboldo, a little town 30 kilometres from Milan. "The vests, in particular, are of a very good quality flannel," says Claudio, with a grin. "They are not white, they're buff, but they are very warm and absorbing. Roche orders them all the time, and several other riders wear them. If you want some yourself, you're going to have to hurry up. Mama is retiring next year; she'll be sixty."

Coppi

So, how exactly does someone like Claudio Chiappucci become a cyclist? It seems his father had a lot to do with it. "I was a runner first of all, I was not bad at long distances. But although I won a few races, I really wanted to be a cyclist. Young lads nowadays want mopeds, but I got a bike and began racing it right away. I was 14. I won my first race when I was 16, in a three-man sprint. Dad was always talking about cycling. He had fought alongside Fausto Coppi in Ethiopia at the war front. They went around together, and even ate out of the same bowl. Coppi was his idol. He dreamed that one day I would be a cyclist, but he never pushed me into it. He thought it was more important for me to finish my electronics course, and that I did. Six months before I turned professional, he died. It's a great shame because I know he would have been unbelievably proud of the way I am now performing, even though they compare me to Bartali - in his day Coppi's biggest rival. Bartali was a fighter, a forceful rider and an attacker by instinct. I bump into him quite often at races and I am sure he can see something of himself in me.

Dad always instilled it into me that you must always give of your best. I strongly believe in that. My whole upbringing was based on it. I was never pampered. My father was very important for my character. To him, it was only good if I showed myself in my best light. I'm a fighter and I will always remain a fighter. I like feeling pain, it gives me a kick. When my father died, I was the only one left to stay at home with my mother. Suddenly I had more responsibility. My two older brothers were already married, so it was left to me to sort everything out. It made me harder as a result."

Battling

Chiappucci's performance in the 1990 Tour has been greatly underestimated. 'A fluke,' it was said. In 1991, however, he won Milan-San Remo, came second in the Giro and third in the Tour. In 1992 he passed over most of the classics. He put everything into the major tours, came second again in the Giro and second in the Tour.

"I can guarantee you, with what I know now, I would never lose that 1990 Tour de France again. No matter what LeMond tried to do about it. I rode like a fool at the time, attacking indiscriminately. When the favourites took off, I couldn't go with them.

I finally reached the top as the result of a long evolution. I had known for ten years that I was a good rider, but now I had the maturity. When I was an amateur I was selected for the national team and I even won stages in races like the Giro delle Regioni. Even then I had the ambition to reach the top. That's why I jumped at the chance to join a big team like Carrera. I turned down offers from the smaller teams, because I was afraid that I would never get out of them.

Everything went according to plan until injuries caused me to lose a great deal of time. In the Tour of Switzerland in 1986, I rode head-on into a car. I broke my collar bone, and worse still, a tendon on my shinbone was torn off. I had to spend the whole of my third year as a pro rehabilitating. I thought my cycling career was over. Then the team decided to call in some of the top specialists. The confidence the team has had in me has been a great pluspoint. I had to have several operations, but I fought my way back. I quietly continued to develop in the shadow of Visentini, Zimmermann and Roche, until my time came. Coming back cost me a good deal of sweat. By now of course, my results in the amateurs were long since forgotten. I was expected to show what I was worth again. Zimmermann left the door open for me. He failed as the team leader and Boifava was looking for a replacement. I made sure my chance didn't go to waste."

Hitting Back

With his infamous Tour exploits in 1990, Claudio Chiappucci was kicking at the shins of stars of the old order. They kicked him back however. "Chiappucci is nothing more than a bandit," said Greg LeMond, after the Italian had attacked when he had punctured during that same Tour. Once, after a criterium, Moreno Argentin was even more forceful, going as far as thumping him. Claudio hit back. "Claudio has the legs of a champion, but the mind of a child," stormed Argentin. Bugno and Delgado called him a traitor after his attack during the Giro when everyone had been summoned to strike action.

"It's to be expected that they won't let me do anything. I stir things up for them during races, so they have to ride harder. I can attack at any moment, so they have to stay on their toes the whole time. I get on their nerves because I'm unpredictable. I can understand why they moan about me. They want to demoralise me because the way I race doesn't suit them. I don't worry about it, though. I don't expect anything from anybody, certainly no favours. I race the way I want to. They all used to liken me to a comet. "He'll soon burn himself out," they said. When that didn't happen, they started to became awkward. They wouldn't sit at the table with me, they rode on my wheel. They destroyed me. Now they are all crawling back. I'm thankful to them for the way they treated me. I turned in on myself to face those situations, drawing on all of my energy to hit back. A sense of chagrin has taken me to the top and has taught me to extend my limits. I suppose I would act in the same way if a new 'comet' were to appear. That's how society is built.

You can see it in the way I race. I am an innovator. I ride according to my instincts, according to my mood, according to the circumstances. The public idolise me, they like me the way I am. I have always been a bit of a character. At school I was. I was rebellious and I was often punished for it. At home I was better-behaved. I had to be. My father was very strict.

Miguel Indurain (left) and Claudio Chiappucci dominated the 1992 Tour.

Cycling is a spectacle. The Tour de France is a circus. But it seems few people realise that. When I attack, I am partly doing it for the crowds. I have no pretensions, unlike some other stars. If I am asked for my autograph, I give it. I was a child myself once. I can just imagine how a youngster would feel if I refused to put my scrawl on his piece of paper."

More Cunning

The antipathy towards Claudio Chiappucci has disappeared in more recent times. The Italian has proved once and for all that he really is a very good rider. It is now accepted that he might attack at any given time. It looks as though Chiappucci himself also seems to have learned lessons from the past. Up until February 1992 he was on the go constantly. He rode track meetings and cyclo-cross. He took part in the cyclo-cross world championship every year, even after he had ridden in most of the classics and the Giro and Tour in the preceding months. Now he has decided to trim down his commitments. In 1992 he was absent from most of the early-season classics.

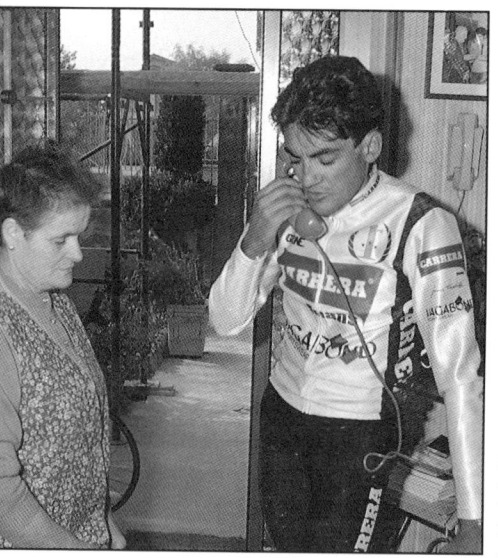

Claudio at home with his mother

"I will continue to put in the serious training, though. In the classics I did ride - Milan-San Remo, for example - I reached 80% of my maximum. The intention was to only reach 100% by the Giro and Tour. I wanted to win both of them. Dear oh dear, it's always the same. Beforehand it was thought it was going to be a good Tour. But I didn't think it was interesting at all. If they don't put a mountain time trial in, it's nothing. A mountain time trial would work to my advantage.

I have one big handicap: I am not a good time triallist. I now know that you don't win the Giro or the Tour in the mountains, because that's where most of the favourites are watching out for each other. It is the time trials that settle things, as Indurain proved in last year's Giro and Tour.

That's the reason I rode in track meetings during the winter of 1991-92;

not for the money, as has been written everywhere. I simply wanted to race better against the clock. All that chasing and pursuing were designed to give me more speed. And that's what happened, though not quite enough, unfortunately."

Marriage

He kept her dangling on a string for seven years, but in late 1992 he finally did it. Claudio Chiappucci got married to Rita. The wedding was one of the biggest media happenings of the year in Italy. Everyone wanted to be there.

"It was no ordinary affair," said the Italian press-corps. "Rita wore a white wedding suit with loose fur. Claudio was wearing a grey suit, a black hat, a chic bow tie and a grey scarf. Anyone living nearby who had a racing bike or a spare pair of wheels stood waiting outside the church. There was a very imposing guard of honour. But the show which they put on after the wedding was even more spectacular. After the service a carriage and horses drew up before the church, Claudio leapt onto the coachman's seat, took hold of the reins and steered the horses and his bride to a nearby 17th century castle where the party continued. It really was something."

Chiappucci is a married man now, but he has not moved house. He still lives with his mother in Uboldo. "There was no need to move," says Calimero. "It is a three-storey house. Mama still lives downstairs, as ever. Her shop is down there, and she doesn't have to climb any stairs. The second floor is where my brother lives, and Rita and I have taken up residence on the top floor. Close to the fresh air, close to the blue sky. We are happy."

So Chiappucci is a rider, son and husband all at the same time, and in September he is taking on another role; that of a father. "Rita recently became pregnant," beams Calimero. "We've done well. The birth is expected to be around the end of September, just before the Tour of Lombardy. I'm now nearly 30, so a child is very welcome. We don't want it to be the last, either, but time will take care of that, and hopefully they'll come no more than one at a time."

MARIO CIPOLLINI

BOUNTY HUNTER

In 1991 it was already becoming apparent: the 24-year-old Italian, Mario Cipollini, was acquiring a growing reputation as the fastest sprinter in the world. The odd doubt about that fact persisted, but by the end of 1992 they had been completely removed, because Cipollini had well and truly confirmed his place at the forefront of the sport's speed merchants. He won stages in a wide variety of stage races. He shone in Paris-Nice, triumphed in the De Panne Three Days and won four stages in the Giro - albeit with more difficulty than expected. After much pushing and shoving, and after the disqualification of Djamolidine Abdujaparov, he also added Ghent-Wevelgem to his collection. In actual fact he beat them all along the way: Abdu, Van Poppel, Ludwig and Museeuw.

Reckless

But Cipollini also had to accept second best, and that again raised questions. In the Giro, for instance, Leoni was quicker than him, twice. It was the Tour, in particular, which was a great misadventure for him. Cipollini had gone to France to win stages, but was sent packing with his tail between his legs. He abandoned the Tour on the stage to Valkenburg, totally drained. That day he had gone recklessly onto the attack, taking a bonus sprint, but he was soon caught and eventually he abandoned. "Now he knows that the Tour de France is the Tour de France," was what was said at the time. "Cipollini thought that he could shine like he did in the Giro, but he couldn't. He was totally confused and disenchanted, and that's when he probably realised that he could no longer stay with it; and that there was still a long way to go. After a brilliant Giro, he felt that enough was enough. He didn't take part in the Italian championship. "Too many climbs and the weather is too nice," said the GB rider, and he took several days holiday. He was made to pay. Hopefully, he will learn one or two things from the mistakes he made. Just before the Tour started, he said that winning stages in France would be easier for him. He now knows better."

Rik Van...

Yet a good performance in the Tour could have made the reputation of Cipollini's fast but reckless legs even bigger. It didn't happen, but he has been given a reprieve thanks to the impressive form he was already able to point to. He has even been known for a while as 'Rik Van Cipollini,' on account of his resemblance to Rik Van Steenbergen, the speedy, strong Belgian who dominated the peloton between 1943 and the mid-sixties. Rik was fast, strong and reckless. He was not afraid to lead out sprints himself, and then took some stopping. Rik liked a laugh and a joke. Cipollini combines these characteristics, with the difference that Rik was a more complete rider and was also a strong rider in classics like the Flèche Wallonne. That is an area in which Cipollini may never succeed.

Class Act

"Cipollini is the classiest act of them all," is the opinion of sports doctor Yvan Van Mol. "I've worked with him for years, and I know his capabilities. Without doubt he is the

Mario Cipollini considers himself to be the quickest sprinter around at the moment.

fastest sprinter in the world, in the style of Freddy Maertens. He is capable of a great deal, but he has one problem: he is raving mad. They always said Eddy Planckaert was mad, but Cipollini makes Planckaert look sensible. He is mad about women, cars and speed. All right, I know you should take that as read, since it is typical of the mentality of sprinters. Apart from that, Mario is also on the lazy side. From June onwards, there is nothing you can do to get him on a bike. The drive and the will have gone, and all he wants to do then is go skimming over the water on his sea-scooter, enjoying the sun, sea and the chance to relax and do nothing."

Playboy

Mario Cipollini is happy living up to his playboy image. He is tall and thin. He usually has two days of stubble on his chin, and his blond curly hair glimmers with gel. He can come up with jokes quicker than you would think possible. And he knows how to liven up proceedings. At the presentation of the GB-MG Boys team, Cipollini stole the show. At the reception held beforehand, a pretty young girl was handing round the glasses for the toast. Cipollini went up to her with his directeur sportif, Abetoni: "Signora, may I introduce you. This is Cipollini, the fastest sprinter in cycling," and he gave Abetoni a hefty slap on his bald pate. Five minutes later, when called to the stage, he made several Indian cries, jumped on his bike and slalomed to the front between the restaurant's covered tables. Five minutes later he went and sat among the musicians and gave his rendition of a trumpet solo. Cipollini knows nothing about music, but he wasn't going to let that stand in his way. "I turned it into a game. It's no more than that. I'm flattered that people call me a joker. It's better than being known as a pessimist, because that's something I certainly am not."

Layabout

Those who don't know him have their own views on Cipollini's happy-go-lucky way of life. To them he must be a lady-killer, a layabout, he must smash up one car after another.
"No way," replies Cipollini. "Me, a lady-killer? Come on. I might be single, but I am engaged to Sabrina, the sister of Taffarel, Fiorentina's former goalkeeper. So I have to stay cool. As far as the cars are concerned, that's a gross exaggeration too. I have written off three cars at most. The way I see it is that I am seriously tied up in my work. Otherwise I wouldn't win 14 races in a season, like I did in 1991; nor would I be the victory king, like I was in 1992. Remember, I also rode the Giro and the Tour in 1992, what more can you do as a rider? What if I did go on holiday afterwards? I had certainly earned it."

Bounty Hunter

Popularity is a game for Cipollini. "I can assure you that there is a big difference between the image you cultivate and your personality. I live one-hundred per cent for my profession. I sometimes find it a struggle, but I don't pull excruciating faces like some of my rivals. Anyway, I like racing. My bike gives me the freedom that I love so much. I work very hard on my fitness, but I am more than willing to, because racing gives me so much back, too. My career gives me the opportunity to live like a gentleman at some point in the future. As well as that, I love everything that is beautiful and enjoyable. If I was not racing and I lived in another age, I would definitely like to have been a bounty hunter in the wild west: as free as a bird."

Self-Confidence

Cipollini is a solid block of self-confidence. He radiates self-assurance. "I'm the quickest. Everyone talks about Abdujaparov, but when has he ever been able to beat me fair and square? His name and reputation are mainly based on his performances in the 1991 Tour and the 1992 Vuelta. Well, I wasn't there on either occasion. In Ghent-Wevelgem in 1991 I might have been beaten, but I was illegally obstructed twice. Abdu stuck out his elbows and veered from his line, and before that Eric Vanderaerden had obstructed me. Dirty sprinter that Vanderaerden, a bandit. Afterwards, at the dope control, I told him what I thought of him. "Next time I'll break your legs." The way that man sprints is sheer madness, just like Abdu when you think about it. They always get to the front too early, and because they aren't strong enough, the only way they have of keeping other riders back is to use sharp practices. That isn't sprinting, it's doing the crawl on your bike."

Well-behaved

Although Cipollini does not hesitate in accusing his rivals of underhand tactics, he himself has a name for being a perilously dangerous sprinter. "He can't keep his hands to himself," says Vanderaerden. "Rubbish," snaps Cipollini back. "He's referring to Tirreno-Adriatico in 1990 when I'm supposed to have pulled Kelly back. Yes, I pushed, because I wanted to get out of the bunch, but I don't pull people's jerseys. I'm more often the victim than the perpetrator in the sprint. At present I am so fast that I have no need to hinder anyone else. If it ever starts going less well, then I can always lash out with the rest of them, but not now. All I need is a little space, then nobody can catch me. The finishing banner is my only point of reference. I don't see my rivals. Abdujaparov always looks round to see who is there when he is in full flight. He can't see where he's going, and that's how he came to hit the advertising post during the final sprint in the 1991 Tour. It was his own stupid fault. He looks under his elbow to see who is behind him and alongside him. And that's dan-

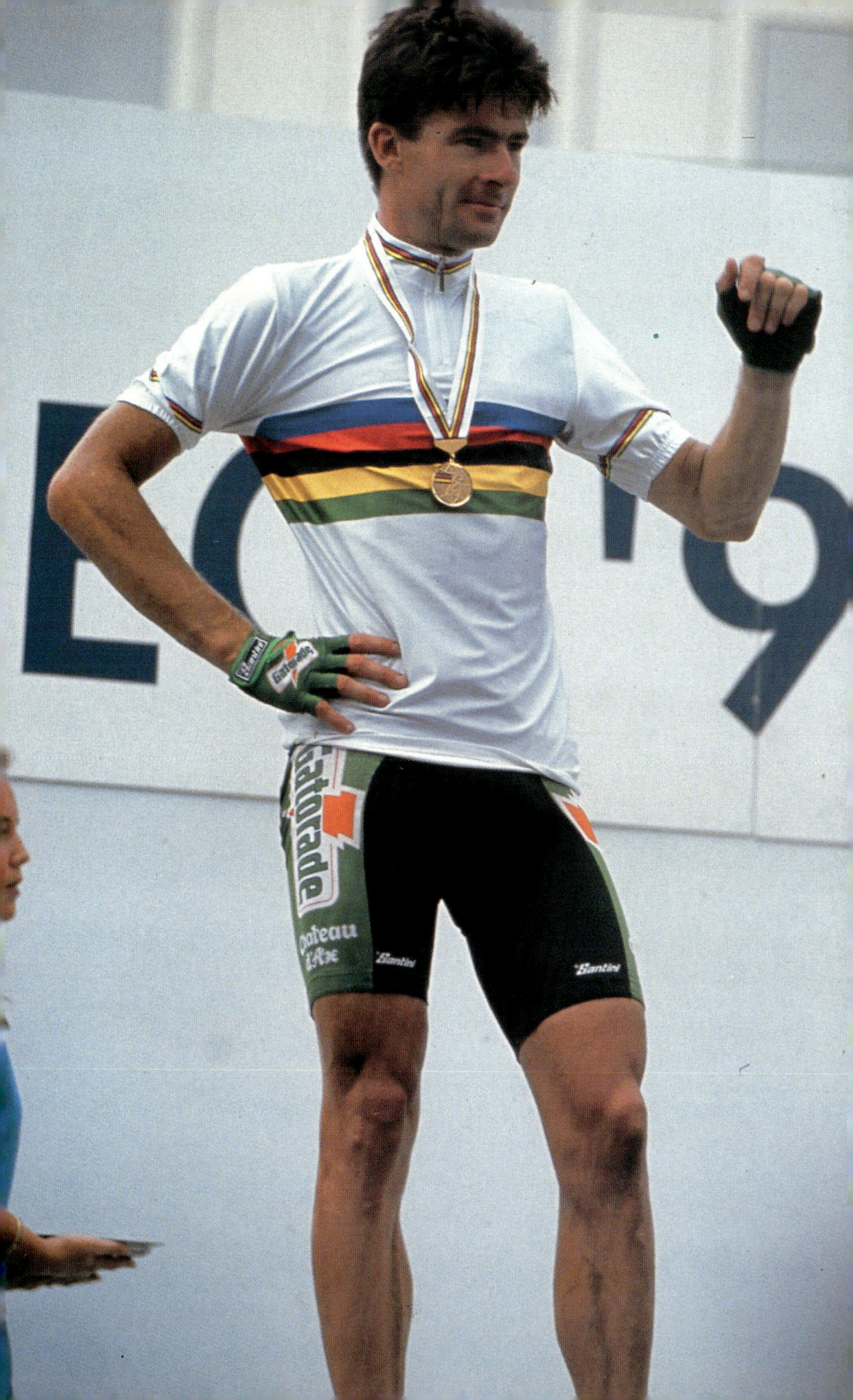
Gatorade
Chateau d'Ax
Santini
Santini

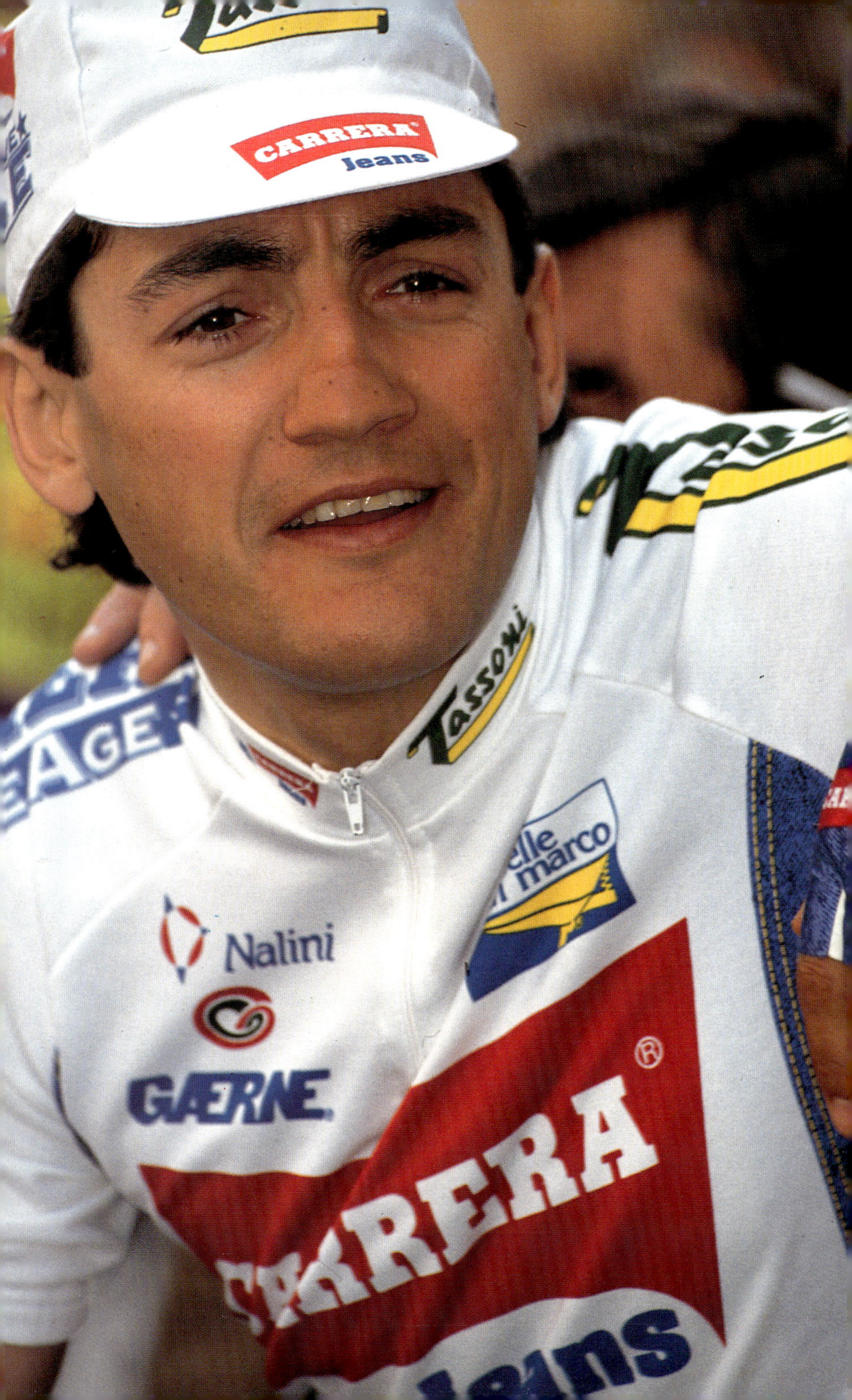
CARRERA
Jeans
Tassoni
Nalini
GÆRNE

gerous. Think of his antics during the 1992 Ghent-Wevelgem. I was sprinting in front, the way was clear ahead of me, but suddenly he was there. I could feel him coming and closed the door following the rule book, but then he only went and clung hold of my shorts. As if all of that was allowed."

Woman

Abdu was disqualified from that edition of Ghent-Wevelgem and Cipollini was declared the winner anyway. Since then things have remained hostile between the two of them. "Abdu is keeping out of my way. In the Giro the riders' union tried to restore the peace. Abdu and I were due to shake hands, and a photograph of it was going to record the moment for all time. I agreed to do it, Abdu didn't. Just before it was due to take place he came along to say that he had to ask his directeur sportif first, but he never came back. At the time some people were urging me to make the first moves towards reconciliation, but I refused. I'm sorry, but I can't help I got the victory in Ghent-Wevelgem. That was decided around the green table. I won't go down on my knees to anyone, not to a woman, and certainly not to Abdu."

Not a Jumper

Cipollini has his own style of sprinting. We will leave it to the man himself to describe it. "My favourite sprint begins 300 metres out. I launch myself from a long-way back and head forward at full speed. The first thing I do is look for Eros Poli's wheel, he is my engine. He is a giant of a team mate, literally and figuratively. He has unbelievable knowledge of his craft, and has incredibly broad shoulders. He protects me from the wind. If he starts making his way to the front, it is just as if the Red Sea was opening in front of us. I know exactly where and when he will drop off the pace, and then I take over. I go straight ahead, no longer looking at anything or anyone, I push the biggest gear, and if conditions are good I go hell for leather. I can keep going at full speed for a very long way. I do miss a certain explosiveness, however. I'm not a jump-sprinter like Basso was in his day, or like Abdu is nowadays, I sprint more in the style of 'the buffalo', Guido Bontempi, or like Rik Van Steenbergen used to. At least that's how Rino Negri, a journalist with the 'Gazetto dello Sport', described it once."

Brother

The quick sprint Cipollini possesses is a family trait. "It must be, because my brother Cesare was fast too. He was a professional for many seasons; he rode the Giro 13 times. When he was an amateur he could sprint quicker than

Saronni, but he didn't have the right mental attitude to make it as a pro. I've been quick from the first day I raced. I wanted to do what my brother did. By the time I was six-and-a-half years old I was sitting in a peloton. Racing was a game back then, and my parents made sure that's how it stayed. I love pleasure, but I had a firm-but-fair upbringing. In Italy young riders have a ticket that has to be punched. Once you have twenty holes in your ticket, you cannot race any more that season. It is done to make sure you don't ride yourself into the ground, and that was very important for my mother and father. The first race I rode, I won. Since then I have totted up about 180 victories, and there are more to come."

Climbs

Sprinters have one big problem: they win many races, but seldom, if ever, the really big ones. Cipollini would like to break this tradition. He would like to win Milan-San Remo one day. "I'm sure I can. If ever a sprinter is going to win that particular race, I want it to be me. For two years I thought that the course was too long and difficult for me. The climbs were too much for me, the Capo Berta, for example, was where I always started to suffer. I used up too much of my energy on the climbs. Since the 1992 season, however, I have known that I am strong enough. During Paris-Nice, on the stage to Marseille, there is a very steep climb. At that point it was the Ariosteas who were controlling the tempo. They couldn't believe their eyes when, after the climb, they saw me sitting their in the group. In 1991 I won a stage in the Tour of Puglia and I'm very proud of it. The finishing line came at the top of a six-kilometre climb. Three of us were out in front: Chioccioli, Chiappucci and me. Two genuine climbers, but they couldn't shake me off their wheels. Cipollini gritted his teeth and did it."

Boulevard

Cipollini is also fascinated by Paris-Roubaix. "Imagine me winning that race, or the Tour of Flanders! It could happen, I'm not dreaming. I want to add quality races to my list of victories, though. If I haven't achieved it before the end of my career, I will be very disappointed. I like racing in northern Europe. With the exception of the Walloon classics, I have a chance in any races held there, something I cannot say about races in Italy. I don't stand a chance in 70% of the races held in my country. When racing in northern Europe, they talk of me as one of the potential winners in nearly every race. The races are lighter and the finish is always at the end of a long, wide, straight boulevard. And that's just how Cipollini likes it."

PEDRO DELGADO

PEDRO CHATTERBOX

The breakthrough of Tour and Giro winner Miguel Indurain has - metaphorically speaking - meant the death of that other Spaniard, Pedro Delgado. After Indurain's splendid victory in the 1991 Tour, that at least seemed to be where it was heading. The power transition was finally completed, more quickly than expected, with Indurain's surprising - it must be said - yet thoroughly deserved victory in the Tour of Italy, followed by its confirmation with his second win in the Tour de France. Delgado could still have kept up appearances and won in the Tour of Spain, where hundreds of thousands of Spanish fans lined the streets to support him in force for one last time, but he had to bow down to Rominger and Montoya. Yet still he started out in the Tour de France as joint team leader with Miguel Indurain, at least until the first time trial when the die was cast. Delgado, however, certainly did not ride badly in the Tour. Indurain won, but Delgado finished a respectable 6th place, at 15'16". A good performance, whichever way you look at it.

Team Mates

In Spain many cycling fans found it hard to accept that the impulsive and explosive Delgado had, at the end of 1991, decided to ride the next two years at the side of his biggest rival. "The explanation is quite simple, though. I had two good offers which I thought were worth considering, one from Gatorade and one from Banesto, who were still my team. To me they were like two identical teams. You see, in both teams there is a big rival: Bugno at Gatorade, Miguel at Banesto. Financially, both offers were about the same. What do you do, then? I knew the mentality of the Banesto team, and all in all I wanted to remain in Spain. Besides, when the contract was signed, it was immediately agreed that we would both be starting the Tour on equal terms. The decision on who would take over as leader would not be taken until it was seen what was happening in the race. The one who was riding best would take the responsibility. If it turned out that it wasn't me, well never mind, I would accept it. And that's what I did. We were also to ride partly different race programmes, in part. Miguel would ride the Giro, because the many kilometres of time trialling would suit him better. The time trials would be decisive and that's ideal for him. I would ride the Vuelta, although I was well aware at the time that the weather can be very bad when it is held. I don't like bad weather, I would always choose the warmth. Unfortunately the weather wasn't always very nice, and that partly explains why I lost."

Leader's Figure

Pedro Delgado is a solid block of temperament, from head to toe. If he thinks it necessary, he shouts, screams, swears at his team mates. "A typical leader's figure," claim the experts. When in 1988 he was on his way to his first Tour victory in the Pyrenees and the Spanish supporters came to exuberantly encourage him with their hundreds of banners, blocking his way through, he swung out angrily all around him with his drinking bottle.

"That's the way I am. I'm aware that Bugno, Indurain and Breukink never get nervous. LeMond, Fignon and I, however, can't sit still for a second. That's a way in which two generations of riders differ from one another. I had known for years that Indurain had what it takes, but because he is so placid he needed more time to break through than others might. If he had my mentality, he would have made it two years earlier. He had the class to be a winner from the first day. I'll never forget the way he came second in the prologue in his very first Vuelta, behind Bert Oosterbosch."

Pedro Delgado and his girlfriend, Lydi, in Segovia

Colleagues

Pedro Delgado is never short of a word or two, he always says what he thinks in a direct way and he bristles with self-confidence. Even Indurain's higher standing cannot undermine it. At the end of 1992, Delgado is still convinced he can win the Tour again. "It is only physically that we are second best. Miguel, Bugno and Breukink are intrinsically stronger. But in a three-week long race, character is more important. You must understand the race, you must ride using your head, and with our experience we are better at it. That's why I think one of us can still win. OK, I'm 32 now, but I still find it as easy to bring myself to go out on a really tough training ride. It is even easier than it was in my first year as a pro. Now I have the experience, I know where I need to start. I lost the Tour in 1991 because the time trials made such a difference, they are my weak point. Miguel is a much better time triallist than me. I have to perform in the mountains, but by an unfortunate coincidence, I had a hard time of it in the Pyrenees on the way to Val Louron, and that's what finished me off. All the fighters failed, in actual fact. LeMond, Fignon and I all missed out, and of the quiet men like Bugno and Breukink and Alcala (who both dropped out), Miguel was the only one who consistently rode at the highest level. Miguel rode brilliant time trials, and he is never nervous. Incredible. On the other hand, in my opinion, he never gets stuck in enough. He should regularly be going all out, but it doesn't happen. Neither have I ever heard him make bold predictions. He never says he is going to win a race beforehand. That's his character, and there's nothing you can do to change it.

We are not friends, but we are good colleagues. We get on well with each other, but our characters differ too greatly to be real friends. Our mentalities are totally different to each other's. Miguel is very quiet. If I say: "Come on Miguel, we're going for a cup of coffee," he goes off to his hotel room. He is very introverted. I do have the impression he is changing, though. At one time all he would say in interviews was 'yes' or 'no,' but now he speaks in sentences."

Distracted

Indurain has his shortcomings, Delgado too. Indurain says of his friend and role model that he is unbelievably easily distracted. "I once missed a plane," tells Indurain, "because Pedro didn't give a thought about when we should leave until it was too late. I would never expect LeMond, for example, to miss the start of the prologue in the Tour, but Pedro would, as he did in 1989." "That's not what caused me to lose that year's Tour," protests Delgado, "it was the team time trial several days later."

Classics

Delgado has not won that many races during his professional career: thirty in all, but they all count. However, a northern classic is still missing from his honours list. "And that annoys me. There should have been a Liège-Bastogne-Liège, Flèche Wallonne or an Amstel Gold Race. In 1989 I came fourth in Liège-Bastogne-Liège. If I had had a 12 gear on my bike that day, I would have made my attack after La Redoute. I am certain I would have won. But instead I had to pedal with a 13, and that's what did for me.

Spanish riders do not really gear themselves for the classics. We mainly ride stage races. Our calendar is full of them. You can count the number of one-day races on the fingers of your two hands. So Spanish riders are primarily stage-racers. In Belgium or Holland, it is the other way round. It seems nobody thinks it necessary to change that tradition, and so things stay the way they are and few Spaniards win classics.

I must say here that I count myself lucky to have ridden two seasons for PDM from 1986. I had just won the Vuelta and I was allowed to join the Dutch team. I think that it was only then that I became a complete rider. For that reason it was also a conscious move for me. All the things I was lacking at the time were worked on: I rode many races on the flat, and more one-day races too, I was given lessons in team tactics, the team managers had a different psychological approach, my character was made stronger; you name it, I worked on it. At the same time, as a stage-race rider, I could follow almost the same programme as always and I was also very well paid. What more could you want? Suddenly I became a better time trial rider. PDM had a special time trial bike built for me. I did a lot of training on it, I came upon my specific riding position and I still think that was the foundation on which my victory in the 1988 Tour was based, by which time I was once again riding for the Spanish Reynolds team."

Sisters

Pedro Delgado-Robledo - to give him his full name - is a nice chap. He lives with his girlfriend Lydi in a lovely house at La Lastrilla, a village four kilometres from Segovia. Delgado is a real chatterbox, quite different from the type of man we expected. He is amiable and very extrovert. "That's due to my upbringing. At home I always had to get myself out of scrapes. My father, Julio, was a lorry driver first of all, then an administrative assistant for the trade union. We weren't very well off. We were ordinary, simple people. We certainly couldn't afford a car; not even a bike. Everything we got we worked for.

Anyway, racing was far from a family tradition. My mother was even outspokenly hostile to it. Far too dangerous, she thought. I had two older sisters, Josefina and Marissa. Marissa never believed I could make it to being a professional. When I won the Tour in 1988, she still said: "Our Pedro was actually a very quiet and shy little boy who cried a lot. I often had to protect him from the bigger boys in his class. Because he was so little, he was tormented a great deal. He was a sensitive lad too, with a very big heart."

I also have a younger brother, and like Josefina he works at the Ministry of Justice in Madrid. My other sister Marissa is a nurse. I also had to study when I was at home. After I had finished at grammar school, I began studying nursing, since that was my big dream. I wanted to work in a hospital. I completed the first year, but then I started to devote all my time to racing. At least I have become competent at languages as a result of my studies: I speak good French, and I can get by in English."

Steering Skill

Pedro saved up himself for his first racing bike. "First of all I played a little basketball, football and did some athletics. When I was 13 I got a job as a paper boy, and with the pocket money I earned I was able to purchase my first bike. Via a school friend I then started racing. He raced for the Monier cycling club and I became a member too. My first race was a hill climb, and I won. I have always been able to climb well. It was not entirely surprising either when you consider that being a paper boy in Segovia meant always going up and down hills. So I was also a good descender, I was very skilled at steering. Climbing is an inborn talent. I have never been a Bahamontes, but compared to other riders of my generation I am among the best. Actually only Herrera was better. I have always had the ability to put in bursts of power in the final kilometres, and few can say that. I never did any special training for it, although I actually had the opportunity. Twenty kilometres from Segovia is where the Sierra de Guadarrama begins, with its highest point the Pico Penalara, a mountain 2,430 metres high. Strangely enough, I always trained in the valley, on the flat roads."

Career

"For me, it really all began in the William Tell Tour in Switzerland. I won the big mountain stage, the points jersey and the mountains classification. With those feats as references, I was signed by Reynolds for their amateur team. In 1982 I turned professional, and in 1983 I rode my first Tour de France. Angel Arroyo was the team leader, and I finished second to him in

the mountain time trial on the Puy de Dôme. For a short time I was second on the general classification, but after some stomach trouble I finished 15th.
In 1984 I was lying in fifth place when, in trying to avoid a reckless Greg LeMond, I crashed and broke my collar bone. In 1985 I moved to the Orbea team and won the Tour of Spain. That year I set off for the Tour with the highest of ambitions, won the stage to Luz Ardiden and finished in Paris in 6th place.
In 1986 I wanted to win the Tour. Due to illness I had only finished tenth in the Vuelta and I wanted to avenge that. By then I was riding for PDM and I felt my time trialling was much better. I won the stage to Pau and was lying in fifth place overall when my mother died unexpectedly. I returned home immediately."

Top Man

1987 was when Pedro Delgado finally made it to the very top. He came second in the Tour to Stephen Roche, losing out to him in the time trial on the penultimate day.
In 1988 he finally did it. Delgado won the 13th stage, and with it the Tour. At the end he had a winning margin of 7'13" over Steven Rooks. In 1989 Delgado, who wanted to confirm his supremacy, arrived late at the start of the prologue, made a mess of the team time trial a few days later and threw away his chance. He finished third. Earlier that season, though, he had chalked up his second win in the Vuelta.
In 1990 Delgado came second in the Vuelta and fourth in the Tour. The following year saw him finish 15th in the Tour of Italy and 9th in the Tour de France, where he was making an all-out effort to help his team mate Miguel Indurain win. In 1992 Perico came third in the Vuelta and once again rode in the service of his team leader in the Tour.

Probenicide

When his Tour victory in 1988 is discussed, the conversation inevitably comes round to Probenicide, a product which was used at that time within sport to neutralise doping. It removes any traces of drug use.
"I'm aware that this is going to be with me for the rest of my life, but I still plead not guilty. The Tour directors put me under pressure to quit the Tour, but I didn't even consider it. I had right on my side. Point one: I used Probenicide for my back. Point two: the product was not on the list of those substances banned by the UCI, and although it was on the Olympic Committee's list, that's not my fault. Someone in the laboratory made a blunder and used

the wrong list. I had been dope tested for five successive days, and yet it was only on the last day that the problem was spotted.

Then a race commissioner gaffed by making the whole affair known, in a drunken fit of temper, before I myself knew anything about it. Just imagine what that was like. For some time after that, my sponsor and I considered bringing a law suit, but for publicity reasons we decided against it. Since then, of course, fingers are constantly being pointed at me, and I think that's a pity. Anyway, I would like to argue for the chance for sportsmen to receive medical supervision. Dope controls should continue to be there to curb excesses, but a sportsman must be given the opportunity to replenish shortages in his body."

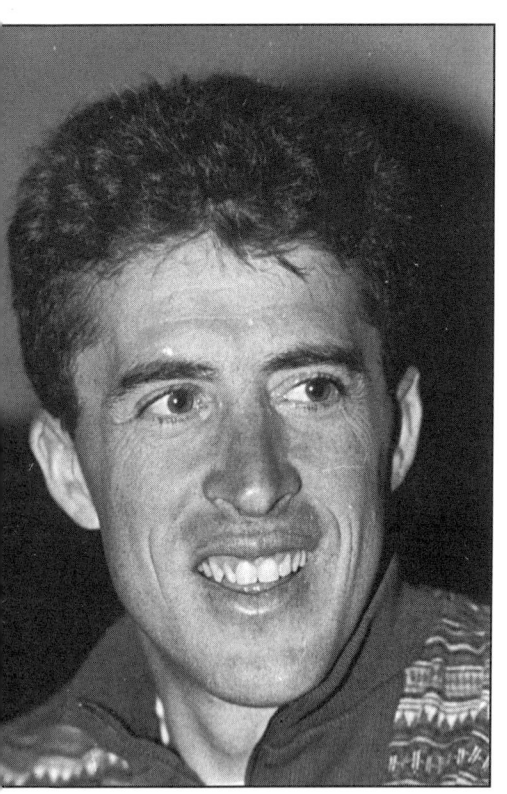

Travelling

Pedro Delgado likes travelling. He could write a book on the trips he has made. At the end of 1991, for example, he went on three long-distance journeys. With his girlfriend, Lydi, he visited Sri Lanka, the Maldive Islands and India. "A land worth visiting, but not a place you would want to live. I like strange cultures. Really I like many things: films, books, concerts. After I won the Tour in 1988, I went to see a Bruce Springsteen concert. The following day I was honoured in Segovia. A rider should not have a blinkered outlook. There is more to life than racing. I also like good food. My favourite dish is sucking pig, a speciality of the region. It is something that riders shouldn't really eat, but it's not a problem for me. I have no tendency to get fat."

Wait and See

"I have always enjoyed cycling. For how much longer I don't know. After the

Tour in 1993 I will decide if I am going to have one more year. One thing is certain, in any case, I will finish my career with Banesto. What I will then go and do, I don't yet know. When it gets as far as that, I'll quietly sit down and assess the situation. I will probably go into business. I already have quite a few shares in companies, one of which is Dinamark, a textile company. We shall see."

Dirk De Wolf

'JEROMMEKE'

Dirk De Wolf is an incredible chap. Those who saw the fantastic scenes after his victory in the 1992 Liège-Bastogne-Liège will never forget them. With a final acceleration up the climb to the finish, he finally rode Steven Rooks, Jean-François Bernard and Davide Cassani off his wheel. It turned out be the race of his life. He had spent hours gritting his teeth with grim determination, but five minutes later, there he was with his child-like good nature, calling to his wife. Dirk fell into the arms of his team manager and threw his winner's bouquet to the crowd. Ten minutes later, with a big white cap on his head and the white jersey of the current leader of the World Cup over his track suit, he was sitting totally relaxed, surrounded by a circle of journalists. "Me, knackered? Come on lads. I've only ridden 270 kilometres today, and I'm used to trips of 300 kilometres and more. I know you're going to say that I was mad for riding for so long in front in weather like this, but that's how I have to do it, it's my style. Anyway, I felt just as strong as I did in the World Championship race in Japan. And it was my kind of weather today. Wolfman likes wolf weather, cold, horrible, wet, it doesn't bother him."

Wolf

His Italian team mates at Gatorade have thought of a pet name for Dirk De Wolf. If they shout 'bandito' or 'lupo' ('wolf'), he looks round. "But they all go to a lot of trouble for me. In the evenings the soigneurs even bring me herbal tea to help me sleep. I get the impression they have put me on a bit of a pedestal. Most of my team mates went home between Tirreno-Adriatico and Milan-San Remo, and I stayed behind in my hotel, alone. Santaromita invited me to stay at his house, but he lives another 240 kilometres further away and I didn't really want to. The directeur sportif wanted the whole back-up team to stay with me, but I sent most of them home. I didn't want anyone around me. "Leave a soigneur here, and give me a pair of spare tyres," I said. "That will be enough."

Pretty

That is typical of the way Dirk De Wolf speaks. He wears his heart on his sleeve, saying what he feels inside. It is usually the first thing that comes to him and if people don't like it, that is their problem. He often plays up to it for the sake of his image, but it never offends anyone.

De Wolf is a concept. He also has his own way of racing. We can't exactly call his style 'pretty': he tugs, pulls, pushes, his tongue out of his mouth, shaking his head. "I know only too well that when I race I don't have the most graceful style and the best-looking face. I realise it looks pretty abnormal. I often watch the big races on video the day after. Well of course photographers will go looking for more interesting riders. Rooks never pulls a face, and he sits there on his bike like a statue. I can't do that."

Milkman

Dirk De Wolf the rider is a little reminiscent of 'Jerommeke', a cartoon character known by everyone in his native Belgium, who is big-hearted, strong and maybe not too bright. But he can always be relied upon to save the day. De Wolf is not a shrewd rider, but he is extremely strong. "That's inborn. My

Dirk De Wolf's finest hour: his victory in Liège-Bastogne-Liège in 1992

father was strong too. He was a milkman. He had a dairy shop in our village. From early in the morning until late at night, he lugged milk churns around. My brother never inherited that strength, but my young son Jelle seems to have it. Strength on its own, however, is not enough. You must also stay healthy. Take me, I'm as fit as a fiddle."

Diary

Dirk De Wolf knows himself very well. He has been keeping a diary since his earlier days. "I started it on the day I became a cyclist, so that means it was about sixteen years ago. I still keep them all. At some date in the future it might be nice to have a look through them. I write everything down, even my getting up routine. I usually get up at five o'clock or half past, at the same time as the mechanics. Every morning I check my pulse rate. It should generally be about 45 beats a minute, but when I'm in peak condition it drops to around 38. I also write down how I feel, what I eat and things that grab my attention. Sometimes I restrict it to a P.S. "It can't get any worse," or something like that. I would be able to tell you precisely how many times I have fallen and landed on my face. About the 1992 Tour it says that Indurain is a flying machine; a computer, and that I have nothing but admiration for my team leader Gianni Bugno. Although he had lost the Tour, he kept on battling. For me, personally, it was a hard Tour, but that doesn't bother me. In another two years - when I'm 33 - I'll pack in cycling."

Rita

Dirk De Wolf is married to Rita. When he moved from Tonton Tapis to Gatorade, she gave up her job at the cultural centre and took on the role of public relations officer for her man. "It's now 1992, and we have been married eight years. We have a son Jelle. I wouldn't be surprised if he became a cyclist too. You should see him when he goes cyclo-cross racing on his bike. Because of Jelle, Rita rings me nearly every day no matter which race I'm riding. It gives me a lift hearing them both. Not that I have a problem with homesickness or anything like that, it's just that I like to hear how things are, and if anything's the matter. At least you find out that way what's happening in the world."

Gas

Dirk De Wolf is a man who knows how to enjoy himself; a pleasure-lover. "But racing comes before everything else. That doesn't mean that I don't appreciate the good things in life.
I like playing cards, any game you care to name: whist, pinochle, anything.

I could play for hours. I also enjoy a lager or a Hoegaarden white beer.
I'm glad I became a racer. It was my uncle Herwig, a rider himself, who got me into racing. I became mad on the sport when I was about 14 because of him. At the time I was still playing football; as sweeper for SK Lombeek. I enjoyed that very much. If I hadn't become a cyclist, I would certainly have become a footballer. My brother is not so sportingly inclined. He is a clerk. He liked going to school more than I did. I followed the mechanics course at secondary school. When I left, I went to work in a factory. My job was delivering gas bottles to customers. Heavy work, but fortunately it was only in the winter that I had to really get my hands out of my pockets and do much. I did that for four years, but I was pleased I was able to make a living by racing as well. Although it wasn't always what I would have wanted."

Guidance

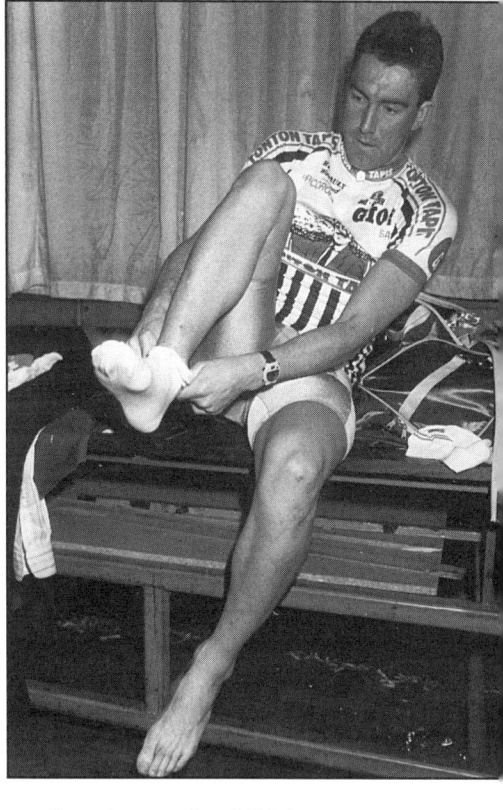

"I was a good amateur, but things didn't go well for me when I first turned professional. Riders like Criquielion knew exactly what they were supposed to do, but others often need the guidance of someone who will give them orders and make sure they are carried out. I'm that sort of rider, and Roger De Vlaeminck was the ideal man for giving me guidance. I'm only sorry that I didn't come across him four years earlier. When I met him in 1988 he said: "Dirk, listen to what I'm going to tell you. You're a good domestique, you work hard for Criquielion; but if you carry on the way you are now, you'll never earn very much money. You turned professional with Boule d'Or in 1983. You've won a stage in Paris-Nice. You moved on to Kwantum, then to Hitachi. What has all of that brought you? You've won a stage in the Four Days at Dunkirk, plus a few kermesses. If you come and train with me for a couple of months, I'll get you up to a higher standard." He opened my eyes for me and turned me into a good rider. In 1989 I came second in Paris-Roubaix, eighth in the Tour of Flanders, and I won four other races. In 1990 I was second in the World Championship Road Race in Japan, I won the Grape Race at Overijse and three kermesses. In 1991 I won a stage in Tirreno, I was third in the Amstel Gold Race, I won the Tour of the Appenines, came tenth in Liège-Bastogne-Liège, eleventh in the Tour of Flanders, tenth in the Championship of Zurich and tenth in the World Championship at Stuttgart. I was now on the right track."

Brown Sugar

From that time Dirk De Wolf has developed certain habits. In 1991, when Roger De Vlaeminck was his directeur sportif at Tonton Tapis, every Friday before a big race, he went on his own to De Vlaeminck's home in Kaprijke. They trained together:

More action from Liège-Bastogne-Liège in 1992

Roger in the car and Dirk behind him on the bike. Afterwards De Wolf went to eat: fish and rice and brown sugar.

"At that time, on the days leading up to a big race, I followed a Scandinavian diet. I rode myself into the ground on a diet of pasta without sugar, and then the body recovers. Then, for the final two days, you suddenly have to start taking in as much sugar as you can, to give you extra energy. I love brown sugar and used to be a real glutton, but I have taught myself to resist it. I'm heavily-built enough as it is and in the winter I effortlessly put on another six kilos. In my peak condition I weigh around 78 kilos, while Ballerini weighs no less than 85 kilos. You know how it is: a reception here, a dinner there. I'm not too keen on all that. At first it was nice, but after a while it gets pretty tedious. I'd rather go to a football match. The problem nowadays is that everyone knows me. If there are 200 people there, 160 of them call out to you. Instead of having two beers, they'd have you drinking twenty."

Dream

De Wolf took on board Roger De Vlaeminck's advice. He trained like a madman, and looked after himself like never before. The results started to show it was worth it. He was on excellent form in nearly all the classics, and at the start of the 1990 season he signed a contract with the Dutch videotape giant, PDM, for a fat salary. Dirk's big finishes included a second place in the World Championship in Japan, behind his training colleague Rudy Dhaenens. For Dhaenens, that victory was the beginning of the end, for De Wolf it was the start of a great run.

"Rudy had a lot of bad luck after that. If he was given the chance to ride the finishing straight again, he might not want to win, so that he would be relieved of the burden of wearing the jersey. I would want it, though, even if I knew that during the following year I would be ruled out for twelve months. You may certainly ride badly in the rainbow jersey, but you can never feel bad wearing it. Not only does it bring a lot of money your way, it is the irrefutable proof that on one particular day you were the best rider in the world. And that's the case with Dhaenens. It is a feather he has been able to stick in his cap once and for always. I don't envy him the rainbow jersey either. I have never dreamed of winning it, I have not had sleepless nights thinking about how close I came."

Popularity

With the money he received from Tonton Tapis, Dirk De Wolf was able to buy himself out of his PDM contract, and move to Roger De Vlaeminck's team. At the end of 1991 he moved on to Gianni Bugno's Gatorade team. According to rumours, De Wolf was signed more for his amiability and being a recognisable figure than for his performances. "If they pay popularity so well, then that's fine by me. The fact is that I had to ride hard for my money in 1992. I have never ridden so many races. By the final day of the Tour de France, I had already ridden 115 races. Some of the Italians don't even reach that figure by the end of the season. I was told it was going to be tough. "What shall I do about it?" I asked my wife. "Don't think any further than April," she said. She would have walked out on me if I had turned down that contract. I only really signed it for the money; I wanted to earn some big bucks. Who doesn't! Don't think that Johan Bruyneel rides for ONCE just for the lightweight bike and the nice yellow team jersey."

Extra Training

Dirk De Wolf rode differently in 1992 than what he was used to. His directeur sportif Claudio Corti and manager Luigi Stanga imposed strict curbs on him. He wanted to do some extra training around the time of the classics, for example, but was not allowed to. "I train not only for my condition, but also for my self-confidence. When I turn up at the start of a big race, I want to know in myself that I have done everything I needed to, and that I am ready for it. I don't like it when there are things I can blame afterwards. I also like to repeat proven good practices. When I came second in the World Championship in Japan, I had trained over 250 kilometres three days earlier. The following season I did exactly the same thing.

The Gatorade management protested, however, and as they are the bosses, I have to listen. The team doctor came to me some time before Milan-San Remo and said: "Lupo, wouldn't you be better off staying at home? Let me just go through your programme again for you." And so he did: Milan-San Remo, De Panne, the Tour of Flanders, Ghent-Wevelgem, Wasmuel, Paris-Roubaix, the Flèche Wallonne, the Scheldt G.P., the Amstel Gold Race, the Tour DuPont in America, the Giro, the Tour of Switzerland, the Tour de France. We would like it if you didn't use up all your energy just yet."

Awake

"I soon found out that with Bugno around, it not easy for you to abandon. The team wasn't big enough to work through a double programme. For Tirreno-Adriatico they had to sign up Pellicioli to bring the team up to full strength for the start. With Roger De Vlaeminck I could occasionally miss out the odd race, but I can't now. I only have time to open my suitcase, empty everything out, then stuff it all back in and be on my way again.

It took some getting used to not having to train so much. I had a sort of guilt feeling, especially since in the past the heavy training had always made me feel good. I now went at it a lot more easily, with the result that I did have more reserves of energy, and that certainly contributed to my victory in Liège-Bastogne-Liège. The year before, they had been used up by the time the classics came round. Roger De Vlaeminck always said that I should not wake up until the middle of March. So, he was right in that sense too."

Wine

One or two things changed for De Wolf when he joined Gatorade. "Now I drink wine with our meals. In the past, that wasn't allowed. I still get up very early - half-past five - at the same time as the mechanics and physios. It's

quiet at the breakfast table at that time, and I have a chat with the men. I was used to going to bed early, and I have continued to do so. My Italian teammates like to watch the television until the final programme has finished. It doesn't disturb me, though. As long as a light is on, I sleep well. At least, as long as it doesn't go on until too late.
I'm happy in the team. The red carpet is laid out everywhere for Bugno, and we all profit from it. I can choose from 22 pairs of shorts. With Lotto you don't have that many after five years. For each special race, I have a special bike. For Paris-Roubaix, I even got a disc wheel with a hydraulic fork.
We always stay in the best hotels. Gianni sets his demands: he doesn't like waiting. Everything is checked too, there are no risks taken. Gatorade is a sports drink, and if a sports drink were to be associated with drugs, it would be catastrophic."

Bugno

Dirk De Wolf now knows Gianni Bugno very well. "He's a smashing chap. He puts an unbelievable amount of his time and energy into cycling. I might talk about something like the carnival season, but Gianni only ever talks about racing. Really he is too nice a man to be a team leader. He doesn't swear, he just lets everyone get on with it.
Apart from that, Bugno is like a computer: he does everything according to schedules. And as far as I'm concerned, that's just fine. I'm happy that I'm still riding for him in 1993."

GILBERT DUCLOS-LASSALLE

ETERNAL YOUTH

In 1993 Duclos-Lassalle won Paris-Roubaix for the second year in succession. He punctured on the first cobbled section, but virtually his whole team waited for him to bring him back to the pack and launch him on a break. "May I put my victory into hunting terms," he said at the finish. "I had brought plenty of cartridges with me, but when I fell I lost them all. Thanks to my team-mates' help, I found one of them again, and in the final sprint against Franco Ballerini I loaded it into my rifle. It was essential that I hit the target. It was all or nothing. I freely admit that Ballerini was the best man in the race and he would have won deservedly had there been no sprint. However, there was, and it was me who was best. I know all about track sprinting. Over the kilometres leading up to the finale, I was dead on my bike, but if there's one thing an old fox like me knows how to do it's to grit your teeth and hang on.

These victories for Duclos-Lassalle on the cobbles of hell are a tribute to hard work and undaunted attacking, two qualities which have made cycling such a great sport. You do not find them so often nowadays. It is also a credit to Gilbert's uncompromising character. He was a winner at 38 with the first grey hairs starting to adorn his temples, but he hammered on as though he was 20. "A glowing example to all racers," was the general view afterwards.

Wife

Outside the showers at the velodrome in Roubaix, we bump into Mrs Duclos-Lassalle, twenty minutes after that triumph. The dope control is just out of the way, and in the showers Gilbert is washing the dust, sweat and exhaustion from his battered body. The warm water is wonderful. "Madame," we ask, "might you be the secret of his eternal youth?" She laughs. "Maybe I am," she says, sharply. "But I don't think you need to look for anything too mysterious in it. I have been married to Gilbert for sixteen years now and he enjoys racing just as much as he ever did. No matter what the weather, he is on his bike at half-past eight in a morning. That keeps him young. At least that's what he says. Oh dear, now I'm starting to well up, yet I'm not normally a sentimental type. I know how much Paris-Roubaix means to Gilbert, though. He has always said he could win this race. That started in 1980 when he finished second to Francesco Moser. After each time he had ridden well he would say: next year I'm coming back here to win."

Head

Gilbert Duclos-Lassalle looks a little like Eddy Merckx: he does not, of course, have an honours list like his Belgian predecessor, but he does have the black hair, the same robust build, the same weight and the same predisposition for Paris-Roubaix. One pertinent fact, however, is that Duclos-Lassalle has had a longer career. The 'Cannibal' retired at the age of 32, while in 1993 Duclos is starting out on his 17th season. In August he will be 39, but retirement is the last thing on his mind. "He is now set up for another ten years," grinned Bernard Hinault, as he watched his contemporary hold a cobble aloft in Roubaix as a symbol of his triumph. "Ten is a little too much," was Duclos' reaction to Hinault's statement. "But another two or three seasons looks a good bet. Please don't put down in the book that I want to break Zoetemelk or Poulidor's longevity records, that my ultimate aim is to do so, because that's certainly not my intention. I will probably be 42 when I pack it in, but then what do I do? I'm quite simply mad on biking. Riding my bike is the thing I most enjoy doing in the world. Don't get me wrong, I have other hobbies. I like to go hunting for pheasants and snipe, and I like horse riding. I'm also involved in local politics and I own a motorbike. But it is bike racing that gives me the greatest pleasure. And that being the case, age doesn't come into it. If it feels right in my head, my legs do what I want. I descend better than a twenty-year old, because I have more courage."

Ambition

Gilbert Duclos-Lassalle may have realised his greatest dream when he won Paris-Roubaix in 1992 and repeated it this year, but the ambition of winning it over again will stay with him until the day he retires. At least that is what he says.

"It's not out of the question. And I don't only intend to win Paris-Roubaix. I'll be going all out for the Tour of Flanders. I once read that Bernard Hinault has said that cobbles are 'pig-shit' and they are unfair. Well I don't think so. He is right when he says that when you start riding them you must feel as though you are going to win. If you don't, you soon feel every single one of them. "Each stone gives you a backlash," says Hinault. "You bounce over them until you are battered to death. Then you've had it."

It's right that you need to have the right attitude. I do. On the cobbles my thoughts are always on winning. It's the magic of the cobbles that does it for me. I suppose Eddy Merckx has something to do with that. When I was young I was an Eddy Merckx fan. My first racing bikes were always in the colours of Faema or Molteni. I even raced against Eddy. At the time his career was drawing to a close, but when he came riding up I moved to one side. Marvellous rider.

My first Paris-Roubaix in 1979 was like a dream. I shared a room with Jean-Pierre Danguillaume the night before. "If you reach the velodrome and it's still open, you've ridden a good race," he told me. I set off and I buckled down to the job and, as it turned out, the velodrome wasn't shut. When I went for a shower I said to Danguillaume: "The little one's here." Paris-Roubaix is what cycling is all about."

Hervé

How does someone like Gilbert Duclos-Lassalle start racing in the first place? He comes from an ordinary family. His father farmed a little land but had another job at the same time, while his mother was a housewife. He has three brothers and one sister.

"I was the youngest of the family. My oldest brother played rugby, one of the others rode bikes and that's how I got started. I was 16 at the time and I became a good amateur: I won the Tours of Austria and Algeria, and they eventually helped me get a contract with Peugeot. My parents always let me decide what I wanted for myself and never put any pressure on me. I started racing because I tried it and found I enjoyed it.

I now have two children of my own. My daughter Margalique likes horse riding and my son Hervé races his bike. At first he played football, but even then I had the impression that he would one day want to become a cyclist. He has the same approach to it as me, first a bit of football and running, then racing. I'm pleased he does it, but I certainly never pushed him in that direction. Of all people, I should know that cycling needs to be a passion. You need to really want to do it or you will never get anywhere. He does have that passion, though. Sometimes we train together. He can always come with me on the last 25 kilometres of my training rides. He really beams with pride when he does. He often watches the video of my victory in Paris-Roubaix in 1992 and you can see his eyes light up. Up to now his results have not been bad. In 1992 he rode three races: he won two of them and came second in the other."

Lucky Stars

Gilbert Duclos-Lassalle has been a professional cyclist for 17 years now. So he has a wealth of experience which he wants to pass on. His younger teammates at Gan say that he is the ideal teacher.

"Do you know what racing is all about? I'll explain it to you. Above all else you need to be in good health; I am. You are either born with it or you aren't. So I have my parents and my lucky stars to thank for that. The rest of it is up to you. Young riders should remember the next piece of advice. Find yourself a permanent trainer and a physio who will massage you every day. I have always had them around. They are worth their weight in gold and the reason why I have been able to keep going for so long. My body is given an overhaul almost every day.

Racing means hard training. I remember Jacques Anquetil. I know he liked a party, but he trained harder than anyone else. That's why he won as much as he did. I also have a great deal of admiration for Greg LeMond. We are companions in misfortune, both of us having been involved in hunting accidents. We both found it hard to get the effects of it out of our bodies, but in both our cases we did it. I will say, however, that in the last couple of years, I don't think Greg has been the best example of how it should be done on the sporting front. He had to do too much travelling and hasn't always had the time to put in the hard training necessary, and that has surfaced as poorer performances over the last couple of seasons. Greg knows that himself only too well. The fact that he has made a conscious decision to stay in Europe during 1993 to concentrate totally on his profession says it all. A LeMond who is operating at one hundred per cent of his capacity is capable of anything. I can see him winning big races again."

Mistakes

There is more Duclos would like to say. "My advice to youngsters is this: don't stay at home when it rains. I have been a professional for a long time now, but I never do. The day the rain makes me stop at home is the day I retire. Cycling should never be a chore. You might catch the occasional cold, but you become harder for it. You also have to know how to handle the media. They say that I'm the friendliest and most popular rider, and God knows what else. I play on it a little by always being prepared to give interviews. All you have to do then is perform well and you've got all the angles covered.

I like working with young riders. I don't tell them before a race that they have to do this or they must do that. No, I wait until they make mistakes and then I correct them. Otherwise they will have forgotten by the next day."

Hunting Accident

Gilbert Duclos-Lassalle may have assembled quite an honours list up to the start of 1993, nevertheless, he has been a domestique for various riders throughout his career. First of all it was with Thevenet, then with Danguillaume, later with Kuiper and for the last few years with LeMond. Along the way, however, he has had a bite of the cake himself. In 1980 he won Paris-Nice, in 1983 the Tour of the Midi-Pyrenees, in 1986 the Tour of Sweden and the Tour de l'Oise. In 1987 he was the victor in the G.P. de Plouay. In 1985 and 1987 he finished second in Bordeaux-Paris, the first time behind Francesco Moser and the second time behind Hennie Kuiper. In 1989 he won the Route du Sud and in 1991 the Midi Libre.

"My career has been steady in the main. Although there have not been many wins that really stand out, I have always performed to a high level. My biggest regret was that terrible hunting accident I had at the end of 1983. It was a stupid business. It happened during a hunting party. The butt of the rifle was on the ground and I was holding it upright when a shot went off. My hand was shattered. I thought that was it and that it would have to be amputated, but in Bordeaux they were able to make sure it was saved by inserting six screws and a plate. You can still see the effects: my hand is still smaller and thicker. There are still 19 pieces of shot buried inside it. You can feel them and you can even see them. The rehabilitation took a long time and it was a long struggle. I was only able to rejoin the peloton in July 1984, and that whole year was a very difficult one for me. 1985 was hard too, but that was when I finally overcame the accident completely. I'm convinced that the anaesthetic I was given at the operation held

Gilbert Duclos-Lassalle has always been eager to win Paris-Roubaix.

back the recovery. As long as I could feel the effects in my body, there was nothing I could do."

Politics

Gilbert Duclos-Lassalle lives in Duros, a small village with a population of 1,200, in the foothills of the Pyrenees, 40 kilometres from Pau. He is a well-liked figure locally. He even has political aspirations. Two weeks before his victory in Paris-Roubaix Gilbert stood in the local elections.

"I am a member of the 'Hunting, Fishing & Nature' party. When the elections were announced they came and asked me if I wanted to be put on the list of candidates and I thought, 'Why not?' I finished in 17th place and I was very happy with that. There was steady voting for me, and that contributed to ten of my fellow party members being elected. I was not elected, but that was never the intention. All I really wanted to do was to underline my love of nature, I will defend it as resolutely as I do cycling. I cannot live without it. I am an ardent hunter for example. I shoot snipes and pheasant and it gives me a great deal of pleasure."

Hotel

Although retirement is still far from his mind at the start of the 1993 season, part of Duclos-Lassalle's future has already been mapped out. "I would like to open an hotel in Le Bearne. I have a business in mind, but that is for later. That is another piece of advice to a young rider: concentrate entirely on your racing. If you get involved in other things, it will start to go wrong. I remember my one-time team-mate at Peugeot, Jacques Esclassin, who in his day was one of the fastest sprinters around. He bought a large cycle concern. As a direct result of it, the last Tour de France he rode was a total fiasco. I remember how he was when we arrived back in our hotel rooms at the end of a stage. Instead of taking a shower, having a massage and being properly taken care of, the first thing he did was grab the telephone to place orders and arrange meetings, and then he would ring his wife because certain things needed to be sorted out. I would never want it to get like that. I certainly want to ride a reduced programme for my final season, to choose certain races I want to ride, while at the same time keeping myself in the limelight."

LAURENT FIGNON

SHOOTING GALLERY

When cyclists become stars they all have different ways of handling their new status and lifestyles. Some riders remain friendly, put the whole fuss going on around them into perspective and look on the glory as something of a privilege. The best example of that is Greg LeMond. Others become moody and arrogant and act as though the world revolves around them.
Laurent Fignon, still deservedly winning stages in the Tour in 1992, has that kind of bad reputation. If something was not to 'Mister Citroen's' liking, he would hit out, push, grumble and swear. "He was always like that," people who live near where he was brought up will tell you. "When he was 16 and went racing, he would sit in the car until one of his companions had sorted out his entry. He was above everyone and everything." "Having a bad character is better than having no character," replies Fignon curtly. He says it is merely a form of self defence. "You have to get rid of stress right away or it gets the better of you. I don't like commotion around me. I have never forgiven the press in France since they wrote me off after my knee operation in 1985. I felt as though I was the target at a shooting gallery. But I was determined to fire back. I didn't get an ounce of sympathy or support from them, yet all of a sudden I was expected to be nice to them. Thanks, but no thanks."

Fingers
There was suddenly a spectacular transformation in the cold, short-tempered, measured Laurent Fignon in 1992. Overnight there was a complete change around in his attitude. It suddenly became sufficient to ask him in the morning if it would be alright to talk to him that night. "He has had his fingers rapped," said colleagues from the French press. "His sponsor has taken him in hand." Fignon's role in the 1990 Tour had been negligible, partly thanks to a variety of injuries. When he eventually abandoned he was cornered by hundreds of photographers, but he turned his back on them all. The ensuing publicity was far from positive, making the sponsor's intervention seem quite warranted. In any event, as a result of it Fignon has become a little more accessible and approachable.

Hamstring

Laurent Fignon's cycling career is closely bound up with his performances in the Tour de France. "I was 21 when I rode my first Tour and 22 when I won it for the first time. Hinault was having trouble with his knee and was recovering in Brittany. My sole function was to try to keep Renault's name among the forefront of the action during the Tour. Pascal Simon played a hero's role that year, but when I took the yellow jersey on the Alpe d'Huez, they might as well have given me a pair of wings, and I was able to win the time trial in Dijon. That first Tour victory is still my most satisfying because it was my first. The following year I won again and that was pleasing too, not least because that time Hinault was riding it. Soon after that I started to struggle with a hamstring injury. In May 1985 they operated on my left leg, and later on my right. They cleaned up the muscle but never repaired it, as was always claimed. When I was finally able to sit on my bike again after 260 days, I broke my collar-bone on the track at Madrid. I had no option but to start all over again. The most difficult aspect of my rehabilitation was that it would not have been good enough for me to become just another rider, I was expected to be the champion of old again. My first practice ride was an out-and-out disaster. I was already tired out after 25 kilometres and was completely dead after 30. But I had sufficient motivation to fight my way back. It took me four years to get back to the same level I had been before, but in the end I managed it. And really, that has been my biggest victory of all."

Kick in the Teeth

Fignon came back because he has a strong character. His victory in the Flèche Wallonne in 1986 was the first indication that he was heading in the right direction. From 1988 onwards, the pedals were once again turning smoothly and he won several major races. For two years in succession, 1988 and 1989, he won Milan-San Remo. In 1988 he came third in Paris-Roubaix, a race he detested, but one he wanted to win at all costs. In 1989 he won the Tour of Italy ahead of Flavio Giupponi. Fignon then wanted to repeat the feat in the Tour de France. He seemed safe in the yellow jersey, but in the final time trial on the Champs Elysées he was beaten by such a wide margin by LeMond that he finally lost the Tour by 8 seconds. A fantastic moment for the American, but the ultimate kick in the teeth for Fignon.

"I never look back. The past is only good for teaching you lessons, that is all. I learned from that defeat that you should have no scruples about finishing off your opponents if you feel strong enough. I should have attacked during the final mountain stage in the Tour that year. I didn't because I wanted to save some energy for the time trial. I lost that Tour because I rode a bad tour overall, with too many off-days. I did nothing in the Alps. It was thanks to two brilliant stages in the Pyrenees that I led the race. In actual fact I don't regard that time trial as a failure, I finished it with an average speed of 53 kph. I have never ridden so fast. I have never dug so deeply into my reserves as I did that day."

Reading

Afterwards Fignon was to regularly repeat that his concentration during that infamous Tour was not at its peak. "I had won the Giro already that season and that put me under pressure. Normally I'm a real bookworm, but I remember that during that Tour I didn't read a single book. I kept on reading the same pages all the time. The writing was on the wall for me. I still say that LeMond won because of his spaghetti handle bar. Let me stress that I have nothing against progress, I'm aware that if we ban research we will end up getting absolutely nowhere. What I do think, however, is that things should be done the way they are laid down in the UCI regulations, and that was not the case.

I think it's hardly surprising that defeat left me totally disillusioned. It took all my inner reserves of strength to motivate myself and put in the hard training. I wanted to ride a good World Championship in Chambéry. I really wanted to win, but it was LeMond's day once again... I would have loved to have won the world title, but you need to be more of a gambler or a chess

player than a cyclist to do it.
The dramatic ending to the 1989 Tour, however, is not my worst cycling memory. It was purely a missed chance. The thing that still really sticks in my throat after several years, is the positive dope test I had after the G.P. of Wallonia, a few years ago. I still maintain that I was stabbed in the back. At the time all I wanted to do was throw away my bike. My urine sample took five days to get from Sombreffe to Liège. Imagine it, I could walk that distance in one day!"

Vet

Laurent Fignon is more clever and intelligent than most of his rivals. When he says something, it sounds as though it has been considered. He also has a few unusual hobbies. "In the winter I do some deep-sea diving. But what I like most is wandering around flea markets rummaging for old books. Anything that looks interesting, I buy. At home I have a very old collection of Flemish Jules Verne stories. I love reading. You know, I was a good student at one

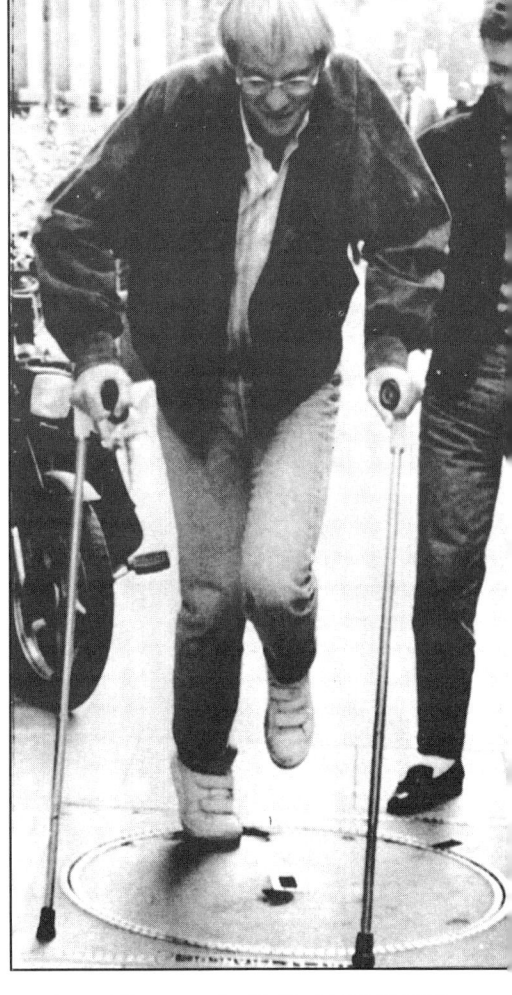

Laurent Fignon was troubled by a knee injury for several years.

time. When I was a little boy I wanted to be a vet, but nothing ever came of that. One of my favourite hobbies, however, stems from that: I stuff animals. After my degree course I went to study science and physics at the University of Saint-Denis, but within six months the dream was over. I wasn't interested in it enough, and by then I was already far too busy racing.
My mother was a housewife, pure and simple. She was no great cycling supporter, but my father was. He was a team leader at a machine tool factory, and when he was made redundant he immediately applied for early retirement. My brother, Didier, was made to study, just like me.
I can assure you that I had to fight to make cycling my career. As an amateur

97

I was nothing outstanding. I was left out of the national team more often than I was selected for it. During that time I rode the Peace Race and finished 31st, 40 minutes behind the winner Zagretdinov. Later on, I started in the open Tour of Corsica, and that's where it all took off. As an amateur I really gave the professionals a torrid time. I won a stage and that was enough to persuade Cyrille Guimard to offer me a contract. For the next ten years we formed a formidable team. I reckon, however, that we stayed together for three years too long. We should have gone our own ways earlier."

Business

In 1992 Laurent Fignon moved to Gatorade, the team which included world champion Gianni Bugno. By doing so, he finally closed the door on Cyrille Guimard. Strange and surprising, because for ten years Fignon and his directeur sportif were as thick as thieves.

"1991 was the worse season I've ever had. Not as far as results were concerned, but for there being a bad atmosphere. Guimard has seen relationships with many good riders fizzle out. He clashes with all riders who have strong personalities: Hinault, Madiot and me, it went wrong in the end for all of us.
We had the same business interests and they contributed to the split too. In reality we were our own employers. The main business concern was a mail order company for triathletes that we ran together. It didn't do badly, either. I think I am quite creative, and when I stop cycling I might go into business. But, for as long as I'm winning races, I'll carry on racing. Once that stops, then that's that. I would never carry on racing if it was only to help someone

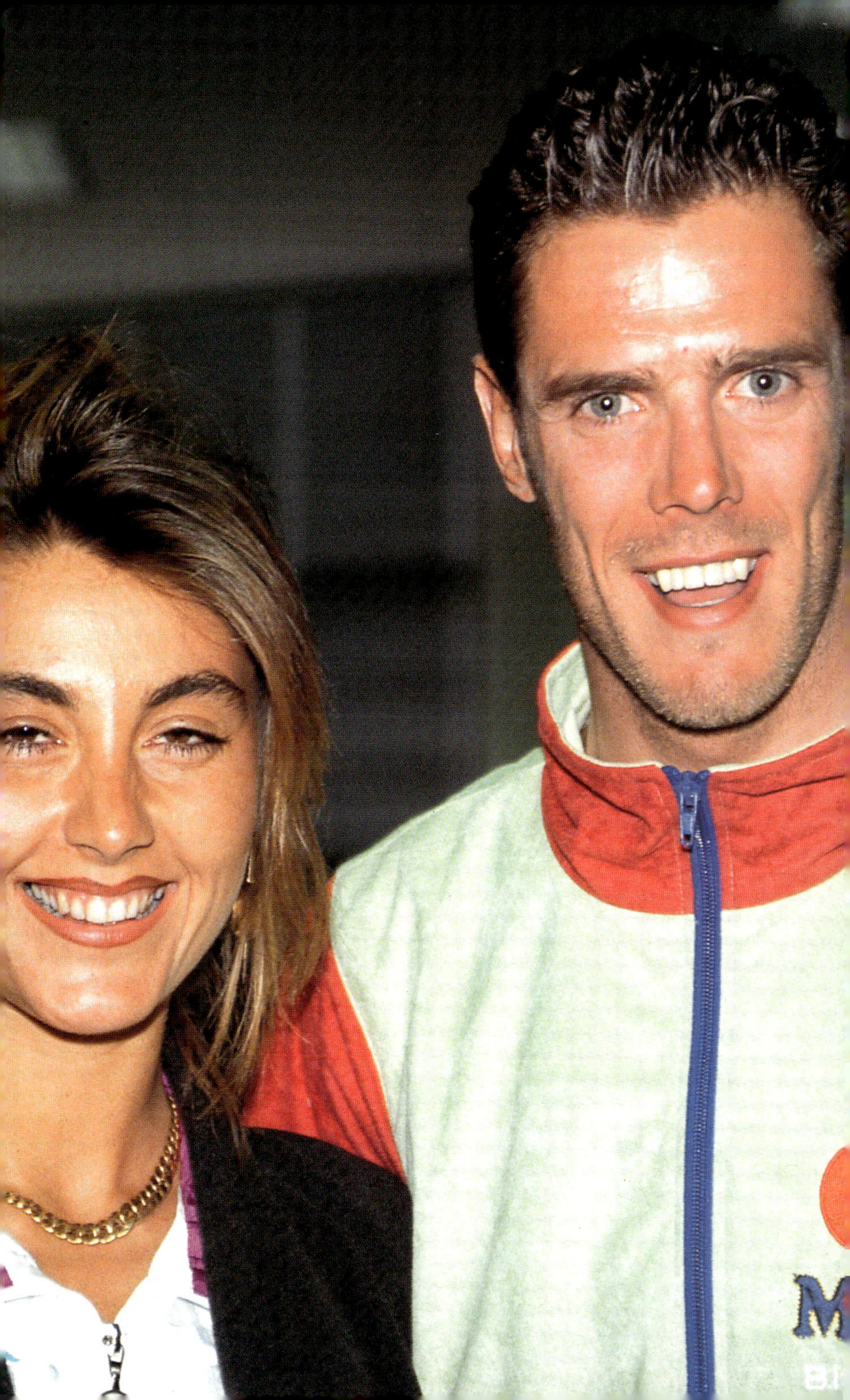
M

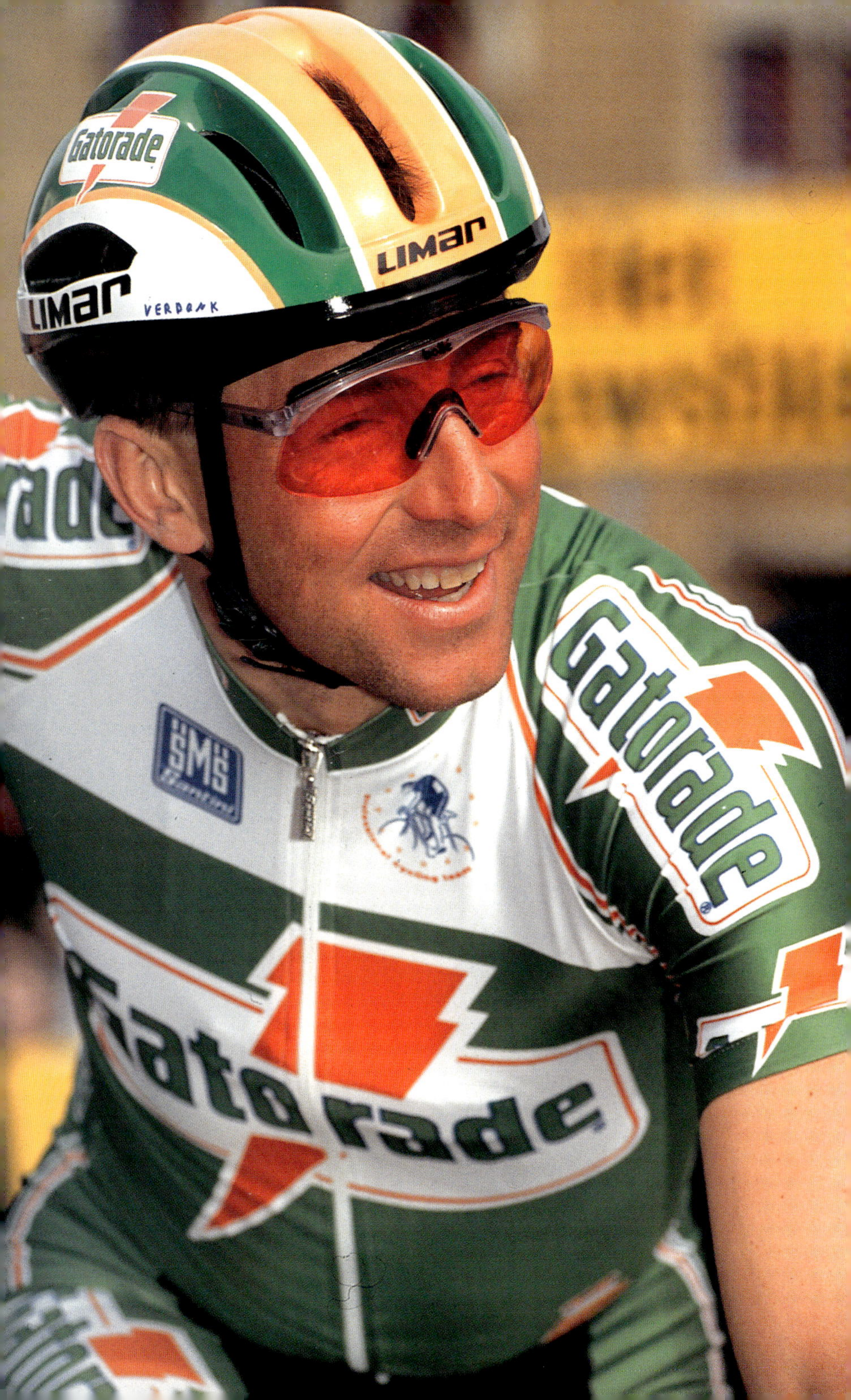
Gatorade
LIMAR
LIMAR
VERDONK
Gatorade
Gatorade

else towards victory. I'm not saying I'm so rotten that I wouldn't help out a team-mate, but just that I prefer winning myself.
Guimard and I also set up France Competition, a company which allowed us to put together our own cycling team. We negotiated contracts with riders ourselves, and then other companies could engage our services. We looked for these sponsors ourselves. My involvement was so great that I even designed the jerseys. Eventually, however, one or two things started to go wrong on the business side, and I accept 50% of the responsibility for it. It makes no difference who finally pushed it over the edge. I'm not blameless, but neither is Guimard. It did, however, make it impossible for us to carry on working together. I want to be happy in the team I'm riding for, but that was no longer the case. In the Tour de France, for example, Luc Leblanc was given priority over me and that was a bad sign for my own Tour.
I also enjoyed many good times with Guimard, however. During our Renault days I earned a great deal of money thanks to him. And I never had a reason to leave, either. What I'd had enough of most last year was the great responsibility I was saddled with. I had ridden for Guimard for ten years, and in all that time it was me who had to clear up everyone else's mess for them. I signed the jerseys, I sought sponsors. If the team failed on the sporting side it was my fault too. Well, I didn't want any more of that."

No Super Domestique
With his transfer to Gatorade, Fignon became a team-mate of the world champion Gianni Bugno. "The Italians will want him to ride for Bugno," was people's immediate reaction, but that is not how Fignon saw it.
"As I still feel I have every chance of winning races myself, I will be going all out for myself. I made that clear to my sponsor immediately. I'm happy to be a team-mate of Gianni, but I'm not going to be some sort of super domestique. When we are racing together and his chances of winning look better than mine, I will have no hesitation in helping him unconditionally. It used to be the same when I rode with Mottet.
Gianni and I have never trodden on each other's toes. Anyway, after Milan-San Remo our paths didn't cross again for quite some time. Gianni rode the Ardennes classics while I rode Paris-Roubaix and the Tour of Flanders. I also rode the Giro but it all went horribly wrong. All of my preparations were geared for a tour to be ridden in nice weather, but there was a lot of rain and that ruined any chance I had.
For the Tour de France we were once again riding together. I didn't sacrifice my chances for him from day one. Suppose he had fallen, what would have

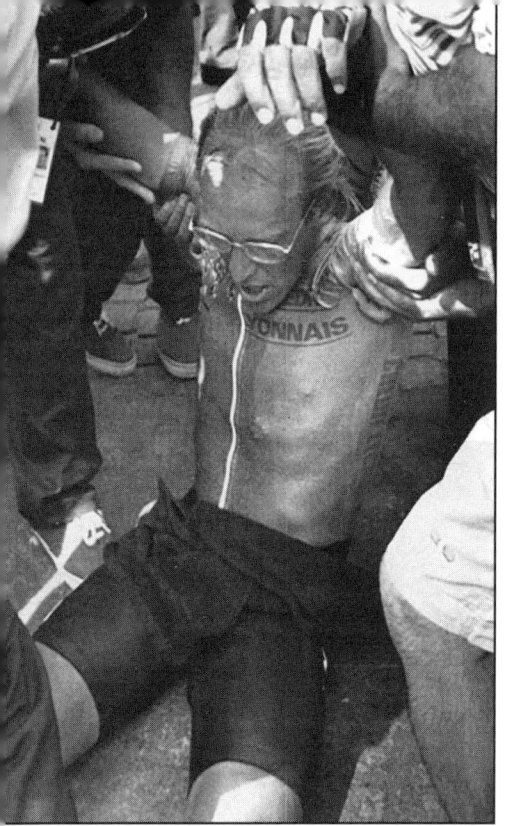

The exhausted Laurent Fignon is not yet aware that he has just lost the 1989 Tour to Greg LeMond.

happened then? Responsibility was shared 50-50. We would then see how it went as the race progressed, and it was clear that Bugno was better. I won a stage and I felt really great about that. It was also good to be given such undivided, enthusiastic encouragement. It was like years ago.

I'm aware that the sponsor is mostly interested in my head. I have an energetic head, it would appear. Right, all the better for me. I'm happy with that because it proves that the company know what they are doing, that they understand how important publicity is. By signing me, they got two birds with one stone: I can win and I'm a media figure. I could have also gone to Peter Post's team. He showed an interest in me and I let him know what my financial requirements were, but it seems they were too great. Then Gatorade came in with an offer which was perfect to help me rediscover my zest for the sport. I was happy because I didn't want to retire. I didn't join them for the money, as financially my family no longer has anything to worry about. I am married to Nathalie and we have two children: a little boy Jeremy and a girl Thiphane. We live in Paris and we are happy. I race because that's what I still enjoy doing. I have always raced for pleasure."

Whining

Fignon keeps on reiterating his love for the sport of cycling. "I was almost done with it at the end of 1991. There was obviously no place for me in France any more. There was no money available for the sport. What a pity that is. You are always hearing how it is the Tour which is swallowing up all the sponsors' money, that the Tour is responsible for all the problems. I think that's a load of rubbish. They ought to be happy that there is a Tour de France, otherwise there would no longer be anything left of the sport in

France. So they have no grounds to moan. We have got to be honest. What other organisation gets so much television coverage? Paris-Roubaix perhaps? If so, it is no coincidence, as that event is organised by the same people, so it's only to be expected. Organisers of other events should make sure that their events are at an equally high standard. Television will respond accordingly. Madame Leulliot has been complaining for years that she cannot find any money for Paris-Nice. Well that doesn't surprise me. She runs it in an unbelievably amateurish way.

I certainly don't feel obliged to play my part in helping in the rebirth of French cycling in the future. I definitely don't want to become a directeur sportif, I would be no good at it. Anyway, I have other plans which are set out in my contract with Gatorade. Above all it allows me to definitely carry on racing until the end of the 1993 season, and then I can stay on as a PR man for the company. I have another year to get used to the work, then after that I have to stand on my own two feet. I would have to have been an idiot not to take up the offer."

Suspense

Laurent Fignon has very few real friends in the peloton. Pascal Jules was a bosom friend but, tragically, he was killed in an accident. At the moment the rider he gets on most with is Maurizio Fondriest. "I once stayed at his house, and he has been to mine. We are on the same wavelength."

Organisers and race officials are not always particularly pleased to see Fignon. In recent years he has had some very strong things to say about the Tour organisation and they have not taken very kindly to it. Fignon accuses Jean-Marie Leblanc and his followers of being primarily concerned with manufacturing sensational situations.

"If they were to let me draw up the stage schedule, the sport would be onto a winner straightaway. I would immediately get rid of all stages with five cols. According to Tour director Jean-Marie Leblanc, it makes no difference. I think that it makes a great difference, though. Have the peloton going more slowly over the first two cols, the riders have to get over them somehow and that uses up energy. Leblanc has gone for maximum excitement. A rider must never take too big a lead, because that might ruin the tension. Come on, people want shows of strength, top performances and dramas. But of course, our opinion doesn't count, never. Do you remember those helmets? All of a sudden we had to wear the stupid things. No one asked us what we thought then, either."

MAURIZIO FONDRIEST

APPLE PICKER

Some people think Maurizio Fondriest is too nice, and others feel he acts too benevolently towards his opponents. Walter Planckaert, his Belgian assistant boss in 1991 and 1992 once said on that subject: "If Maurizio rode someone off his wheel and the wind was blowing straight into his face, he would wait for him. He would never consciously make anyone suffer. I'm afraid that's the sort of mentality that would be more suited to women's racing. He is going to have to change his attitude or he will never do anything. We discussed it between ourselves at the time. I hope he took the hint."

Maurizio Fondriest did indeed learn the lesson. At the end of the 1992 season, he was forced to leave the Panasonic team of Peter Post and Walter Planckaert, much against his wishes. The reason for that was that Post's budget with his new sponsor was 40% lower than for the previous season and it was felt that Fondriest was too expensive to keep. But on joining the young Italian Lampre team, Fondriest seems to have rediscovered his motivation. He had taken on board many of the lessons he had learned, and it resulted in his marvellous victory in Milan-San Remo. On the day his daughter Maria-Vittoria was born, he shot up the Poggio like a rocket. Nobody was able to get back up to him. The first person he telephoned from the maternity hospital was Walter Planckaert. "I'm ringing to thank you for what you've done for me," said Fondriest. "I've become a real cyclist thanks to you."

The brilliant victory in Milan-San Remo had been signalled by an equally impressive win in Tirreno-Adriatico just before, in which he also claimed two stage victories. But these triumphs did not satisfy his hunger. He went on to win the Flèche Wallonne, finish third in Liège-Bastogne-Liège, fourth in the Amstel Gold Race and eighth in the Tour of Flanders. Not surprisingly all these great performances put him at the head of the world cup standings on the completion of the spring classics.

Crown

Talking of a metamorphosis. Up to the end of 1992 Maurizio Fondriest was mockingly known as the 'King without a Crown.' He had won the World Championship in Ronse in 1988, but he had never been able to follow that up with performances to confirm his new standing. When he won the World Cup series in 1991 without having won one of its races, they even changed the points distribution for the following season. "The overall winner must have won at least one of the World Cup races himself," declared the man behind it, Hein Verbruggen. That statement didn't give Maurizio Fondriest the credit he deserved because, whatever else, he was the most consistent rider throughout the season. Only the crowning glory was missing and he was only too aware of that. "I'm like a king without a crown. That is the greatest disappointment of 1991. Next year I want to do better."

In 1992 Fondriest did try to do better, but his plans didn't entirely work out. He did well in some of the spring classics. In the Tour of Flanders he came fourth. In the Amstel Gold Race he launched an attack, was pegged back again, and then chased so hard in the final kilometres that his team mate, Olaf Ludwig, took the first classic of his career with the minimum of trouble. However, the big win remained elusive, and for the time being the Italian still remained primarily known for his World Championship victory in

Fondriest, world champion too early in his career?

Ronse in 1988, when the whole of Belgium felt that Claude Criquielion had been robbed of the title. The Walloon rider and the Canadian Steve Bauer got tangled up with each other. Criquielion fell and Bauer carried on riding with his legs hanging down. All it was left for Fondriest to do was to cross the line for victory.

Heavy

It goes without saying that the Italian didn't let the chance slip. It seemed as though he was destined to become the next big thing in Italian cycling in rapid time. Bugno, Argentin and Chiappucci, however, built their reputations ahead of him and he continued to struggle to live up to his promise. The press did not neglect to make something of it, of course. "Fondriest was far too young to win the world title." Comments like that made him touchy. "I was young, obviously, 23, but at least I did win it. Better to have been world champion once than not at all. Other riders spend their whole careers chasing such a victory. I can tell you now, that jersey was heavy, very heavy. Due to illness and a knee injury, I didn't get the chance to show what I could do either, I wanted to push myself too hard. I still feel, however, that I deserved to win that jersey, no matter what is said. Even without the fall I would have won. At the time, the whole affair between Bauer and Criquielion was a great irritation. When I stepped up on to the podium I was very frightened. The entire crowd was standing there, booing and shouting, and no one applauded. Yet they had seen that I had done nothing wrong. I hadn't pushed Criquielion.

It has been said that I had already given up when Steve Bauer stuck his elbows out, but that was not the case. Do you think I would have made the same mess of things as I did a few months earlier in Milan-San Remo, when Fignon left me trailing in his wake? On that day I was riding with a gear far too big, while Fignon was riding on a cog lower. I had taken that lesson to heart. In Ronse, although I was lying three metres back at the moment it happened, that was all part of the plan. I wanted to have a clear road ahead of me and I didn't want to be blocked off by anybody. I kept calm, with the intention of going for it hell-for-leather over the last fifty metres. Anyway, I knew the finish. I had spent time between the Tour of Flanders and Paris-Roubaix getting to know every inch of the course."

Character

Sports doctor Yvan Van Mol knows the Italian riders well and has worked with Maurizio Fondriest for several years. "It is not surprising that Maurizio's professional career had such a difficult start. Of the crop of young riders who turned professional at the same time as him, he was the only one who went straight in as a team leader. He had to be a star when he was anything but ready for it. It was just when Moser's career was drawing to a close, and Saronni's best days were also behind him. In consequence, Maurizio did not have the time to mature gradually, and by the end of 1991 he had paid the price. In 1992 he finally put it behind him.

What Fondriest certainly did have from day one, however, was a strong character. He is moody and slightly pampered, and that doesn't make it easy for him to fit in to a team. He doesn't know his own capabilities well enough, otherwise he could have become another Argentin. He has the same qualities: bursts of speed, commitment and motivation. Fondriest is not a natural sprinter and he doesn't have enough strength to make long solo breaks. He should be able to compensate for that and prepare specifically for certain races. Argentin is a master at that, because he knows his limitations, Fondriest doesn't. That's how Maurizio threw away half of the 1990 season by gearing everything towards Paris-Roubaix, even though his constitution is far from ideal for it. You need to be well-built to be able to ride on the cobbles, like Moser or Ballerini. Those two riders have the right body for such a demanding race, while Fondriest has to rely on the strength of his character.

One thing you must say for him is that he puts everything into his profession, up to the point of being fanatical, even. What he has yet to realise is that he can achieve better results by getting plenty of rest. He allows himself to be influenced by too many people."

Guts

The very least you can say about Fondriest is that he has guts. When he turned professional in 1987 he could have joined Bianchi, at that time the biggest of the Italian teams. He turned them down, however, and signed for Alfa Lum, a much more modest outfit.

"I wanted to be the team leader from day one, I didn't want to be led. Dancing to the tune of Moser or Saronni did not appeal to me. I wanted to learn the job under the best possible circumstances. A big team would never have taken me on as a leader, but Alfa Lum did. My attitude was not appreciated at the time - Saronni was angry, and Moser too - but I survived it and at the same time I had come much further than other first-year professionals of my own age. I'm glad I took my chance. The only disadvantage to it was that I was always expected to perform well.

I adopted a negative attitude to the 'big names' of the time, and that had its consequences. I only live 35 kilometres away from Moser, yet we never trained together: Francesco never wanted it. I still admire him, though, certainly for his character and his enthusiasm for his work. As a person, however, he has a lot less to offer.
I have also had serious head-on clashes with Saronni. The reason for that was that I used to ride my race and not worry about what other people's intentions were. "There will be no attacking today," Saronni once said to me. I im-

mediately attacked, against the star's wishes. You should have heard what he had to say afterwards. I was an utter bastard. "I don't give damn about Saronni," I said at the time. "I don't speak to stupid people." He's a rider I have never wanted to emulate."

Respect
A rider for whom Fondriest does have a great deal of respect is Moreno Argentin. "We are similar sorts of people. Up to the start of 1991, Moreno handpicked his races perhaps a little too much. He limited himself to those races that he felt he had a chance of winning, and didn't take the rest that seriously. That is something to do with the fact that Argentin does not have the physique of Moser, but if he wants something, he does not let anything stand in his way. He is very intelligent. When we raced against each other in the juniors, we often trained together. When we slogged it over the climbs, we looked for each other. We are still good friends. We both like skiing and often go to the mountains together. I have a lot of respect for anyone who accepts me for what I am. When people find it impossible to do so, I can be unpleasant. My favourite races are those in which you have to battle, the very hard ones; ones in which only the best riders have a chance of winning. That is the reason I enjoy racing in Belgium so much."

Grandmother
Maurizio Fondriest comes from Cles, a small village 45 kilometres from Trento. From San Michele al Adige, the road slowly winds its way uphill. You make your way between two gentle ridges until the landscape suddenly fans out into a plateau. At the end of the valley is Cles, 658 metres above sea level, and clearly a very old village. In his lifetime, the Roman emperor Claudius left an edict lying somewhere around here. When it was found, Cles was made immortal. The population of the village is about 5,000. Fondriest and apple growing hold its honour high to the outside world.

"My father Cornelio is an apple grower. A poor harvest for us would still produce 130,000 kilos in a year. The region is famous for the quality of its apples. We mainly grow Golden, and we receive about 35 pence per kilo for them at market. The apples they grow in Trento are only worth a third of that. During the picking season, my father has 25 pickers working for him, out of season there is only him and my brother. I myself have been up and down the ladder thousands of times in my time when I should have been at school. Nowadays my help is no longer required. Anyway, I don't want to take the risk of taking another tumble.

My love of cycling comes from my father. He even used to race himself, until my grandfather put a spanner in the works and made him work. Then he got married. My brother Francesco was born first, two years before me and that obviously brought with it new responsibilities and concerns. After that, Dad was to old to take up racing again. "Do something else within the sport," suggested my mother, and he became a race commissioner. He did that for fifteen years. On Sundays I was allowed to go with him, and we would ride in the car behind the race. We made a note of the numbers of those riders who dropped out, and he wrote out the result of the race. Weekends could not come quickly enough for me."

Posters

Fondriest started racing in 1975, when he was ten. "In my very first race I came third. My grandmother got me my first bike. It was an ordinary bike with racing handlebars, but slowly I converted it into a proper racing bike. In those days when I won races it was always by big margins. I would attack 10 to 15 kilometres from the finish, and I was gone. The older I got, though, the faster I found I could sprint. As an amateur I could suddenly ride time trials, too.

When I was a boy I was always an Eddy Merckx fan. I still have posters of him hanging above my bed. Eddy could handle all kinds of terrain, and that was how I thought the ideal rider should be: a champion must be able to do it all. I thought it then and I think it now.

I was pleased with my career as a youngster. In 1985 I won the Tour of Greece, I came fifth in the World Championship at Giavera del Montello. In 1986 I won 14 races. I won the Tour of Lombardy for amateurs, I also won a stage in the Tour of Hainaut, and I came seventh in the World Championship at Colorado Springs."

Glasses

Although Maurizio Fondriest is undeniably Italian, he doesn't look like a typical one. He has paler skin and fairer hair than his compatriots. In his own country he undoubtedly cannot get a word in edgeways, because he is very quiet and doesn't like a commotion. "Maurizio is an intellectual," some say. He is cultured, he often wears glasses and in late 1991 he got married to a graduate, Ornella, who studied economics and speaks fluent French. "He is too nice," say others'. Yet he does have a strong personality. To him black is black and white is white. It is as well that he has a strong character otherwise, as an Italian, he would never have dared to join a Dutch team. In Fausto Coppi's day, it would have been regarded as sacrilege. Apart from Marco Giovannetti, who went to Spain as a domestique but came back a team leader, he is the only Italian rider in living memory who has made that move. That happened at the end of 1990 when Fondriest moved from the Del Tongo to Peter Post's Panasonic team.

"When it comes to organisation, Post is a master. Furthermore, I rode the programme I wanted to myself, and really it was left up to me. They say that Post puts his riders under pressure, but right up to the time I left, it was something I never noticed; quite the contrary in fact. Towards the end of the 1991 season I was in a state of total nervousness. I was leader of the World Cup, but I wanted to win one of the races to show I was worthy of my first place. "Keep calm," said Post. In that year's Amstel Gold Race, I had come second and would have won but for a series of mistakes. Maassen had hindered me in the sprint and I allowed myself to be caught. If I could ride that particular race again, I would definitely win it. But everything has to be in your favour. Post was the first person to make me realise that.

With Del Tongo I really was under pressure, even though I rode thirty races a year less than with Panasonic. My schedule was too 'Italian-orientated,' and didn't really suit me. Now I rest if I need to rest, and I race if I want to race.

With Del Tongo I went at it all-out until June, and then I was left with nothing to do for three months, even though I would have given anything to ride in the Tour de France. By the end of my first year with Post, I had won three minor races; a stage in the Tour of Sicily and two in the Catalan Week, but as a rider I had made more progress than in all the previous years put together. In 1992 I made the next step. In spring I rode a good Milan-San Remo and came fourth in the Tour of Flanders, but I didn't win a classic. Olaf Ludwig may have won the Amstel Gold Race, but it was, in part, a victory for me. I had very good legs that day."

Cobbles

Fondriest certainly isn't afraid to say things his countrymen would rather not hear. Last year he made no secret of the fact that he would rather win Paris-Roubaix or the Tour of Flanders than Milan-San Remo.
"I never said that I don't want to win Milan-San Remo. Obviously I do, I came fairly close in 1988 for that matter, when I came second to Laurent Fignon. Milan-San Remo is a superb race, but on the cobbles you can prove that you are the best, and to me that seems more important. I made that choice a long time ago. As a young boy, I saw Francesco Moser win Paris-Roubaix, and I have never been able to forget it. I was a fan of Eddy Merckx, and I could have spent hours watching Moser hurtling through the 'hell,' and I wanted to emulate them both. I was captivated by it. I remember that when I was an amateur I was very keen to ride the Tour of West Hainaut in Belgium, because I knew we had to ride over cobbles."

Coppi

Italian cycling history has shaped Fondriest's outlook. "Magni and Coppi were, in my opinion, the best Italian riders of all time. Where do you think they made their names? Paris-Roubaix, where else? If I could model myself on anybody, it would be those two gentlemen. Many riders from my country hate northern Europe: it's too cold, it rains too much, there's too much wind. But I love it, because it really sorts out the men from the boys. A softie will never win the Tour of Flanders. It could well be that at the end of my career, it will have been shown that I gave in too easily in races, but even that won't change my opinion.
I now know that I don't have the right build to ever win Paris-Roubaix. It has meant that I have had to aim for new goals. Because I want to get to the top, I will mainly be concentrating on races I think I can do well in, such as the Tour of Flanders and Liège-Bastogne-Liège. I'm having to let my head rule

my heart and admitting that Paris-Roubaix is not for me. From now on I'm going to have to give it a miss so that I can recuperate, but if ever the day comes when I have won my two target races, you will see me rattling my way over the cobbles again."

Bursts of Speed

People who know about such things say that on the short climbs in particular Fondriest is able to produce incredible bursts of speed. "It is something you are either born with or you're not. Unfortunately there aren't many finishes where I can demonstrate it. As far as other aspects of my ability is concerned, there isn't really anything at which I am especially good. I'm an all-round cyclist, but my weakness is in the mountains. Yet that should not really be the case, when you consider that I live in a mountainous area. The Stelvio is 100 kilometres from where I live, and I have often ridden up it. I have worked hard at it, and it is now starting to bear fruit. The fact is that I want to do even better. In my opinion, you are only a great rider if you can escape on the big climbs.

My character is my strongest card. They say that I'm a fanatic, but I don't agree. It's just that I have chosen the perfect profession. Racing is not a job. It is more like a game.

Fondriest at home on the rollers

I actually train in the old-fashioned way. I have my own trainer, Volney Vasquez, a Chilean and what he says goes. His most important principle is that I should not use too big a gear. I am supple, and in the long run, that will be my principal weapon. Volney says that I will be at my best when I'm 27. That's the age I am now, and I am gradually getting the feeling he is right. I believe in giving as much attention to training as possible. They say that I do too much and that I don't get enough rest. I have tried to do something about it. As far as that is concerned, the 1990 season taught me a great deal. It brought to light one or two weak points. I have to take into account that I am not at my best when it rains. I'm also aware that I have let myself be influenced for too long by the wrong people. I've put an end to that, though, and peace and quiet has returned."

Sports Freak
On 9th November 1991, Maurizio Fondriest married Ornella and being a married man has clearly had its effects on the rider. They both love music. "Just give me a couple of Phil Collins CDs and some reggae music and I'm happy to sit back in my chair and relax. At the moment cycling controls my life. I have invested quite a bit of money into my own cycle business, but it is my brother who runs the shop. As for the rest, I am very much a sports freak. I often go swimming, since it is good for cyclists. I also go skiing and cross-country skiing regularly, and sometimes I ride my mountain bike. I like to go to watch football; I'm an AC Milan supporter. I also like fast cars, but I'm not a playboy. Laurent Fignon is someone I have a good deal of time for. He has visited my home in Italy, and I have stayed with him in Paris. He does not beat about the bush, and that is something I set great store by."

MIGUEL INDURAIN

NATURE LOVER

With his victory in the Tour of Italy in 1992, Miguel Indurain became the first Spaniard to ever win that prestigious stage race. Thanks to the FICP points that wearing the pink jersey brought him, Indurain also jumped ahead of Gianni Bugno and became the number 1 ranked rider in the world. His Tour de France victory in 1991 had already created a big impression, now he was regarded as a demigod. The Spanish prime minister Felipe Gonzales immediately sent him a telegram congratulating him. Suddenly the Giro was swarming with Spanish journalists, and present on the final stage to Milan was Javier Gomez Navarro, the Spanish minister of sport, governor of Navarre and mayor of Pamplona. The winner's father, mother and three sisters had gone over to Italy for the first time to celebrate the occasion. Spanish flags waved and there was overwhelming enthusiasm all around. Spain worshipped its hero.

Tour '92
Indurain's triumph in the 1992 Tour surpassed even the Italian victory. The Spaniard is now one of a select band of riders who have won the Giro and the Tour in the same year. Eddy Merckx managed it on no less than three occasions, Hinault and Coppi twice, Anquetil and Roche once. 500 Spanish supporters had travelled to Paris to celebrate their idol's second successive Tour victory. They banged their drums. they cheered and they chanted the name of Indurain until their throats were sore.
Indurain's second Tour de France win was achieved in a different way to 1991, when he made such a forceful break on the second Pyrenean stage to Val Louron and confirmed his supremacy in the following time trial, from then on riding in yellow. In 1992 the Tour was Indurain's from the moment he won the time trial in Luxembourg. From then on he only had to defend his lead to be able to take the winner's jersey home with him. In the final time trial between Tours and Blois he underlined his supremacy again. "I had to approach it in a tactical way. It was never my intention to win the Tour purely by winning the time trials, though. Anyway, I can assure you that doing

that in itself wouldn't be enough. Winning means that you might have to ride at the front for 21 days."

Record Books

The 1992 Tour de France will go down in the record books as the quickest edition of the race ever. The riders rode right to the limit. Yet throughout the fight, Indurain looked as solid as a rock. By the end of the race there had only been a couple of occasions when he looked slightly uncomfortable. "The first was in the stage to Brussels, because of the rain. Rain is what I hate most. On that day I was almost racing blind. It was pure guesswork on whether I could get past riders to the left or right. It was an even money chance that I would ride into the kerb-edge. The only thing on my mind was reaching the finish safely. On the stage to Sestriere, 2 kilometres from the line, I suddenly died and could go no further. Fortunately for me, the finishing line wasn't far away."

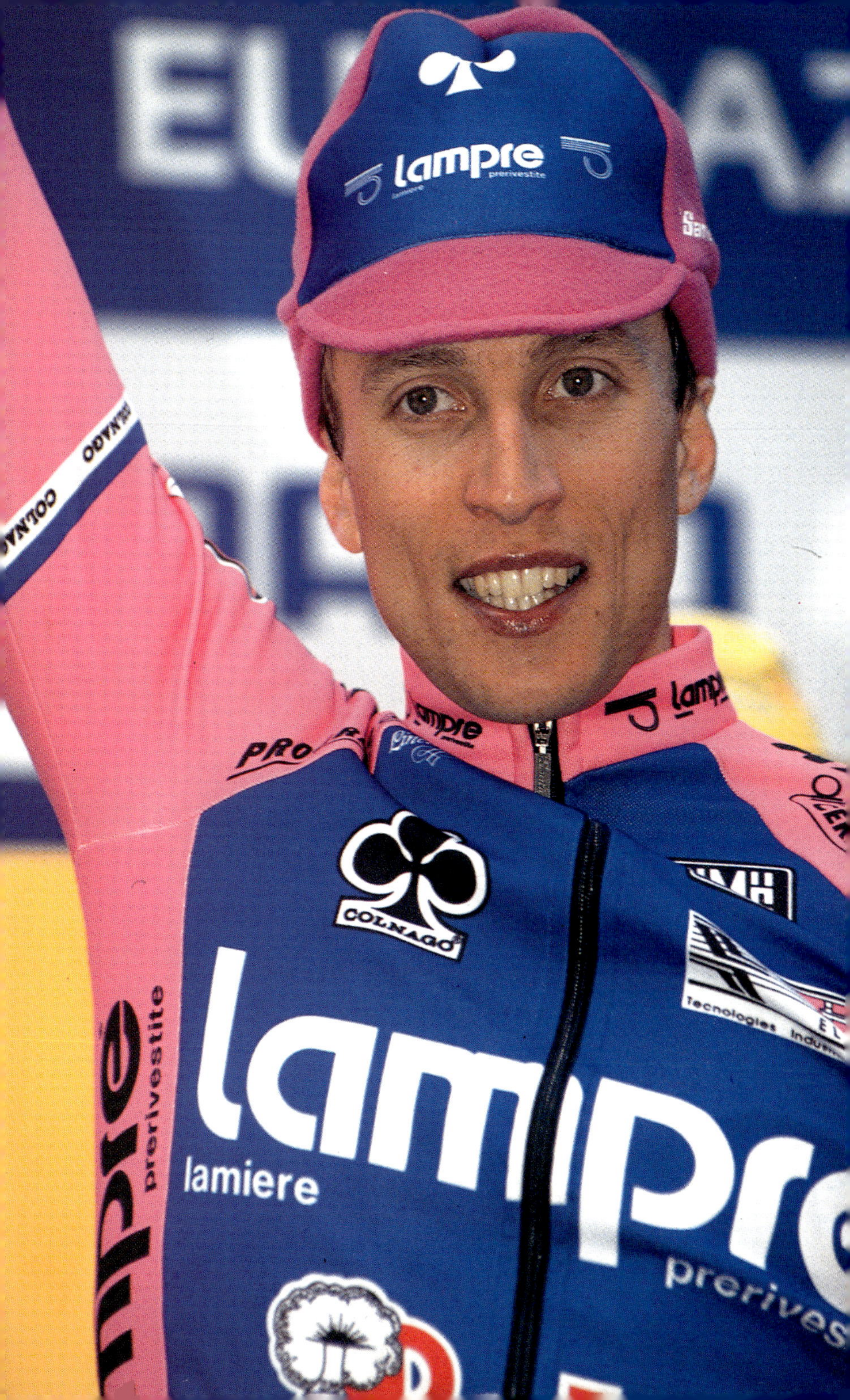
lampre
prerivestite
lamiere
COLNAGO
Tecnologies

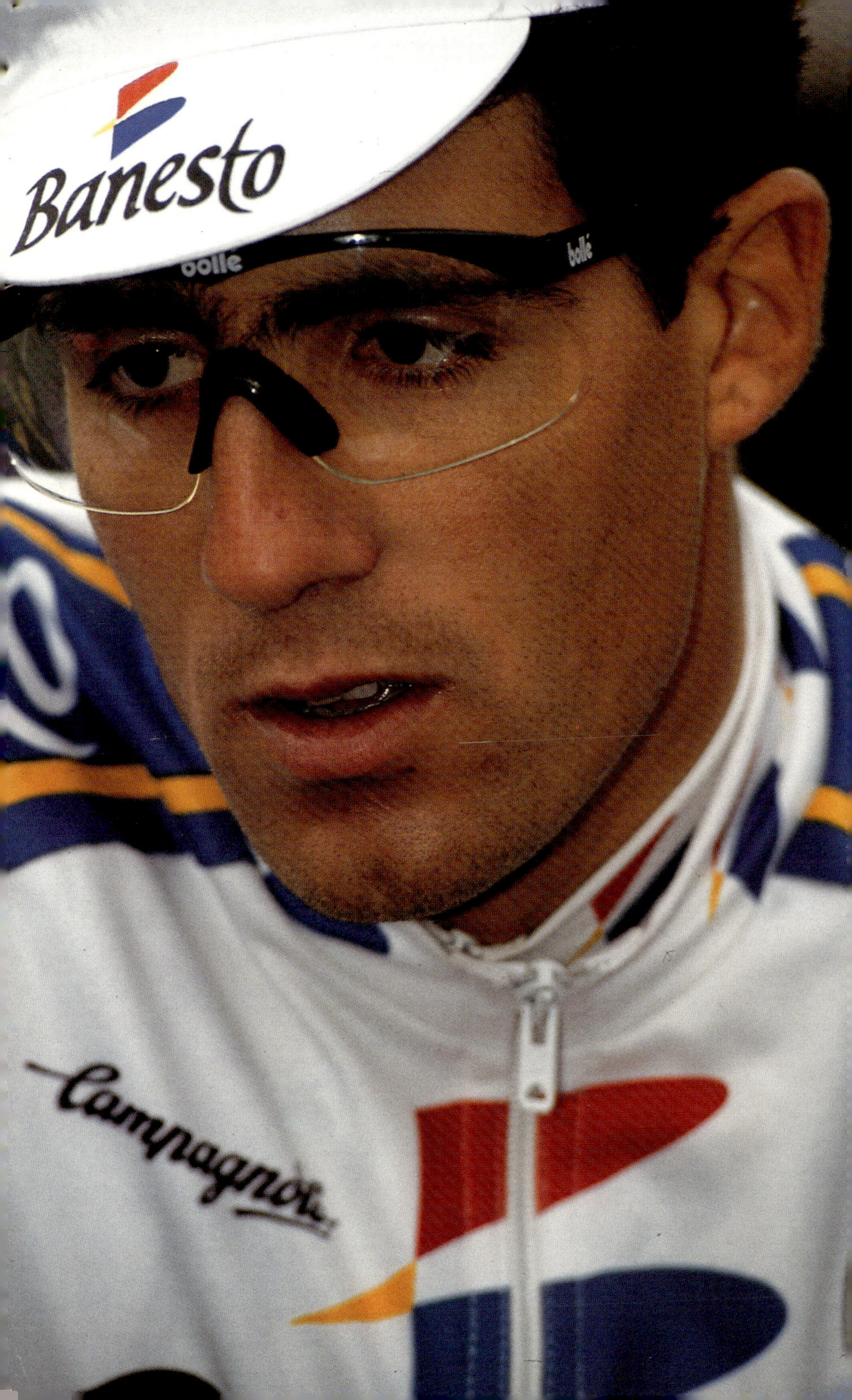
Banesto
bollé
bollé
Campagnolo

Champion

So 1992 was a marvellous year for Miguel Indurain. Not only did he win the Tour and the Giro, but also his national championship. He does not wear his champion's jersey, however. "For publicity reasons my sponsor won't allow me to. I had asked the Spanish federation's permission to do this before the race. Had I not received it, although I would have started, I would not have ridden to win. But I did, so I went all out for it. Another dream was to win the world championship and I gave it my best shot. The course in Benidorm could easily have been designed with me in mind, it was so perfect, but the plan misfired. The race wasn't hard enough. When all is said and done, I'm not really a one-day racer. I'm more a typical stage racer."

In spite of all his success, Indurain remains stoical. He has a singular way of living with his popularity. Being the sort of quiet man he is, he finds it easier to withdraw into himself. During stage races there is never any sign of him until, five minutes before the start of that day's racing, when he suddenly emerges and then immediately takes up his position in the middle of the pack. If his team mates go for a walk after their evening meal, he stays in his room, phones his girlfriend Marissa and gets some rest. "Miguel is rather introverted," says Pedro Delgado. "I must have asked him a dozen times if he would like to come with us, but the answer is always no. He shuts himself off and avoids contact with others."

Big Mig

And yet Indurain is an extremely popular rider. He thinks much of the interest the public show in him is precisely down to this mysterious aura he has created about his person. The farmer's son from Villava reveals little and guards his emotions, and it is that which they find intriguing and which attracts interest. People also like the underdog, and until he was 27 and in the shadow of his team leader Delgado, that is what he was. Furthermore, Miguelon, 'Big Mig', is tall, dark and handsome, with the look of a charmer, and it is this which no doubt impresses the señoritas. On top of all that, add the class and style of a gifted rider and you have all the ingredients for a complete success story.

Mandela

Spaniards are usually fiery and boisterous, but Indurain is not. He is, though, charming and friendly, smiling every now and then, but no more than that. Referring to himself, he says that outward appearances do not interest him. Last winter he was overwhelmed by all the honours he received, only two of which he considers important. "I really appreciated being voted the sportsman of the year for 1992 by the Italian newspaper, the Gazetta dello Sport," says the Tour winner. "Chiappucci had told me before that I was highly-rated in Italy, but I didn't expect anything like that. My happiest recollection, however, was the presentation of the 'Premio Principe de Asturias'. In Spain there is no higher honour. It is not so much the honour that goes with it, but the fact that I was standing on a podium alongside Nelson Mandela and Liz Taylor. It was because of Mandela in particular that made me so proud.

Farm

Villava is 4 kilometres from Pamplona, a town 60 kilometres from the border with France, not far from the Pyrenees. On the corner of a dirt track is Indurain's parental home; a large, tall, white-painted house. On the other side of the road there is a paper mill. Cars and lorries come and go constantly. The traffic jams, the smell, the noise, the dust: at first sight it is not a very attractive environment for a champion. Until he married, Indurain lived there with his parents, his brother Prudencio - six years younger than Miguel, and already a professional with Banesto - and his three sisters, Isabel (29), Maria Dolores (25) and Maria Asuncion (22).

Miguel is a rich man, but that wouldn't be apparent from looking at the farm. "Dad doesn't breed cows or pigs, no livestock is fattened up on the farm. We grow grain and all the money goes into materials and equipment as it always

It is not only the time trials Miguel Indurain wins in the Tour. In 1990 he won the stage to Luz Ardiden.

has. We would eventually like to buy some land, but I'm afraid it's impossible. The business does not belong to my parents alone. My uncle and cousin are also involved in the business and that makes it more difficult. There isn't a great deal of land available anyway. The paper mill has meant that there is no longer any chance of expanding in that direction. So Marino Lejarreta and I have put some money into a supermarket for sports clothing. It has been going so well that we now sponsor a cycling club."

Two Houses

Miguel Indurain was married late last year to Marissa, his long-time sweetheart. Getting married has led to one or two changes in their lives that might have been expected. The couple moved house, for example. Indurain has enough money, so he bought two houses. "I liked living on the farm, the only thing wrong with it was the disturbance you got from the paper factory. Every morning and evening there were traffic jams outside my front door and I didn't like that. The first of the two houses is five kilometres from my parents' house, just outside Pamplona, the capital of our province. The other one is in Benidorm, very close to last year's world championship course. We switch between the two regularly. One day we are living in one, the next day in the other. Actually, it depends on what sort of training schedule I'm working to at the time. If I am taking in climbs we stay in Benidorm."

Driving Forces

You could set your watch by the rhythm Miguel Indurain has developed turning his pedals. In time trials his legs turn at a pre-determined rate from the very first metre onwards. His rhythm and style are very impressive. It is not surprising that a young man with a build like Indurain would want to cycle. "My parents never put any pressure on me, not even to work on the farm. They just let me do it. I obviously used to lend a hand - and still do in the wintertime - but school work was regarded as the main priority. I went to a technical school and I am qualified to make moulds, as I have a certificate as a turner. I enjoyed studying maths, but I hated history because I am no dreamer. My father was thankful that I was so sporting. He accuses me of being lazy, but my brother Prudencio is much worse.

I rode in my first race when I was 11. I was a member of the local 'Club Ciclista Villavas' from our village and I came second. I was pleased about it, but at that time I wasn't yet sure what I really wanted to do, and I went back to playing football. After that I played basketball for a short while, but team sports didn't interest me as much. Some players don't work as hard as others, and I didn't think that was fair. I wanted to do something that was down to the individual. I was still too young to put everything into racing, and so I did some athletics for a while. I was pretty good at the 400 metres - I was even champion of Navarre in the discipline - but cycling would not let me go. My next race came when I was 16 alongside lads of the same age from our region - Inaki Gaston, Riduara and a young Gorospe."

Hour Record

Any rider who considers himself among the select club of top riders at any given time must show an interest in attempting to break the world hour record. LeMond is contemplating making an attempt. Time-trial specialist Indurain would have a good chance but he has no specific plans. "At some future date I would like to have a go. We shall have to see how my career progresses. You'd be best trying an hour record when you are about 31 or 32. For the time being, however, I am concentrating 100% on road racing. I know that I would need at least six months to get used to riding the track, and at the moment I haven't the time to do that. You can never do two things well at the same time. I do have some experience on the track, though. I once rode the Madrid Six Days, the year it was won by the Hermann brothers. I have also taken part in the Six Hours of Euskadi, I know the track at Barcelona. It went quite well."

Delgado

Delgado used to be his leader and is still a team-mate. 'Perico's' part in Indurain's career is well documented: Miguel got his chance to develop further in Delgado's shadow. "We're not bosom friends, because we're too different from each other. I do go and visit him at his house, but not that often. I do appreciate Perico, though, very much so. He used to receive all the attention and had to face the pressure, while I was able to develop as a rider. That's the way it had to be because, when all is said and done, I was very young when I turned professional; only 20. When you're that young and you are not given the opportunity to develop, you will go astray. Pedro was not an idol to me, but a good example to follow. He can look forward to a race. When he is riding really well he can put in incredible bursts of speed and he has an enormous amount of drive in him. I don't have that. I'm more level-headed; not as nervous or tense, and personally I think it is an advantage. I don't get excited very quickly. I put things into perspective. I'm really happy that I'm a good racer, but I realise that it has a lot to do with good fortune."

Medical Supervision

Indurain patiently bided his time and developed into a superb rider. "I had good help. The first one who pointed out my faults was Dr Conconi the Italian specialist who also supervised Francesco Moser. Not that I followed his schedules, but I did listen attentively whenever he had anything to tell me. I had just won the Tour de l'Avenir, but I felt that I was still short of what I needed to be on the climbs. Echavarri, my directeur sportif, sent me to see him, simply to see what he had to say. "You have unlimited potential, but you are far too heavy," he said. "If you want to be good you will have to lose 5 kilos." I was 6'2" and weighed 83 kilos at the time. My ideal weight for the Tour is now 78 kilograms.

They say that patience is my most important quality. I don't waste energy. In the 1992 Giro I never went on to the attack myself. I could make up for any time lost in the time trials. In the mountains it was up to my rivals to trap me. I rode on my guard, defensively.

I'm a realist and I can thank Eusebio Unzue, my very first trainer for that. "You must not try to run before you can walk," he always said. That explains my slow but steady progress. I had been a professional for seven years when I won my first Tour, I took that time to do it. I was a good young rider, but nothing special. In 1983 - the first of my two years as an amateur - I won the national championship. The title was my very first victory in the category. Then Unzue took me under his wing and that brought me quite a bit of success. The next year I won 15 races. I took part in the Peace Race, the Olympic Games in Los Angeles and I won two stages in the Tour de l'Avenir. "Now's the time to turn professional," he said, and that's when I did. It wasn't really a difficult decision since Reynolds, my first employers, already sponsored the amateur club of which I was a member. The company comes from my own area.

Looking back on it, perhaps I turned professional too soon. I knew nothing about the pro scene, and I was never in the hunt for anything. I had everything to learn. In fact Echavarri, my directeur sportif, held the same principles as Unzue. "Steady growth," he ordered, and that's how it has been. In 1985 I wore the leader's jersey during the Tour of Spain for four days and I won the Tour de l'Avenir. Every year the target was set a little higher. As Pedro Delgado was coming up with all the success the team wanted, it was no problem at all."

Modern

Since then, when it comes to popularity, Miguel Indurain has overtaken his former team leader. He is now the top man in a Banesto team which includes Jean-François Bernard and Pedro Delgado. Indurain has less panache than Delgado, but he gives the team a greater chance of winning things. At the same time, though, it has also been said of Indurain that he is a little lacking in ambition, that he is not strong tactically, and that occasionally he needs to be given a good shake to wake him up. "I race according to the way I feel. I don't waste my energy. The foundation for all my stage-race victories are the time trials. In the 1991 Tour I took the yellow jersey at Val Louron. I attacked and was then told by my directeur sportif to wait for Chiappucci and together we closed the gap. At that moment I still didn't realise I could win the Tour. It was only that evening in my hotel room that it dawned on me. I did have a bad time on the Alpe d'Huez, but my rivals didn't capitalise on it. I found it really hard trying to stay with Bugno. Luckily Bernard was there to help me do it.

I think of myself as a modern racer. Spanish cycling greats of the past were mainly climbers. I am principally an all-round hard rider. I know my limitations. I don't get involved in bunch sprints because of the risks they hold. In sprints against about twelve men, I would fancy my chances. For a long time I was also not up to scratch as a climber because I was too heavy, but I eradicated that defect. I did a lot of power training and trained a great deal in the mountains. I'm still not one of the best climbers, but I am doing more than just coping. I will certainly never be able to shoot away on climbs."

Supporter

A rider Miguel Indurain always greatly admired is Bernard Hinault. "Hinault was a brilliant rider and he was the boss; he had something special. There is no leader like that any more. I can't do it. There has been a levelling-out at the top. Many of us are at a similar level.

I used to support Hinault, but I never idolised him. I don't idolise anyone, that's not how I was brought up. At home I was taught to keep my two feet on the ground, the way all farmers do. Their harvest depends on the weather, on enough sun and rain. Many things can go wrong, therefore, that you can do nothing about. You must take everything as it comes. I stay calm through it all. I never scream or shout at my team-mates. Aggression does not make me a better rider. After all, everyone makes mistakes, I do, and you must be able to forgive each other. You will achieve more by having several good friends around you."

Catching Colds

Indurain has reached the very pinnacle as a stage-race rider, but in the classics he has not really done anything special up to now. He has won the San Sebastian Grand Prix, but that's all.

"To each his own. In normal circumstances I should do well in the Flèche Wallonne and Liège-Bastogne-Liège; I actually did finish fourth in the latter race in 1991. The weather is so changeable, though. When the sun shines everything is fine, but if it rains or gets too cold, I lose 50% of my potential. I have one weak spot, I catch colds very easily, and for a long time that has had an effect on how my career has gone. The early season has repeatedly been a wash-out for me, particularly when I first turned professional. While everyone was out on their bikes, I sat at home sniffing, coughing and sneezing. All it needed was a shower and a little wind and that was it for me. I try to avoid it when I can. I like Paris-Nice - I have won that stage race twice - yet I have opted to ride Tirreno-Adriatico now because the weather is nicer. The reason I chose the Giro in 1992 instead of the Vuelta is partly to do with that. The weather can be really bad during the Vuelta. Tony Rominger could tell you something about that. He's a hay fever sufferer, but he has never had any trouble with it during the Vuelta.

Some of the classics don't appeal to me at all. Cobbles scare me off, so I will never ride the Tour of Flanders or Paris-Roubaix. I would probably get over them quite smoothly as I am rather heavily built, but that still won't persuade me; I simply don't like cobbles. Neither do I feel very comfortable in the commotion you get at the foot of a climb. Any typical stage racer finds the same problem. I'm also frightened of falling. I once broke my wrist and when I ride on cobblestones I can still feel the pain. In 1990 I broke my collar-bone and now I would rather not take any risks."

Mattress

Miguel Indurain now earns around £1 million a year, around three-times as much as he did before his 1991 Tour victory. The team sponsor, Banesto, is the third biggest bank in Spain, and it mainly thrives in the area around Madrid. In Villava, the village in which Indurain lives, there isn't even a Banesto branch. "I suppose Villava is too small to have one. But in Pamplona, a few kilometres away, there is one. Anyway, the sponsors are more than happy with the response they have had because of Pedro Delgado and me.

Last year the team generated a total of £10 million worth of publicity. That doesn't mean that everyone has suddenly gone and entrusted all their money to Banesto."

Future

In general, professional cyclists can carry on until they are about 35. As far as his own future is concerned, Indurain has no definite plans.

"I'd like to race for another four years and then I'll retire. I'm certain I can win the Tour one more time, but not five like Merckx, Hinault and Anquetil. My Spanish supporters should not raise their hopes for that. What I will go and do after that, I don't yet know. I don't like to look into the future. You hear it said that no good comes of putting things off until tomorrow, but I'm not so sure about that. By the time I retire, I will want to have earned enough money to allow me to lead a nice comfortable life. I am and will remain a nature lover. One of my favourite pleasures is wandering through the woods on my own.

It was not my upbringing that made a champion of me, it was inborn; if it not have been I would have given up a long time ago. I used to eat a sandwich and drink a Cola or a Fanta when I went out racing, and I still don't ride with my head in the clouds. I can assure you that it doesn't make much difference to my parents that I am a star on a bike. All they ever wanted was the best for me. My bike was a means of getting out to the fields. My father was extremely disappointed when I interrupted my education to go racing. The bike was no necessity, nor was it something which could be used to hold me back. I would have found it hard to deal with if that had been the case. People say that it is precisely this necessity, this pressure which creates great champions. I disagree with that. I am sure that I would have been able to make my way in life without cycling. If, for whatever reason, I suddenly had to give up the sport next year, I would be sorry, but it wouldn't be the end of the world for me."

LAURENT JALABERT
WHITE DOVE

Laurent Jalabert, the best French rider in 1992, looks a little like his role model, Bernard Hinault. Well at least he has the same black hair, and the same, smallish, build. But his eyes are different: they contain mystery, they are somewhat more sad. Neither is Jalabert the same sort of natural-born leader that his illustrious predecessor was. Hinault would speak out when something was not to his liking, often leading protests and demanding action. Jalabert is quieter, he knows exactly what he wants and sets out to get it. What the two of them do possess is that same single-mindedness that turns riders into champions. At first sight, Jalabert looks rather reserved, but that is only an illusion. He is more waggish, more sociable than that. He is not afraid to pull your leg, tweak your ear and share a joke with you. He makes sure there is a lively atmosphere wherever he is. At least that is what they are saying at ONCE, the team he is riding for again in 1993.

Temperament

Not only does Laurent Jalabert look like Bernard Hinault, but he is following in his footsteps to a degree. "I never had posters of him, that wasn't the sort of thing I did anyway, but I did admire him. I thought the way he used to win his races was a delight to watch. He always won so easily, as if it had been no trouble. Winning was just a game. Bernard had a very strong temperament, and I'm pleased that I have, too. I once read somewhere that Hinault had said that I could become a good rider. It gave me a great deal of pleasure finding that out. What a compliment to get! I'm a fighter, the same as he is. Although most of the races I've won as a professional have been in sprint finishes, I can assure you that wasn't the case when I was an amateur. Back then I used to win many races by big margins. I rarely, if ever, waited for the sprint. I attacked. I looked for the toughest races because they were the ones I could dominate. I still go for the toughest races, for that matter."

Cool Customer

Jalabert is no fool. They do say that he doesn't race intelligently, but that's not the same thing at all. As an illustration of this, when we asked him where he lives, he told us the following about it. "Mazamet is 50 kilometres from Carcassonne," he starts. "You may have heard of Carcassonne, it is the town in which there is a fully preserved walled section. Do you know where the name Carcassonne comes from? According to legend, the town came under heavy siege centuries ago. When the soldiers advanced under cover of nightfall, they were spotted by a certain Madame Carcasse. The brave woman immediately began ringing the alarm bell. Within five minutes the whole town knew what was happening: everyone was alerted."

White Dove

"Jalabert is the white dove of the team," beams ONCE's directeur sportif Saiz, when you ask him to describe his French protégé. "He's a comfortable rider and he's very easy to motivate. He lives for cycling and he has the legs to win any kind of race. At the moment he is a specialist in the classics and the World Cup, but I'm looking forward to finding out in two year's time whether Laurent can reach a higher level, because he's a very good climber. From now on it is not important for him to sprint quickly, but it is important for him to climb well."

Brother

Laurent Jalabert comes from a working-class family: his father works in a steel plant, his mother makes leather suitcases and handbags. He has one brother of whom he says: "Frederic is a rider too. At the beginning of the 1993 season he was 20. I'm certain he has the qualities needed to become a professional. Even though he doesn't climb as well as I can, he can get the better of me in sprints. I will eventually help him come by a professional contract. He has what it takes to make it: he certainly has the temperament and the ability.

129

As long as he is prepared to train and work hard, he could do it. But it's up to him to make sure he does."

Sylvie

They say that the partner has a significant impact on a professional cyclist's career. She makes him or breaks him, the saying goes. A rider needs to be well looked after, the wife must iron out his problems, and she must be one hundred per cent in her support of his profession. Jalabert is married to Sylvie and she is a tough customer. Early in the 1992 season Laurent was sitting at home fretting because he was sick when the season began and his form had yet to return. "On your bike," she said. "It isn't that bad. You don't know what it's like not to be able to get anywhere. Things could be a lot worse than they are now, you know."

"I met Sylvie at a race in Salsigue, the village where my grandmother lives. That morning I had taken part in the French national championship team pursuit at the track in Carcassonne. We didn't ride badly, but we had been knocked out. I knew that there was going to be a road race that afternoon in Salsigue. My grandfather was a member of the festival committee and he had asked me if I wanted to ride in it. So I headed there as soon as I could, and Sylvie was there too. She was there to hand out the bouquets, and as I won, that's when I got my first kiss with her. That same evening there was a banquet and I came across her again. After that, one thing led to another. We eventually got married when I was 21. We now have a baby daughter, Pauline, and she is the apple of my eye. At home we rarely talk about cycling. When I get home I tell Sylvie what has happened that day, and that's the end of it."

Climbing

Much of Jalabert's reputation is founded on his performances in the World Cup, on his second place in the World Championship, and on his stage victory and battle against Johan Museeuw for the green jersey in the Tour in 1992, and on his three stage wins in the Tour of Catalonia. At the start of 1993 he was 24. If he can point to such an impressive honours list at that age, then we can expect a great deal more to come.

"Museeuw is a good sprinter and is very versatile. He climbs well, but not as well as me. Everyone says I'm a sprinter, but I don't actually agree with that. In normal sprints I don't stand a chance against the really quick men: I get beat by Museeuw and by Abdu, Van Poppel and Cipollini. I am only quick at the end of a demanding race. My kind of sprinting, then, has nothing to do with speed, but is all about strength. I compare myself a little with Sean Kelly. At first he didn't win that many races, either, but that eventually changed. Anyway, I don't want to sprint for my whole career. I'm trying to become less and less involved in them. That's something you will already start to notice in 1993. For the next two years I'm going to improve my climbing. There is a lot of work to be done in that area. My time trialling also needs to improve to a higher standard. I'm not yet able to ration my efforts from beginning to end, I have trouble keeping the rhythm going."

Rugby
Another of Laurent Jalabert's pleasing qualities is his realism. He doesn't live in the clouds, he keeps two feet firmly on the ground. He even says that many people in his village do not know his name. In view of his achievements in 1992 and 1993, that is pretty remarkable.

Winner of the Tour stage to Brussels in 1992

"But true, nonetheless: in France you have to have won a great many races before you're considered a star," he explains. "And as yet, I've not reached that point. And anyway, cycling is not particularly popular in our region. People aren't interested in it. Football is played a little, but it is rugby which is the main sport. It is like a religion, everyone follows it. I once played myself, but I plumped for an individual sport. A cycling coach lived in our street, and every weekend he held a gathering on his doorstep. One day I went along myself, and I returned the following week, too. I rode my first race when I was eleven. I wasn't a fanatic, though. Racing was purely for fun. There was no money in the club, no resources, everything was done in a simple way, but that didn't matter.
I was not an ardent follower of cycling. I suppose at that time I knew more about rugby. But that didn't stop me going with my parents, when I was 15,

to watch the Tour at the Aubisque and Guzet-Neige. The Pyrenees were magnificent. What has stayed with me from that day is that Greg LeMond was wearing the rainbow jersey, Hinault made an impression on me and Robert Millar won the stage. Millar was riding for Peugeot at the time, but I can't remember anything else apart from that."

Clubs

The young Jalabert had ability. He won his first race at the age of 17, and won a further 12 races that year. He did even better the following year.

"I rode 35 races and won 19 of them. Then I left my local club and joined one in Montauban. I was a junior at the time. They must have seen something in me because that year I was chosen for the World Championship in Casablanca, where I finished 17th. Those World Championships were my first trip abroad. After that I raced in Switzerland and then in a stage race in Canada. I won two stages, beating that year's world champion in the process. That was the day when, for the first time in my life, I thought that I just might make it as a rider.

In the meantime I had discovered that the club in Montauban was not right for me. They wanted me to ride on the track, but I wanted to develop my career in road racing. Then came an offer from some people in Narbonne. I knew the president of the club, but then spanners started to be thrown into the works from different sources. The result of it was that the move got drawn out so long that the transfer period expired and I was no longer able to leave. I was forced to stay with Montauban, something I was very much against. A cycle dealer from Toulouse then intervened to secure a move for me to the Blagnac Guidon Sprinter Club."

Yves Hézard

Laurent Jalabert was only 19 and a half when he turned professional. At the time Yves Hézard was the team manager at Toshiba, and he showed an interest.

"I knew Hézard and he knew me. He had known me since January 1988. I was part of the provisional squad for the Olympic Games, and Hézard was the coach. One of our first activities was a training camp in Mégève. I remember us having to go cross-country skiing. I knew nothing about it, I had never done it before, and Hézard gave me my first lessons. One day we had to go on a 15 kilometre hike. I stood there on my skis. Every fifty metres I fell over, and after ten minutes both my heels were covered in blisters. I assume it was because my ski shoes were a couple of sizes too small. So I then went to Hézard to explain to him what the problem was. "Forget about it, and carry on," he said. And carry on I did: on my own in the wide open space, on my own through the woods. Marvellous. I love the countryside, everything was a lovely white, winter was at its most beautiful, but my whole body was hurting. It was already getting dark and everyone was long since gone, no one having waited for me. I struggled on further until I got to the hotel, but when I got there they were amazed to see me. Hézard could not believe his eyes. He thought that I must have done an about-turn on the way. Nothing of the sort: giving up is a term you won't find in my dictionary. When I turned professional he remembered that."

Quiet

Laurent Jalabert has also come a long way as a person. As a young boy he was rather timid: he did not say much, he did listen attentively and joined in the laughter. But he never took the initiative. As a rider, though, he does display a strong personality.

"I am not naturally very open. I am rather quiet, but my biking has changed all that. I have made an effort to change. Everyone is friendly with me, so I'm friendly with everyone else. Cycling is definitely a man's game. The weak go to the wall. Those who use their elbows get through, it's as simple as that. In my early days as a pro, I was led astray a little. I really should thank Philippe Leleu for taking me under his wing. It was Hézard's custom to have his young professional riders share a room with one of the old pros in the team. In my case this was Philippe. He showed me the ropes. Some riders acted like real big-heads in front of young riders, but he didn't. I count myself very lucky in that respect because as a young professional I knew nothing about the ins and outs of the sport, and he gave me a foundation course in it. He taught me the ABC of the bike. I have just as much admiration for him as I do for the top riders from my early days. As a pro, you should never feel as though you have made it. In fact it is a continuous learning process. I can assure you that I picked up more from the three weeks of the 1992 Tour than I did in the three previous years. It must also be remembered too, however, that without those three years of acclimatisation, the three weeks would not have been so good. Racing is a vicious circle."

Hate

Speed merchant Jalabert is a very good climber, and that makes him the one rider who can win any of the classics, whether it be Milan-San Remo or Paris-Roubaix, the Tour of Lombardy or Liège-Bastogne-Liège. "I'm an all-rounder, I'm good in all disciplines, but I'm still only young. I still lack strength and experience. The classic which inspires me the most is the Tour of Flanders. That one is the best, the one in which the legend still buzzes. In that context I count myself lucky that when I turned professional at 20, it was with Toshiba whose top man was Jean-François Bernard. Before then I had never seen a cobble. When I was an amateur I had won the green jersey in the Tour de l'Avenir. At first in the pros, I went for the smaller events. Every weekend I would ride the smaller races in Belgium. At first I was scared of all the cobbles and of the kerbstones, and I frequently fell. I didn't reach the finishing line very often, but eventually I learned how you are supposed to race on them and things started to go right. Now I feel at home on the cobbles. There is really only one race I hate: the Amstel Gold Race. If it was up to me, I would never ride it again. I could win that race, but at what cost? I broke my collar bone on it early in the 1992 season. There are cars all over the place. At about every fifty metres there is a left-hand bend. Awful, and not up to world cup standards."

Gourmet

Laurent Jalabert loves Bordeaux wine, owns a Harley-Davidson on which he rides endurance races, he does not watch television, but enjoys eating in restaurants.

"I'm a gourmet. I love duck pie and I love chocolate; anything that has sugar on it in fact, and cakes too. After a race I like eating steak and chips with mustard. I know the Belgians love eating chips: one of my wife's cousins lives in Brussels and we have been to see her there. But when I need to take it seriously, I do. Then I'm totally wrapped up in my profession and have to avoid all that sort of food. When there is free time, I love to go out on my motor bike with Moncassin, a good friend of mine who I have known since we were together in the juniors. I reckon we must have raced against each other once a week in those days.

I'm the sort of person that likes doing things up. I have just finished some building work, so my hands are always full. I know quite a bit about it, having followed a course to become an electrician when I was at school. Although I left school when I was 17, there are certain technical things that have stayed with me."

Disqualified

Laurent Jalabert is the rider who finished second to Gianni Bugno in the 1992 World Championship at Benidorm. "On that day he made the mistake of not starting the sprint from the front," says his directeur at ONCE, Manolo Saiz. "I obviously wasn't strong enough," says the rider himself. "But it was still a nice souvenir to collect. I was beaten by the better man on the day. Bugno started the sprint himself, but I really thought I could catch him in the final few metres. I failed, though. I never lost another single metre to him, but neither did I take any back. The two metre lead he had when he started the sprint was still there at the line. My wife and parents were standing alongside the course that day and they were pleased with me. I was disappointed, because I came so close, yet also content to have finished second. It's up to me to do better in the future. Everyone says I am still young and that there will be other chances."

Jalabert was disqualified after winning the sprint among a chasing group on

Bugno is world champion. Jalabert is beaten in the final sprint in Benidorm.

the stage to Luz Ardiden in the 1992 Tour, and saw it given to the Belgian Johan Museeuw. "I did nothing wrong that day. Even Museeuw's directeur sportif, Vandenbroucke, came up to me after the race to say that he couldn't understand why the jury had reached its decision. But if that was the case, why did he lodge a complaint in the first place?"

Ambition

Jalabert also has things in common with Eddy Merckx. He has the same desire to win, the same passion for fiddling about with his bike. "In the past more than now, but certainly during training I always carry my spanners with me," he admits. "I change my shoes and I adjust my saddle position. But I have now found my ideal riding position.

I'm also ambitious. I love bikes and I love my job. I'm aware of the fact that nature has given me certain gifts, and I try to use them. If I only win a classic and the green jersey in the Tour this year I will not be satisfied. I want to win the World Cup outright, and I want to win a stage race more than six days long. Apart from that, I'll be working on my climbing and time trialling. I think I can win the Vuelta one day. And if I make as much progress in the next five years as the five previous ones, who knows what I might do in the Tour. Five years ago I had never seen an Alpine col."

SEAN KELLY

KING KELLY

On his passport it says 'John' Kelly, but to avoid confusion with his father, the family called him 'Sean', the name by which the whole world knows him. This same Sean was the rider of the eighties, the King Kelly of the present professional peloton. Sean turned professional in 1977 and is still racing in 1993.

It took quite a while before his first big race win was under his belt. That came in 1983 when he won the Tour of Lombardy, and it was the start of a glittering sequence. Kelly eventually won the Tour of Lombardy three times, the Tour of Switzerland twice, Paris-Roubaix twice, Liège-Bastogne-Liège twice, Milan-San Remo twice, the Tour of Spain and Blois-Chaville. On top of that, he finished seventh overall in the Tour de France in '83, fifth in '84, fourth in '85 and ninth in '89. He won the green jersey four times. If we were to list his 'minor' victories, it would take up quite a lot of space.

Kelly has the reputation of being the most professional rider of his generation. Ferdi Vandenhaute worked with the Irishman at PDM for a year: "When he left us at the end of 1991 and went to Lotus-Festina, we were losing a really great rider overnight. Kelly combined class, determination and professionalism. He was an example to everyone, whether it be minor or big-time riders. I will give you an example. I have always felt that during the period in which the classics are being raced, riders must put in additional training. The question is: how do you drum that into riders? If you tell them yourself, it sounds like you are ordering them. In situations like that you bring in Sean to help. He would tell others, of his own accord, that he did some extra riding. And if Kelly thought extra training was necessary, then the rest followed without question. Sean never complained, either. His hotel room was always to his liking; the water was always warm or cold enough."

First Communion

Sean Kelly grew up in Carrick-on-Suir, a small town on the banks of the River Suir, as the name suggests. In the town there is a 'Sean Kelly Square'. "Carrick-on-Suir is a small farming town in south-east Ireland. Tipperary is not that far away. My parents were farmers but I was more interested in my bike. I got my first bike on the day of my First Communion. I can still remember coming out of church and, with tears in my eyes, nagging my mother to let me go for a ride around the town. I had already promised, without any prompting, that I would make sure my clothes didn't get dirty. She was dumbfounded.

For years and years I dreamed of being able to ride my bike to school. I was really fascinated by the hill I always had to ride over on my way there. In the Tour de France it would be classified as a category 4 climb. I might have been gasping when I got to the top, but I was screaming as I flew down the other side again. There was no better feeling in the world."

Sunday

"Two years later, when I was 14, I started racing. My brother Joseph raced too, and I followed in his footsteps. The best thing was that most races were ridden on a Sunday and that meant I didn't have to work on the farm. My first race was a 'handicap race'. The better you were, the longer you had to wait before you could set off. I got a three-minute start because I arrived at the start line with a rickety-looking bike. Nobody managed to catch me, though. On the next occasion I had to start with the last group. How my bike looked did not come into it.

It was at these local races that I met my wife Linda. Her father was the chairman of the local cycling club, the Carrick Wheelers. He organised many races and I won quite a few of them. There wasn't much competition in my own country and fortunately I was soon being selected for the national teams. Those first contacts with international racing were hard but priceless. I will never forget my first Milk Race. I didn't have a clue as to how I was supposed to ride in the peloton. I had a real job reaching the finish within the time limit. My legs shook with fear, so afraid was I that I might puncture. I would never have been able to get back up to the group. Nonetheless, I won the penultimate stage. I was a bit lucky to be in the decisive escape but I beat everyone in the sprint."

South Africa

"The most crucial point in my cycling career was my suspension in 1976. I was an amateur, racing because I wanted to see the world. That was really the main reason why I was in the Irish national team. I never thought about turning professional. The travelling was great and I didn't really know anything about cycling. I received an invitation to a stage race in South Africa and I was determined to take them up on it. I gave myself a pseudonym and made my way there. It was, of course, against rules and I was suspended. My world was suddenly turned upside down and because I still wanted to race, I went to France for four months. I came across Jean de Gribaldy and he spent hours going on at me about how I should turn professional. But I was only 19 and thought I was far too young. Jean kept telephoning, three, four times

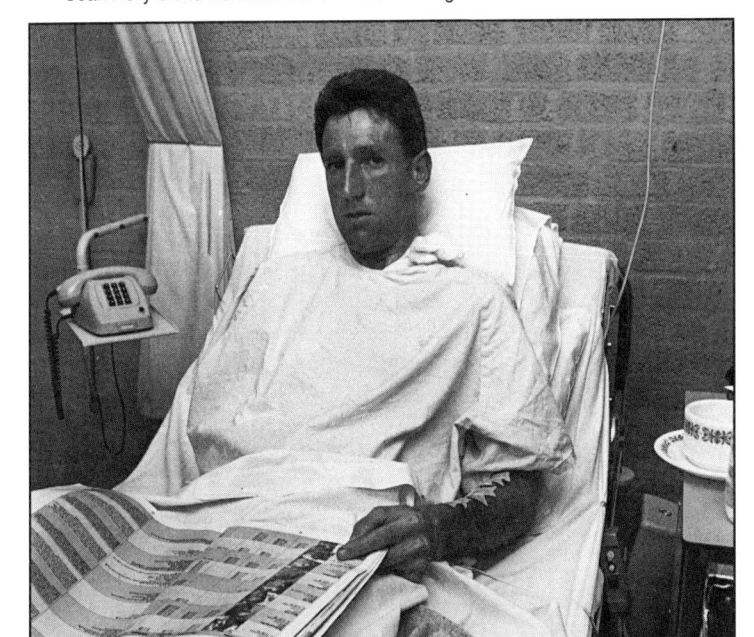

Sean Kelly broke his collar-bone in 1990 and again in 1991.

after another, but I wouldn't listen. "In that case I'm coming to Ireland myself," he said. A taxi brought him to our front door. I put my signature on the contract just to put an end to all the nagging.
It's not true, however, that had it not been for him I would never have turned professional. You mustn't forget that I had won the Tour of Lombardy as an amateur. Besides, I was due to join a cycling club in Metz which had many professional connections, anyway. As it turned out, then, I became a professional with Flandria."

Musketeers

"At that time, Flandria had the three musketeers riding for them: Freddy Maertens, Michel Pollentier and Marc Demeyer. Actually I don't have the happiest of memories of those times. I was too often in the shadow of those three, and I wasn't allowed to ride races the way I wanted to. Looking back on it, it was a good place to learn the trade.
If I wanted to become a real rider, however, I knew I had to get away from there, and I moved to Splendor. A fine team, but the internal jealousy became so widespread that I found it hard to settle. I did get on well with Claude Criquielion, though. We were both brought up on farms, so when we shared a room, we at least knew what we could talk about. We also both enjoyed peace and quiet. My wife Linda still says that I am too quiet.
At that time Berten De Kimpe was directeur sportif at Splendor. He left me to my own devices. His training methods were outdated, but his strict bearing and discipline made up for much of that. Obviously, it was Jean de Gribaldy who I remember most. We worked together for eight years, eight years of continuous education. He taught me everything he knew. In 1987 he was killed in an accident."

Mason

"I'm quite a sensitive person by nature. I hate human problems such as the political situation in Northern Ireland. I think it is terrible that people with families are being mown down.
If I hadn't become a bike rider, I would have been a mason. Before I moved to the continent that's how I earned my living for two years. At school I was no high flyer. My favourite subject was history but I didn't like Gaelic, which was taught in our school. I would rather have learned German or French, I felt I could have put them to better use. I thought Geography was interesting, too.

When I retire from cycling, I would like to do a lot of travelling. I like Spain and America. I only have one hobby: in winter I love hunting pigeons, pheasant and deer. It is great spending hours in your shooting boots, trekking through the woods."

Mistakes
"I have made many mistakes as a cyclist. The biggest one is that I have raced far too much. I won't ever do that again. That was Jean de Gribaldy's fault. According to him a rider could never race enough. For years I rode 200 races a year, no problem. If there was any criticism of it, Jean used to protest. "You only get tired in your head," he would say, "not in your legs." The result was that during my best years I was always tired when I started the Tour de France. I was never fresh and, therefore, I never stood a chance of winning it. Compared to the name I made myself in the classics, I never did enough in the Tour. I won five stages and stood on the podium in Paris wearing the green jersey four times. I finished fourth in 1985 and fifth in 1984, but only ever wore the yellow jersey for one day, in 1984 in Pau. I have never been considered as having a serious chance of overall victory. My climbing was never good enough; my bone structure is too heavy. In top condition I weigh 72 or 73 kilos and that is too much. Against the out-and-out climbers I have always lost out."

Romanticism
"It is said of me that I have a thoroughly professional attitude, and that I am

easy to work with. To me everything is fine, the bike, the hotel room, the food, the hard training, the rain, the sun. You may call that professionalism, I don't. That's the way I was brought up, I have got that sort of mentality from my parents, it's the way I live.

The youth of today are different, they are more demanding, more relaxed and pampered, and that's not good for them. I went to school and after I'd finished I had to work very hard. That attitude has kept me in the peloton, at the age of 36. The romanticism of cycling was always an alien thing to me. I had hardly heard of the Tour de France when I was a young lad. The newspaper reports gave only the bare minimum of details: Merckx won that stage on that day, it rained and X remains leader. I didn't even have a clue how long a stage race like that actually lasted."

Bad Seasons

"1990 and 1991 were terrible years. I broke my collar-bone twice: the first time on the cobbles during the Tour of Flanders, and the following year during Paris-Nice. On top of that, the PDM team abandoned the Tour en masse. Later on, my elder brother Joseph was killed in a training accident. A car ran into him at a corner. It came as a terrible shock. I didn't, for one second, think

'John' Kelly and his wife, Linda

about retiring, however; Joseph would never have wanted that. He was a hard bloke, just like me. All those years ago we started out cycling together and we both went to the continent to become amateurs. Joseph lacked certain qualities, but he spurred me to keep on going. It was he who made a cyclist of me.

The Intralipide affair in the Tour hurt me deeply. I had worked bloody hard after breaking my collar-bone to be ready for the Tour. I wanted to do really well in it; I wanted it to make up for my season. But through the fault of the team doctor, it all went wrong. All the effort was in vain and there was nothing I could do about it. I was totally innocent, and that was the reason why I didn't pack it in before the '92 season. I refused to take any of the blame for it because I was not in any way responsible."

World Champion

"I have won most of the races that I have wanted to at some point, except for the Tour de France and the World Championship. In the 1990 World Championship at Chambéry I missed the chance of my life. I should never have lost to LeMond. A year later I had another go, and in 1992 in Benidorm I tried again, but I fear that by then it was already too late. I blame myself for my defeat in Chambéry. LeMond sprinted with a twelve, and I didn't have that gear on my bike at all. "You won't need it," I thought to myself. It was a gamble that carried a great risk: the sprint could not be started from a long way out or from the front, otherwise I stood no chance. LeMond must have sensed that. At 800 metres from the line he went after Fignon. I knew at once that I was beaten. Fortunately I had already signed a contract for the Tour of Britain the following week, otherwise I would have never climbed on to a bike again. My spirit was shattered, I couldn't see any reason to carry on. I just wanted to crawl into my easy chair."

Six Days

"Believe it or not, I have never ridden a six-day event in my life. At the end of the 1989 season there were hectic negotiations to get me to ride at Paris, but I didn't let myself be talked into it. In the winter I rest, end of story. At the end of October I always go back to Ireland. The countryside is a beautiful green. That's when I go hunting, I ride my mountain bike and spend more time with my wife and the twins."

Last Gasp

"1993 is going to be my last season. I'm going out with a massive party. I have made it clear that I only ride the classics, and under no circumstances the Tour. When I broke my collar-bone during Paris-Nice in 1991, and for the second year in a row had to miss the spring races, I thought about retiring. "Don't do it," my wife said. "You'll be sorry if you do." I have to say she was right. I watched the classics on television and I can assure you that I felt more pain sitting on my settee than I would have done sitting on my bike. I'm glad I kept going, that I fought back one more time. I have even won the Tour of Lombardy and Milan-San Remo since. In Lombardy I profited from my experience and battled right to the bitter end, and in Milan-San Remo I once again took a descent at a hellish speed. If you think of your wife and children at a time like that, you've lost."

School Friends

"I'm getting older. My hair is already turning grey. During a stage in the Ruta del Sol, I went to ride alongside Jo Planckaert, the youngest member of that family. I told him that I had once ridden with his father Willy and with Walter and Eddy. I joked that it was about time I retired too, but I didn't mean it. I still love the bike. If I see my old school friends cycling to work and coming home at night, then I see how I could have been. I have earned a great deal of money, I have travelled the world, and they are things they can only dream about."

Black Hole

"I'm aware that cycling in Ireland will be in a vacuum when Stephen Roche and I retire. Our amateurs don't have a great deal to offer, there is no one ready to take our places. Thirteen Irish youngsters are now touring throughout Europe, but they aren't winning much. Conor Henry won the Milk Race, a straw to which we are going to have to clutch. It isn't easy in the professional ranks. Paul Kimmage once finished 6th in the amateur world championship, but he never made it as a pro. As an amateur Martin Earley won 20 races, but as a professional he is still, what you might say, somewhere in mid-table. I hope he can keep interest alive for a few years to come, until new talent breaks through.

In the meantime Roche and I have created something of a cycling tradition. When I started racing all those years ago, there were at most a thousand riders, now there are five thousand. When I retire there will probably be around seven thousand. It is a healthy base from which to build. If the Irish federation approach me, I would be happy to work with the youngsters. I will never become a directeur sportif, you can be sure of that. I don't want to be catching planes fifty times a year. At a local level I'd like to do something. Beyond that I don't know what the future holds. A few years ago I wanted to buy a farm, but that idea has gone out of my head again."

GREG LeMOND
MILLIONAIRE

Greg LeMond is the most talked about, the most celebrated but at the same time the most criticised top rider of the last fifteen years. The American has never taken it to heart: whatever the circumstances he keeps on laughing and thinking positively. Even after he eventually retires, there will be signs indicating how much he left his mark. Edwig Van Hooydonck has introduced the half-length shorts and Moser a whole series of technical gadgets like the disc wheel. LeMond has tried out countless types of handle bar, inspired by the triathlon bike. He also introduced the idea of gearing your whole season towards the Tour de France. LeMond had his own outlook on everything from food to the season's schedule, but if he wanted something, he didn't let anything stand in his way. One notable and surprising exception was when he abandoned the Tour during the 13th stage in 1992.

Cowboy Hat
No one knows Greg LeMond better than Otto Giacome, the man in the cowboy hat who waits for Greg at every finish with a sponge, towel and drinking bottle. For fifteen years they have been almost inseparable.
"I am paid to do everything for him. So I even clean his room, as he is quite untidy. A few years ago he couldn't even find one of his yellow jerseys. I look for his shoes and I pack his cases. I drive him to the airport at Zaventem and I pick him up again. I also take his children to school. When the family is away I keep the house clean, I vacuum, I do everything. In every race Greg rides, I'm there. Racing is my life. My job is not so demanding, but I am away from home a great deal. I'm aware that I am out and about with Greg more than I am with my own children. I feel guilty, but my wife puts a brave face on it."

The Person
Otto has known LeMond since the American was only 17 years old. That means he knows what sort of person he is dealing with. "I got to know him at races in northern California. My son raced then too. They rode together in

youth races. Because his father was still racing with the veterans, Greg needed someone to massage him and hand him his drinking bottle. That was me. Greg is pure class; I knew it from the first time I saw him ride a bike. As a junior he had such thin legs, but he could pedal incredibly hard. He was small but strong. No matter how steep it was, he used the biggest gears when he rode uphill. I once saw him make a break and he lapped all his rivals, not once or twice, but three times. The only thing he said after the race was that it had been really tough."

Cancer

"LeMond is a smashing fellow. He is also very human. After Steve Bauer's altercation with Claude Criquielion following the 1988 World Championship at Ronse, he went looking for him to give him a few words of encouragement. Last year a woman asked him if he would autograph a book. "For my young son," she said. "He has cancer and is in hospital." Greg jumped into his car and delivered the book personally. At a later date it was arranged for the youngster to follow a stage in the Tour. After his victory in the 1990 Tour de France, Greg bought a gold watch for every member of the team personnel and every team-mate. Even Pensec, who had by then already signed for a Spanish team got one. So too did Greg's sister and his brother-in-law, Patrick Blades, who was the one who had wounded him when they were out hunting. He had enclosed a note: "Without you I would no longer be racing. My batteries are now recharged. Do not have any worries about me."

Acrobatic Skiing

Greg LeMond the rider has it all at his fingertips. He has every facet of the sport under control. One area in which he stands head and shoulders above everyone else is descending. Greg bends forward, looks straight ahead, puts his hands on the bend of the handle bars, and flies downhill like a kamikaze pilot. "There's nothing I prefer doing. When I was young I used to ski a lot. I loved acrobatic skiing: into the air, one or two somersaults, then back onto the skis. Fantastic. I wasn't afraid of a high-speed downhill race either. I wasn't bad at it. Perhaps I could have gone further in the sport. At that time, however, I lived in Nevada, a place where it never snows in winter. My skiing coach ordered me to do a lot of cycling to maintain a high level of fitness. In the end I found I enjoyed the cycling more."

Turkey

"In the States most children are mad on baseball. But I felt much more attracted to bikes and anything to do with them. A cycle dealer near to where I lived came from Italy. Whenever I went to his store, my eyes were drawn to all the photographs and posters on the wall; of Eddy Merckx in his yellow jersey, for example. I was intrigued by the colour. Even then I dreamed of one day riding in yellow. I was also a big fan of Merckx at that time. Above my bed I had posters of him and of the Tour. I often used to just sit there looking at them.

My first race came when I was 14 years old. I had a yellow bike and wore an old-fashioned yellow shirt. I was Merckx. At the start they all took the mickey out of me. "Turkey!" they shouted. So I was pretty vexed when I set off. I was determined to show them. I won the race by a full minute."

LeMond Senior

"One of my most important qualities as a rider is that my capacity to recuperate is excellent. I rarely, if ever, have a real off-day. In fact, the longer a stage race lasts, the better I ride. The only time it was different was in the 1992 Tour, and that's because I wasn't fit when it began.

I have inherited my ability for rapid recuperation from my father. The previous generation can count themselves lucky that he wasn't a racer himself. He was very strong, but as America had no cycling tradition, he never thought about the sport. When I started racing, he got himself a veteran's licence. We often trained together and he rode really well, even though he had had little or no practice.

Sport was always important to my family. My father and mother were both clay-pigeon shooting champions. That was their great passion. I grew up with it, and I thoroughly enjoyed doing it myself. Where did you think my love of hunting came from? I was already joining in when I was twelve.

I also have two sisters. The older one in particular was very athletic. She was a champion gymnast until she seriously injured her back. And just like me, she too had incredible stamina."

Educational Background

"If I had not gone into racing, I would certainly have become a businessman. I would have gone into real estate, like my father and grandfather. From the very moment I had decided I wanted to become a rider, everything else became a side issue. I wasn't a bad student, but it didn't interest me. It didn't worry me too much to fail algebra but I did enjoy studying English. During my final year at high school I was absent quite a lot, as by then cycling had taken preference. I completed my studies through a correspondence course."

Children's Room

"During all that time I had only one aim: I was determined to go to Europe. But at home, things didn't exactly fall into place for me. In order to get some money I used to do odd jobs. I mowed the neighbours' lawns, and I parked cars for a nearby hotel.

Kathy and I first spent a little time in Switzerland and Belgium, and a year later we went to France. We weren't married back then. I won the junior world championship and a cycling club in Créteil contacted me. If I joined them they would look after everything. They had promised us our own apartment, but it turned out to be a children's room in a family guest house.

We had $2,000 and we didn't speak a word of French. For the first few days it rained non-stop. After two months we were on our knees financially. We had a very hard struggle, but we came out of it stronger."

Tour

The list showing Greg LeMond's results in the Tour de France is certainly impressive. He has ridden it eight times, he has won it three times, come second once, third once and seventh once. In 1992 he abandoned. "First of all I want to say that ever since I rode in my first Tour, I have started each time hoping to finish in the first three. If I thought I couldn't, I wouldn't have bothered to start. My first victory - in 1986 - should have been a time of celebration, but the whole of France wanted to shoot me because I had beaten Hinault. He was out to convince everyone that I had tricked him, that I had betrayed him. He really hurt me at the time. No one knew better than Bernard that I had been the stronger of the two of us. He kept on attacking, even when I was wearing the yellow jersey, but I survived it, and that gave that victory a particular cachet in terms of sporting achievement. It is not true that I was out for revenge, though. There are one or two things I could accuse him of, but I must say of him that he definitely had the strongest character of them all. He is a case apart. I deal with things a lot more rationally. When I want to attack, I wait for the most suitable moment. Hinault acted on instinct, he responded to impulses."

Victories

"The main value of my second victory - in 1989 - is that it marked the comeback from my hunting accident. Yet there was criticism then, too. Before I beat Fignon in the time trial on the Champs Elysées they felt that I was being far too lackadaisical. Fignon made all the running. Obviously, I still wasn't ready for it physically. I really didn't know beforehand, how far I had come, or how the Tour would unfold.

1990 may have been the year of Chiappucci's stunt, but it was me who gave the race its colour. I did what I had to do, and on Luz Ardiden I went on to the attack. The difference with previous years was that a lot more riders were in contention for overall victory. No one really stood out. I really do think I controlled the race. I was stronger in the mountains. In time trials I couldn't go flat out because I had an injury on my bottom. I only had one really anxious moment, that was on the stage to Pau when I punctured and Chiappucci attacked. It was my first puncture of the season."

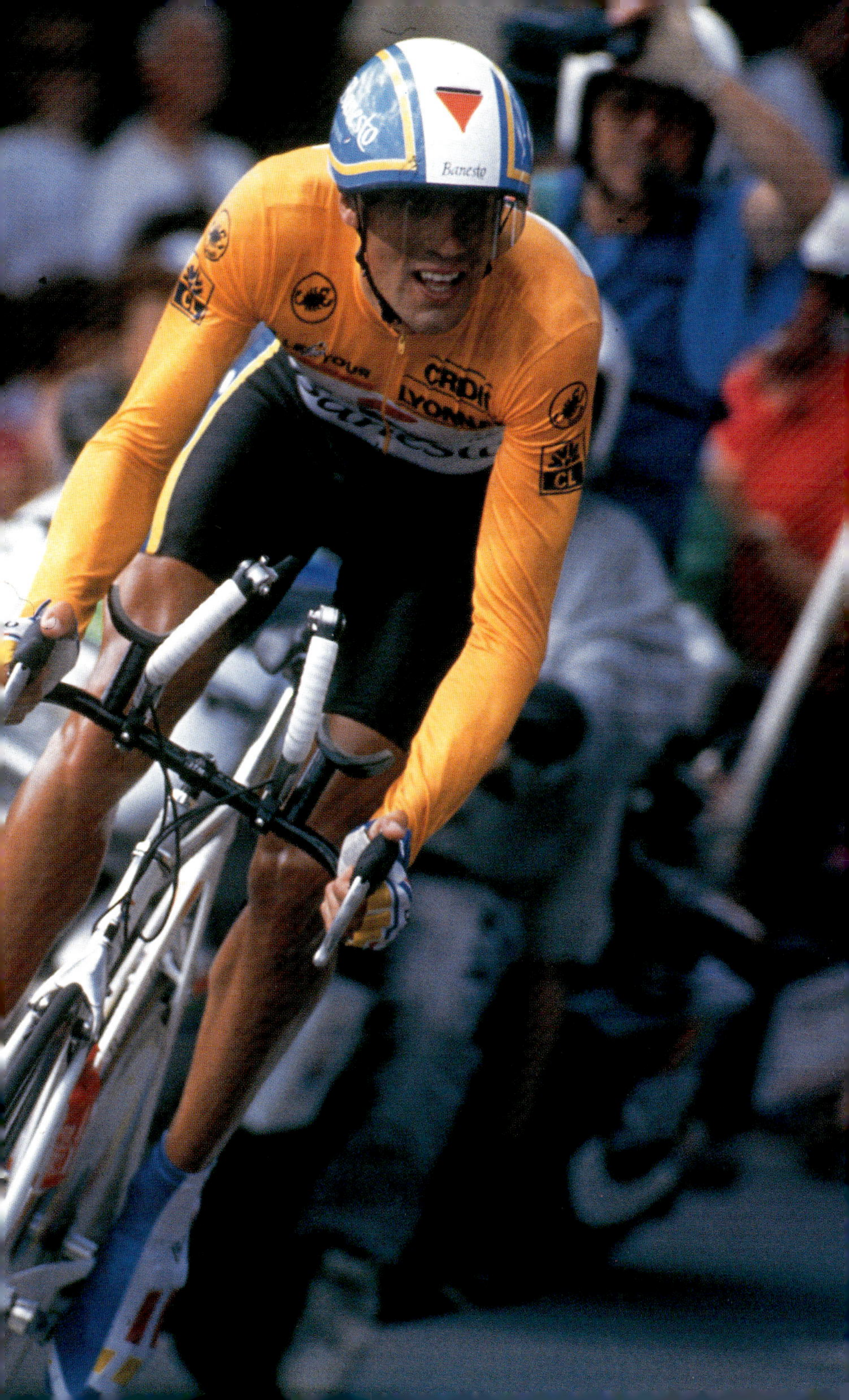
Banesto
CRÉDIT
LYONNAIS

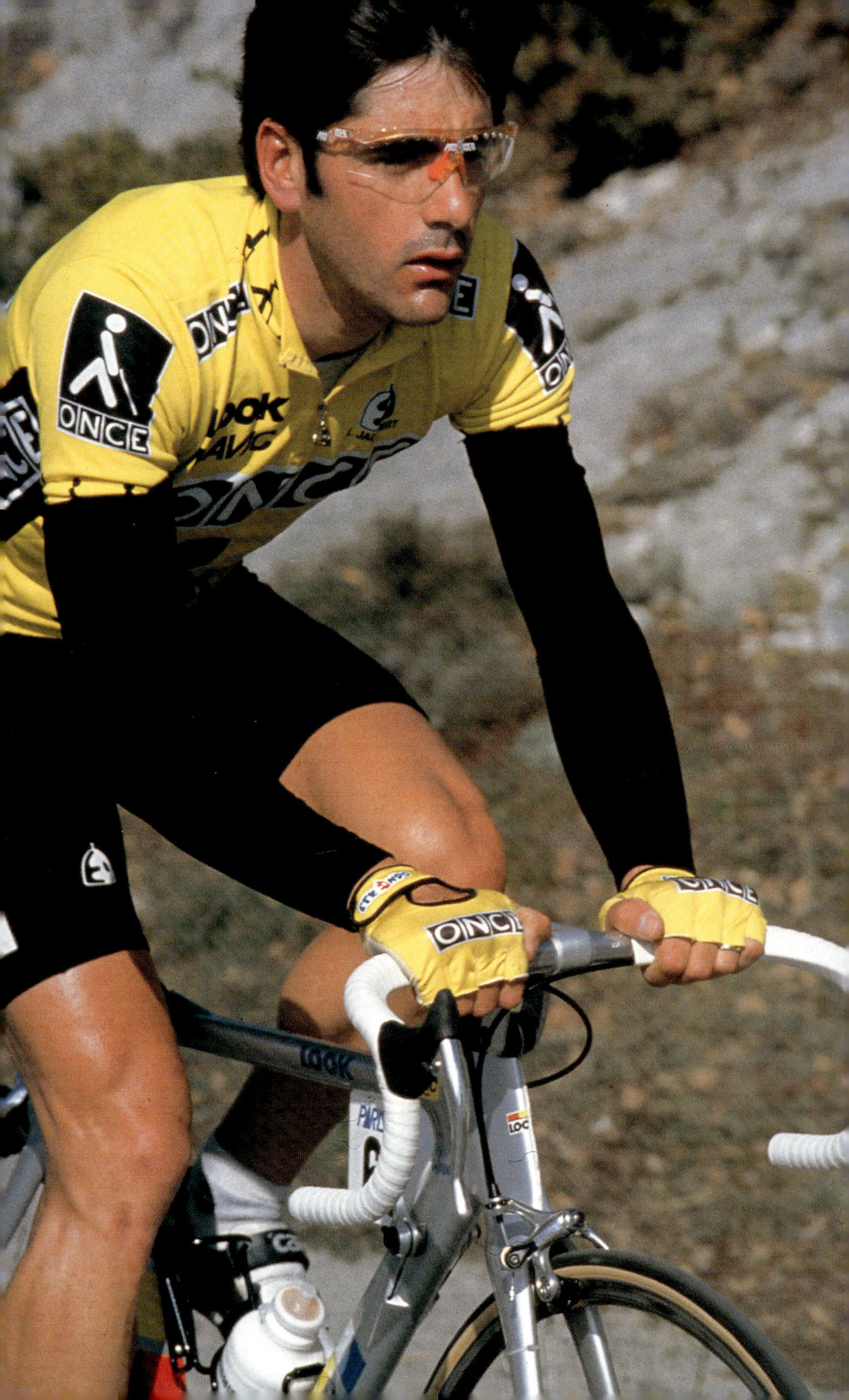
ONCE

Defeat

Greg LeMond had to make way for a superior Indurain in the 1991 Tour and finally finished seventh.

"I was very disappointed afterwards, and still am. If I don't win the Tour, it means the season goes down as a failure. I'll always remember it, though: that Tour was a flop not because I wasn't the strongest rider, not because Indurain was so much better than me, but because I was not fit on the mountain stage to Val Louron. A blood test had already indicated that I had a bacterial infection. I took antibiotics for four days, with all the effects that brings. I was having such an unbelievably terrible time that I even feared I would have a reaction. The next day I wanted to give up, I was dead on my feet.

I don't want to use that as an excuse for my defeat. I also made tactical blunders during that Tour. In the first stage I attacked with Breukink and that was a mistake. From that moment on, I had the weight of the Tour on my shoulders. It also made me realise that it threatened to be a difficult Tour. Everyone was looking out for me, waiting for me to crack up so they could finish me off. Indurain was gambling on me having an off-day. Fortunately I heard about that. Before that Tour I still thought that losing would be scandalous. I was even sure that my career would be over, but, of course, that's not true. Defeat is not a crime."

LeMond introduced the 'spaghetti' handle bar into professional time trialling.

Catastrophe

The 1992 Tour was a total catastrophe for LeMond. He was never, at any

time, in the race. On the stage to Sestriere, Claudio Chiappucci rode at such a hellish pace that the American lost 49 minutes. The next day, on the stage to Alpe d'Huez, he abandoned, together with his super domestique, Gilbert Duclos-Lassalle.
"I was completely drained. My legs wouldn't take me any further, I was totally exhausted. I had started that day in the hope that the pace would be a little slower, but on the first climb I lost the wheel in front. By the second feeding-stage it was already clear that I was not going to reach the finish within the time limit, so I abandoned. It seems that what had happened to me the week before in San Sebastian was the cause of my problems. Because of the blasted blockades on the French autoroutes, it took me 36 hours to get from Kortrijk to San Sebastian. At the very time when a rider should be resting for the Tour, I was wearing myself out. As well as that, the first few days of the race were ridden at such a blistering pace that I didn't get chance to recuperate. I was tired and it was only getting worse. On the flat stages it was going well, so much so that on the stage to Brussels I even went on the attack with Chiappucci, but in the mountains it's a lot harder to conceal. If I had ridden a good Tour, I would have attempted to break the world hour-record. I immediately scrapped those plans, but I haven't ruled it out completely. I will be retiring from cycling in 1994. Keep an eye on me, though, I'll be back.
The first weeks after me abandoning the Tour were terrible. I was totally drained, unable to give anything else. On top of that I was suffering from stress because my negotiations with a new sponsor were put on hold for quite a while: no less than six weeks in fact. That obviously affected me too. It even went as far as me wanting to quit cycling altogether."

Classics

Greg LeMond will go down in history as one of the best stage race riders of all time. There is, however, one blemish against his prestigious career record: he has never won a top classic race. LeMond has been World Champion twice, winning at Altenrhein in 1983 and Chambéry in 1989. In 1992 he rode a marvellous Paris-Roubaix for the Z team, in 1984 he finished fourth in Liège-Bastogne-Liège, in 1986 he even came second in Milan-San Remo and in 1990 was also second in the Championship of Zurich. Eddy Merckx has never been able to reconcile himself with that and once spoke out strongly: "LeMond is no real world champion. A world champion stands out the whole year round; in the spring, in the tours, in the autumn. LeMond only rides well in the Tour, and there is nothing difficult about that."
LeMond reacts fiercely to that: "Pure jealousy. It's because my bikes sell well

in the States. Merckx should mind his own business. I used to really admire him. He once came to my house; we were almost friends. I don't understand why he says something like that, then. I'll tell you this: Merckx would never win nowadays, the way he used to. In his day, he was the only rider to make the most of professional supervision, while today everyone does."

Heat

Greg LeMond has not been able to dominate a single one-day race. "After 13 years as a professional cyclist, I know that I perform best in the heat. So in the spring I am never at my best, it's as simple as that. I'm not cut out for that sort of race, either. If I wanted to win Paris-Roubaix I would have to begin training for it in November, because I need to do as much as possible. If I were to do that, I also wonder whether I would be able to ride a good Tour. And the Tour de France is the race for me. A Belgian grows up with the Tour of Flanders, and an Italian with Milan-San Remo, but when I was young I had never heard of the classics. I would lie awake thinking about the Tour de France, though.
I know myself. No matter what I do, I am only at my best in June and July. With the best will in the world, I find it impossible to do any more than I do in March and April. My confidence grows as conditions improve. The better I ride, the more self-confident I am, and the deeper I can dig into my reserves. In the meantime I am also getting older. In the early stages of his career even Hinault chased everyone down. Later he became more selective, of his own accord. In 1985 and '86 I wanted to shine in every race, but in the end I failed to clinch a major victory. Which is the most important, then?
Another factor also comes into play in autumn. In September I always want to go home. It is an irresistible urge; a biological clock, the same way a pregnant woman has to give birth. If you were to organise the whole cycling season in America and send all the Belgian and Dutch riders there, I'd be interested to see how they would be after two months."

Money

The all-American Greg LeMond has his own, somewhat unorthodox ways of doing things. He is not afraid of eating hamburgers during the Tour and he loves spicy Mexican food. LeMond also brought big money into the cycling world. At the height of his career, Eddy Merckx earned £500 a month, maximum, LeMond has a fixed monthly income of almost £100,000. And that is taking no account of his publicity contracts.
"I'm not embarrassed about earning so much money. It is ten times more than

President Bush, I know. On the other hand, something like 100 American baseball players get more than I do. And how much money has the boxer Mike Tyson made? I have never asked for that much. Whether these sums are justified I don't know, you'll have to ask the sponsors. But I doubt whether those people are idiots. Even when I lose, I generate publicity. Besides, for the most part I pay for myself, because through me a great deal of money goes back to the sponsor. Some companies will shell out thousands for you to ride on their tyres. In 1992, half a million pounds was totted up that way."

Fishing

In previous years the American - who in 1993 is riding for Gan - has got a lot of people's backs up by frequently stepping back a little from racing during the season and going hunting or fishing or playing golf. "European riders think about nothing else but cycling. American riders have not been brought up in the same environment."

Fly fishing is his greatest hobby and he has a subscription to several special-

Greg LeMond after his first Tour victory in 1986, with Bernard Hinault

ist magazines. Former president Jimmy Carter is also a keen fly fisher.

"I have always been able to get stress out of my system. Spending a single day with my wife and children has always been an ideal escape valve for me. My rivals can count themselves lucky that I don't get the chance to go fishing during the Tour. If I could disappear for a while to a mountain river with my rod, I would return completely rejuvenated.

Music is also relaxing. I'm a fan of Talking Heads and the Rolling Stones. I know Mick Jagger personally. When I was 19 I sat at the same table as him. After a basketball match between the Cosmos and the Giants I went to the dressing room and saw Jagger sitting there. In the winter of 1989 I met him again. Alan Dunn who is the Stones' tour manager and also the vice-chairman of a London cycling club, invited me to come and see them. Backstage at the giant rock venue they were playing at in Minneapolis, we were introduced to each other. Jagger told me he knew Francesco Moser. By coincidence the Stones were in Mexico City when Moser was tackling the world hour-record and Jagger went to watch."

Hunting Accident

Easter Monday, 20th April 1987 is a date Greg LeMond will never forget. Greg was out hunting for turkeys with his uncle Rodney Barber and his brother-in-law Patrick Blades. The cases were already packed and ready for his return to Europe. "We had camouflaged ourselves, so that we could move about inconspicuously. It was a stupid accident. I was standing near a tree, when a turkey suddenly appeared and Patrick shot. Shooting a turkey when it is on the ground is something you must never do. Pat shot as a reflex action, however, and I took the full force. I was bleeding very heavily, but we had to wait for a Highway Patrol helicopter to fly over to take me to the Davis Medical Center in Sacramento. Nearly an hour had passed before we arrived there. The operation lasted about two hours. There were shot wounds to my small intestine in two places, and one in my diaphragm. My collar-bone and two ribs were broken and my liver and kidneys were damaged, something made worse by the fact that I had lost three-quarters of a kidney in an accident when I was a boy. On top of that I also had two small holes in my right lung and a whole series of wounds on my back and side. The rehabilitation dragged on for months. On the final Sunday in August of that year, I rode my first comeback race at Wielsbeke. The organisers reduced the race from 100 circuits to 75 especially for me."

ADR

"The road back was an unbelievably long one. A year later I suffered so incredibly during the Giro that I thought my cycling career was over. I could no longer do it. A medical examination showed that the level of a number of materials in my blood was too low. The shortages were replenished, I was ready for the Tour and I won it. I have to say I was lucky that the ADR team found a place for me that year. Besides that, however, I have few good memories of my time there. The team-mates and team management were great guys, but the sponsor was a gangster. The things that man told me and the promises he made; he never kept a single one of them, however. He still owes me an awful lot of money."

God

"Even after all these years, I obviously look back on my accident every now and then, but only in a positive way. It will actually extend my career a little, because it happened at a time when my morale was having to take several blows. You then rest a while, recover, reload your batteries and your enthusiasm comes back.

The effects of the accident will never completely go away. There are still a few gunshot pellets in my shoulder. My self-knowledge has also been upset to a degree, because since it happened my body has reacted in a different way to various forms of exertion. The problem is that I don't know how. My vision of life has also changed. I believe in God and I enjoy life a lot more."

Friends

Greg LeMond is a good-natured, jovial fellow. He laughs a lot, he is friendly and he seems to have time for everyone. Like so many Americans he has a strong, uncomplicated, independent personality. He values a certain degree of freedom. His directeur sportif Roger Legeay, nevertheless, keeps a tight rein on him. "I don't have many really close friends: Johan Lammerts, Vincent Barteau and Otto Giacome, my Mexican physio. Otto is my alarm clock, my cook, my guardian angel, my odd-job man. Cyrille Guimard claims that he has always got on well with me but that is a lie. During my first year as a professional with Renault, the team management had arranged to make a house available for us, but it wasn't ready. We had to make do without any hot water, with bare walls and a studio couch. It was winter and freezing cold, and the heating didn't work. My wife Kathy had no option one day but to reluctantly go to the Guimard's for help, but Mme Guimard just sent her away. "We know about it," she said. "I asked someone to repair it weeks ago but he hasn't turned up yet. Sorry, but I can't help you." Kathy wasn't even allowed inside. She came back in tears. At that time I was earning £400 a month. After the telephone bill had been paid there was only enough money left for food."

Souvenir

After his 1989 Tour victory, Greg LeMond earned £1.1 million per season with Z for three successive years. Greg stepped onto the podium with his young son in his arms, something which probably brought a tear to the eye of millions of women. And with that, the link with the children's clothing producers Z had been established.

LeMond is very much a family man. "Kathy is very important to me. I knew one of her girlfriends. After a race in Wisconsin - I was 16 at most - I was sitting in a terrace bar. We got to know each other and it seems it was love at first sight. A wife is very important for a rider. I find it enormously reassuring that I can always turn to her. Kathy knows what she wants. She is totally behind me."

Moving House

Greg LeMond is certainly not a one-house man. It would take more than the fingers of one hand to count the number of times he has moved house. As a young man he regularly came over to Europe.

LeMond comes from the baking heat that is the state of Nevada. He moved first to Reno in California, but because everyone wanted to talk to him about cycling, he decided to leave. He moved across the States to live near Minneapolis, where he bought a beautiful villa in Wayzata on the banks of Lake Minnetonka. "Minneapolis, Minnesota, is a huge city, but I know little about it. Around my house is 40 hectares of agricultural land. Prince lives opposite but I never see him. 'The land of the 10,000 lakes,' the tourist leaflets tell you.

Last year they counted the lakes and it appears there are 15,509. The woods are full of bears and deer." LeMond found what he needed there: harsh, cold winters so that he didn't have to acclimatise every year when he returned to Europe. He also found space, tranquility, wonderful natural surroundings with rivers and lakes where he can go hunting or fishing. LeMond still has a house in the south of France and one at Marke, near Kortrijk in Belgium, too.

"I only spend at most three weeks a year in Kortrijk, but I like it there. Belgium has the smartest movie houses in the world. The cinema managers keep the original soundtracks and then subtitles are provided.

When you look at it more closely, I live an awful life. I live from one period of jet-lag to another. I never thought I would have any trouble with it, but I was severely disappointed. No less than 230 days of 1992 were spent in hotels. I'm finding it increasingly difficult, because really I'm a nature lover."

Retirement

Sean Kelly says that he and LeMond could probably keep racing until they are 40. "Greg is as fit as a fiddle and has always raced clean, so it will be quite some time before he's finished." LeMond has somewhat different plans, however.

"I originally intended to retire at the end of 1992, but now the Olympic Games in America in 1996 looks like an appropriate occasion to stop. We shall see. If I quit at the end of '94 I will have been racing for three years longer than I promised my little son Geoffrey. He is interested in cycling, but like so many children in the States, he likes trying out many sports. After four weeks of baseball he tries something else."

Restaurant

"I have a make of cycle which carries my name, and I will certainly become more involved with that. I could go into real estate, like my father: buying land, setting up and developing projects, I like the idea of doing that. There is also a chance that I may do some studying first, not for a qualification, but to make me more competent in business and bookkeeping. I already invest part of my income, and I will have to start something with it. My brother-in-law Scott Morris, Kathy's brother, and I have recently opened a restaurant in France Avenue in Minneapolis: the 'Tour de France' a fashionable establishment with room for 65 diners. Scott is the chef and he prepares new American cuisine. I don't get involved in the daily running of it."

Homesick

LeMond will probably never turn his back on cycling completely. "I would like to work with young riders and amateurs, but not professionals. I will never become a directeur sportif. I would like to promote races, though. I would also really like to travel with my wife and children. It may well be physically possibly for me to carry on until I'm 40, but it is getting harder and harder to leave my family behind. My wife and the children, Geoffrey, Scott and Simonne, don't see enough of me. Not that I become filled with guilt about it - it is, after all, simply part of the job - but I do get homesick more quickly and more often these days."

Intentions

Greg LeMond began the 1993 the same way as he did two years ago: five kilos overweight and in poor condition. He abandoned in the Tour of the Mediterranean and withdrew from Paris-Nice before it started.

"I didn't do much training during the winter. I wanted to be in action by January, but didn't make it in the end. Firstly my wife was sick and I had to look after the housework. Then there was the team presentation in Paris which lost me ten days training with all the travelling. But there's no use crying over spilt milk, I have good intentions for the season. I'm going to build myself up very gradually, the way I did in 1990 when I won the Tour: the way I did in 1991 for that matter.

So I'm gearing myself towards it as I have in the past, riding the Giro again as a form of ultimate preparation. Anyway, when I did it differently, nothing startling happened. Last year I started training earlier, but what was the result? I was flying in Paris-Roubaix and from then onwards it went downhill. After the Tour of Switzerland I was tired, and when the Tour de France began I was dead. Why do you think I abandoned? I just could not go any further.

I want people to remember me as a multiple winner of the Tour de France, becoming the first non-European winner in the process, and as a double world champion. On top of that, every non-European knows how to tackle the sport over here and succeed thanks to me. And besides all of that I have helped change the sport; I have made it possible for riders to earn more money, and I have made cycling more popular over a substantial part of the world. The triathlon handlebar in time trials was introduced by me. The Japanese have become interested in it because of me. No, they won't forget me in a hurry."

FRANS MAASSEN

MIDFIELDER

The 1989 edition of Milan-San Remo is a race which will long stay in the memory. The clouds hung low, it was raining and it was freezing cold. The Capo Berta was out of the way, the Cipressa was approaching, and in the distance the Poggio was waiting, more threatening than ever. The PDM team with Kelly, Alcala and Rooks had been keeping a firm grip on the race up to that point. Suddenly Frans Maassen, stood up out of his saddle and left the group containing Jan Gisbers' men hopelessly floundering. "I'm going after him," shouted Laurent Fignon, and he sprinted like a frisky foal, his pony tail flapping in the wind, until he got up to the Dutchman. Fignon didn't hang about. He increased the tempo a little. Maassen bravely fought to stay with him, but Fignon's determination and class would break him near the top of the climb. Fignon looked round, saw that he had done it and bore down for his second consecutive victory in the Primavera. The Frenchman revealed later that he was dead. "It was make or break. I had to shake off my fellow escapee, or he would have beaten me in the sprint. With pain in my legs, I went again and that time it was Maassen who seized up."

Marvellous stuff by Fignon, good riding too from the 24 year-old Maassen who, with his second place, was halfway to a total breakthrough. "I now know I have it in me," laughed the curly headed man from Ittervoort, afterwards. "And I will do everything I can to make sure that whatever talent I have inside comes to the surface."

Silent Force

It is generally true to say that it seems to be mainly hotheads and jokers who make fast bike riders. Exceptions only serve to confirm the rule. Frans Maassen, Jan Raas's protégé, is a silent force, yet that doesn't stop him pushing the pedals with much style. If that were not the case, he would never have won the Amstel Gold Race, a stage in the Tour de France, the Wincanton Classic or the Dutch championship.

His team-mates call him 'Snacks'. "That's a souvenir from the Tour of Sweden a few years ago. I was leading at the time, but in the stage in question my legs were bad and I lost my leader's jersey. That day one of the Elro Snacks riders rode a good stage, and in the evening he was on Swedish television. The lads took the opportunity to make a few jokes about him, while having a playful dig at me for losing my jersey. Since then I've been known as 'Snacks.'"

Priest
Frans Maassen comes from the Dutch province of Limburg. A few years ago he lived in Haelen, but then went to live with his girlfriend, Margret, in Ittervoort, the last village in the Netherlands before the border with Belgium. "Soon after we moved in we had a visit from the parish priest. The good man came to tell us as soon as he could that it was the sort of village where everyone gossiped about each other, so he advised us to get married rather than live together. Since then, the priest has become a good supporter of mine. When, later, I won a stage in L'Etoile de Bessèges, he even sent me a card congratulating me.

Football was the first love of Frans Maassen (front row, second from right).

Margret and I have since married, but only because that's what we were intending to do all along. Margret is a physiotherapist. She has her own practice and she has to work hard. Her working day is very long. At first we had trouble adjusting to it, or at least I did. When I came home from a big race I wanted her to have a meal ready for me, but that wasn't always possible. I now understand that she has to keep part of her life to do her own thing. I am away a lot of the time, after all."

Football
It is actually quite surprising that Frans Maassen ever became a cyclist. Maassen senior used to be an estate agent-cum-building contractor - as he sold houses - but alongside that often did architectural work. Business, however, didn't do that well and he changed jobs and became a damage expert. Frans has a sister four years younger than he is. An aunt - a sister of his dad - once played in the Dutch national handball team.
Round the dinner table, however, the number one topic of conversation was football. Maassen senior had played football, so his son would too.

"I was interested in cycling, but not greatly. I only ever watched it on television when the Tour de France was on. That was something I didn't want to miss. In those days we often used to go to France for our annual holidays. We once went to Pau and another time to Brittany, and if the Tour ever came near to where we were staying we would watch from the roadside. Joop Zoetemelk was riding for Miko back then. Happy memories, but no more than that, because my number one hobby was football. I used to play in the centre of midfield for FC Haelen, our village team. Most of the players were 30 or older, and I was about 16 or 17, but I was still good enough to get into the first team. There was too big an age gap between me and the rest of the team, though. I took it fairly seriously, while my colleagues enjoyed going for a beer or two after matches. I wanted to play at a higher level, but it was not to be. A sort of sports festival was organised in our village, and our football team took part in it. We all had to try out a different sport. "I'm going to try bike racing," I said."

In 1983 Frans Maassen won the Tour of Landgraaf for amateurs.

Individual

Frans Maassen entered the bike race and it went well. "I didn't win, but I did beat someone who was a top rider in the region at the time. "You'll have to become a cyclist," they said. And that's what I did, even though I received offers from two top non-league football teams. But the pleasure had gone out of football for me, and I never took them up on them. I was fed up of competing against those older players, taking all those knocks and fighting against relegation.

I started cycling and I said to myself: "If I am dropped during a race, I have only myself to blame." That individual aspect of cycling greatly appealed to

me, the being one hundred per cent responsible for yourself.
You mustn't come to the conclusion from this that my love of football has completely evaporated. I once read in a magazine that in his spare time, Piet Den Boer (the former KV Mechelen striker) prefers watching a film to a football match. Odd is that, when you think how great a match like Real Madrid versus Milan can be. Many professional riders are mad on football. Jan Raas is not so keen on it, though. "Don't play football," he says. "It is bad for a rider." A couple of years ago we even managed to get him to play in a match. During the game, he brought down his then team leader, Rolf Gölz, with a heavy challenge. That was typical of Jan, he never likes to lose."

Mister Zoetemelk

Any rider with six years as a professional behind him has already covered quite a lot of ground. Frans Maassen started with the juniors and had won five races in no time. "In the last race, Van Katwijk was coming to watch. That was pretty important because he ran a sponsored team. He wanted to sign me and I fought for all I was worth. That day I made two separate attacks, but on both occasions I was pegged back. "It makes no difference," he said. "I have seen that you can ride a bike. Here's a contract, if you want to you can join Mindex." And that was, of course, what I wanted. My eyes were opened by what I saw then. It was like entering another world. For instance, that year we were riding Eddy Merckx bikes and they were real gems. I used to stand there looking at them, admiringly.
I did my very best. I was a good amateur, nothing out of the ordinary, but I still hoped to turn professional. I even quit the law studies course I had registered for at the university of Maastricht. I never took it up and really that was for the best because I would rather have followed a sport-oriented course, but I wasn't good enough at gymnastics. "No more law," I said, there and then. "I'll spend a year putting all I've got into cycling." In my head I already had it all worked out.
When I wanted to turn professional, I was determined to join Jan Raas. The problem, however, was that I first of all had to be spotted by him. It was the Tour of Sweden, an open event, that did it. Frenchman Duclos-Lassalle won the event overall, but I finished second and Joop Zoetemelk was third. I even impressed myself.
Two men who had always impressed me as riders were Johan Van Der Velde, because of his wonderful style, and Joop Zoetemelk, for the way he inspired such awe; even when we rode together for Superconfex. I was always inclined to say 'Mister' to him, I never dared address him as 'Joop.' Actually, I

165

still have trouble with it. I don't suppose he has ever noticed anything himself, he never really said that much."

Roller-Coaster

And Jan Raas did indeed come knocking after that Tour of Sweden, and the Maassen roller-coaster has been at full speed ever since. "If I had signed for Peter Post then, my career would have taken a completely different course. I was not a brilliant amateur, Peter Harings, for example, always got the better of me. Peter opted for Post, but he is now burnt out. A young rider must be able to grow, because the switch up to the pros is very demanding. You can ride badly in the amateurs and still finish in the first three. With the professionals, you can still lose the wheel in front even if you're riding really well. In my first Paris-Nice, I discovered that. Nothing I did worked. On gentle climbs I was having to push myself as hard as I could, just to stop myself being dropped. I'll never forget seeing Fignon slam on his brakes, get off and pee by the side of the road, before leisurely joining on again five minutes later. At that moment my tongue felt as though it was hanging down to my spokes. Five days later I was home again. It took me a month to get over it. I sat doubting whether I would ever make a decent professional. Fortunately my dad gave me his full support. "You must allow yourself two years to find out," he said. I immediately fought my way back. I now know that it is like starting from square one when you turn professional: your past counts for nothing, but you shouldn't panic."

Step by Step

Frans Maassen goes through his professional career: "My first pro year didn't produce that much, I needed time to adjust. I won two races and that's all there is to say about it. In my second year I won 13 races including the Tour of Belgium. I also won the red jersey in the Tour de France as the best intermediate sprinter and that was very important for publicity. In my third year I came second in Milan-San Remo and I won the Wincanton Classic and the Dutch national championship. The breakthrough was on its way. In 1990 I won a stage in the Tour de France, I won the Tour of Belgium again, the G.P. Eddy Merckx and the Flèche Brabançonne. Each year there had been an improvement. My sprint victory against Maurizio Fondriest in the Amstel Gold Race in 1991 was a new high for me. I then went on to win the Tour of the Netherlands and two stages of the Four Days at Dunkirk. By the end of all that, I was nearly at the top. Only the Tour de France was disappointing, and that's because I was sick. 1992 should have topped the previous year. I won the Three Days at De Panne and thought that I had arrived once and for all, but in the big races I didn't have the best of luck. I finished fifth in the Tour of Flanders, but as an end-of-term report for the early part of the season, it was not good enough."

Plus and Minus

"When you reach a certain standard, you are no longer paid to win lesser races. Unfortunately it is not easy winning a big race. I'm now at a point where I am physically at my peak, but nowadays they won't let me slip away in an escape, unnoticed. Although I may have reached my maximum in terms of condition, mentally I haven't yet. They are always saying that I'm too nice, but I'm not so sure of that. I'm one of those people who immediately want to talk about problems when they arise. I don't let anything lie dormant. I do sometimes wonder whether I can put up with enough suffering. The problem is that I don't know how my colleagues feel that pain, so it's impossible to make comparisons. I do know, though, that I can hide it away when I'm exhausted. I am also good at assessing races. The way I see myself is that I don't have as much class and capacity as some riders, but that I make up for that by my insight. I can analyse a race. If that was not the case I would want to be as strong as an Edwig Van Hooydonck."

Mistakes

Frans Maassen is a realist. He rides with both wheels attached firmly to the ground. "In seasons gone by, I have made many tactical mistakes. The first big one was in that Milan-San Remo with Laurent Fignon. It still breaks my heart that I wasn't able to sprint against him that day. I should have hung on to his wheel. He was a star, I wasn't. I shouldn't have taken on any of the lead work. Somewhere in me, though, I have a sense of fair play, and for that reason I did.

Another incident which continues to haunt me is that first, so important, stage in the 1990 Tour de France. I was in the escape with Bauer, Chiappucci and Pensec, which turned the entire Tour on its head. Although I won the stage, I was the only one of the four who never got to ride in yellow. In the morning I was as pleased as punch that I'd won the stage; by the afternoon I was at a low ebb. I was certain we would win the team time trial, that I would take the yellow jersey and that I wouldn't have to relinquish it until

Frans Maassen is one of the true breed of hard riders.

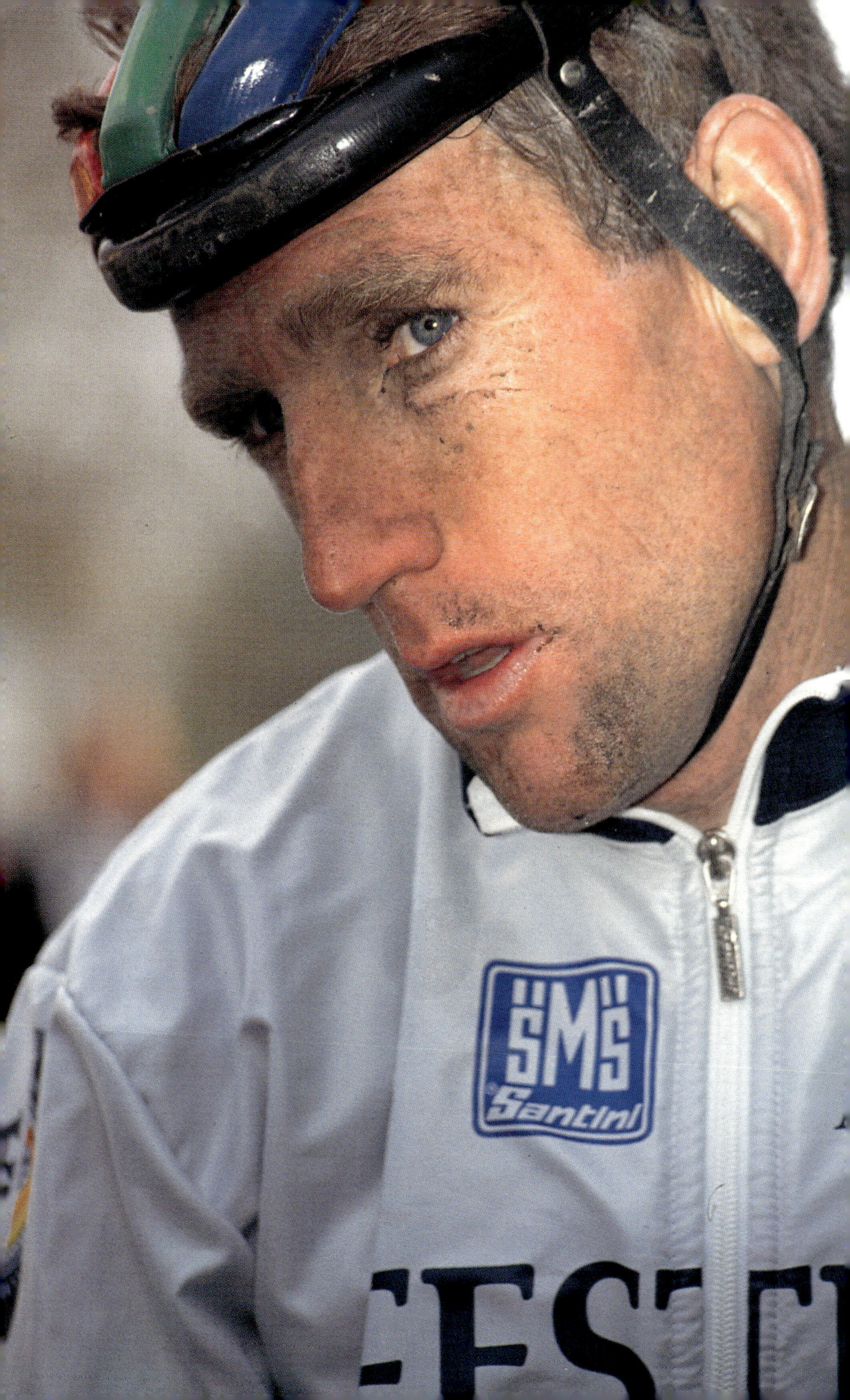
SMS
Santini

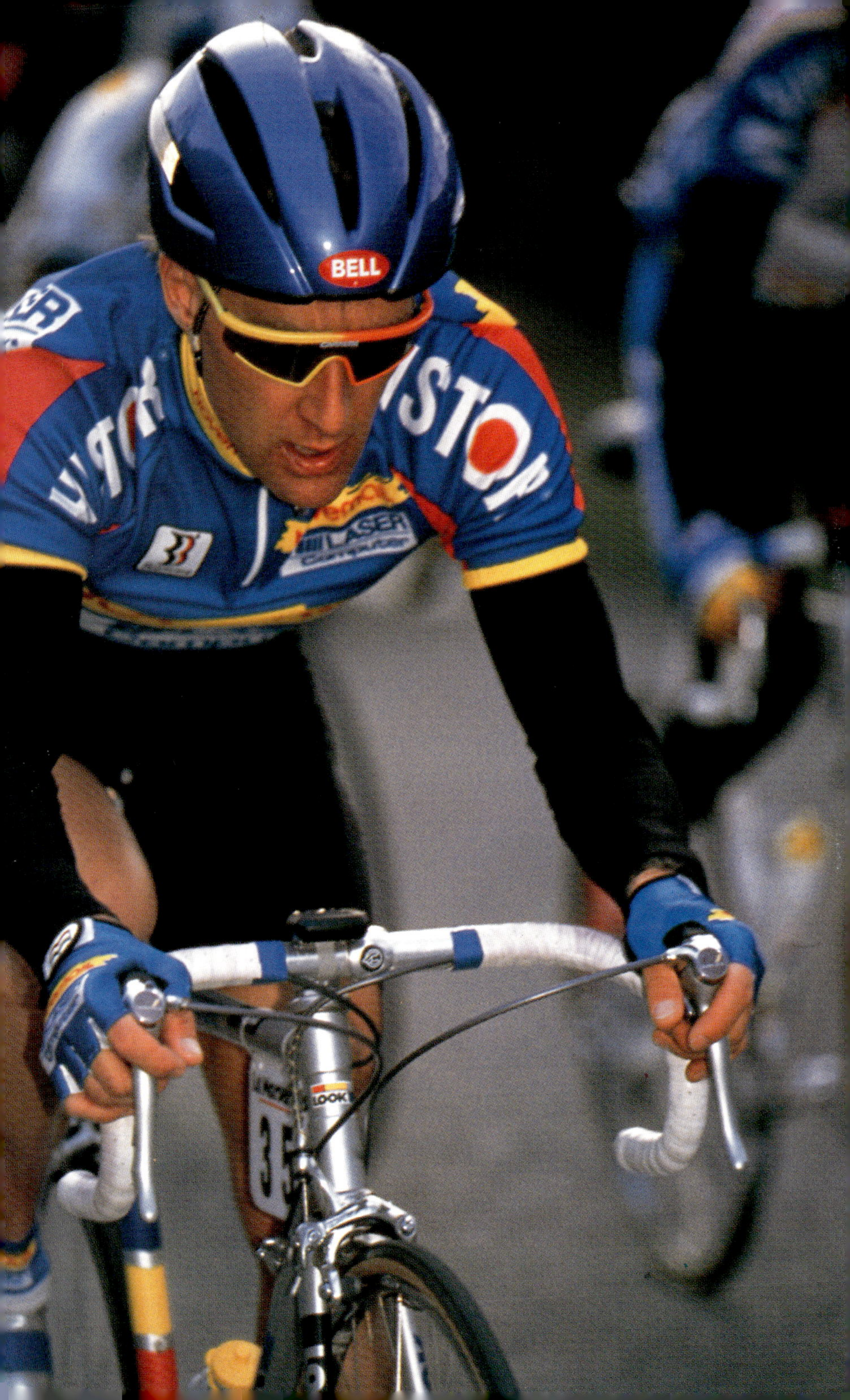
BELL
LASER
LOOK
35

ten days later. In the end it was the Canadian Steve Bauer whose team shone, not the Bucklers. I don't look back on that day with any pleasure."

Fighter

Frans probably doesn't look back on the stage to Montluçon in the 1992 Tour with any affection, either. He was leading with Marc Sergeant and Jean-Claude Colotti. Theo De Rooy ordered Sergeant to stop doing any work. When Colotti attacked, Sergeant didn't react, and neither did Maassen and the stage was thrown away. People put it down to the feud between Raas and Post raising its ugly head again. That might have been so, but the victims were the two riders. "I think it's a shame that it is Maassen and Sergeant who had to pay for it," said Post. "They are both fighters and neither of them deserve to be labelled the way they have."

Frans Maassen was deeply unhappy afterwards. "I love my sport. I am a sportsman, one hundred per cent. But what happened today is a disgrace. Raas and Post must get round the table, because this cannot be allowed to go any further. Would you like to get them together? I told Jan this morning that I was going to attack. I was determined to win this stage. I even added that I hoped a Panasonic rider would go with me, as otherwise I would never be able to get away. I was glad that Sergeant had hitched up his wagon. He knows how to ride at the front. If there was one rider I would choose to ride the Baracchi Trophy with, it would be Marc. The way he can push the pedals. We were working well together until Theo De Rooy called his rider back. I immediately asked Marc if he would check with his directeur sportif again. He did, but he was told not to work."

Superstition

Frans Maassen drives a BMW 520 I. He is interested in a wide range of other sports, and claims that he knows a lot about them too. Apart from that, he likes watching films, he loves nature and he likes skiing. In contrast to many other riders, he is not really a music lover. He likes Fleetwood Mac, but pays little attention to it beyond that.

Maassen is superstitious, though. "I always wear a small crucifix around my neck. If I'm not wearing it, I'm nervous and unsure and everything goes wrong. I prefer not to ride wearing number 13. I have raced in it twice in the Grape Race at Overijse, and I had to abandon on both occasions, something that's unusual for me, as I always try to reach the finish in every race I ride. I don't like abandoning out of pure laziness; honestly that's the truth, it's because I don't like training hard. When you abandon you have to go out on a hard training run on your own, and I'd rather not. I don't mind training on my own at seven o'clock in the morning, as long as it's quiet, and preferably without any touring cyclists around. I'm happy to let them ride with me, no problem, but if they cling on to my wheel, I ride them off it. I hear that most of my colleagues do the same."

CHARLY MOTTET

RUCKSACK

If he were not such a great rider, you probably would not even notice he was there. Charly Mottet is an inconspicuous, modest figure. They do not even gossip about him. His appearance is, nonetheless, distinctive: short legs, a robust upper body and a sturdy head. He is smaller than his rivals, but that makes no difference to him. "It's always been like that," jokes Charly. "My parents thought and hoped for a long time that it would change, that I would suddenly start to grow. I remember getting my very first racing bike and them discussing the size that the wheels should be. "We're going to save money by buying you a bike that's a couple of sizes too big, so that you'll be all right with it in one or two years time," said my father. Dad worked for the post office, and my mother has mainly been a housewife for the last ten years. So at home money didn't grow on trees. That first bike is still there at my parents' house, and it's still a couple of sizes too big."

Professional

Mottet has the reputation of being a difficult, annoying and self-willed little man, but that is refuted within the Novemail team. At the end of the 1992 season, at the age of 30, he signed a contract with a non-French team for the first time in his career, after five years with Cyrille Guimard followed by four seasons with RMO. Despite the adjustment, he was accepted from the very first moment. "Mottet, a difficult bloke? Nothing of the sort," says Novemail team manager Peter Post. "Professional certainly, but that's an entirely different thing. Mottet knows what he wants, he also knows what we want and it clicked between us immediately. The fact that he went out and won the Tour of the Mediterranean in February 1993 is proof to us that he takes his profession very seriously indeed."

Rugby

Over the many years he has spent racing, Mottet has built up a reputation as an all-round rider. He is a strong time triallist, a good climber, and he is not afraid to attack. Not bad for someone so small. "I'm small I know, but I've never let myself be pushed around. For instance, I played rugby for a long time. There was a pitch 400 metres from where I lived. It's a game in which players of all sizes can take part, big lads and little ones, so that meant me, too. I loved the game and I wasn't a bad player. Up to the age of fifteen, I knew everything there was to know about rugby. I ate, drank and slept the sport.

Cycling was something I followed more from a distance. I can still remember our village being the feeding stage on a stage of the Dauphiné at one time. That has stayed with me. Actually I could never sit still. I always had to have something to keep me occupied. I liked cross-country skiing and swimming. I knew nothing about cycling, but that gradually changed. I have a brother who raced for two years, and my uncle was particularly interested in it. He lives in Montelimar and he took me all over he place to watch it: camping on Alpe d'Huez to watch the riders go by, attending the Grenoble Six Days. And very enjoyable it was too. Don't get the impression that I was totally disinterested up to that point, when I was 12 I was already riding a bike. I remem-

Charly Mottet and Philippe Crepel, the PR man of Peter Post's Novemail team

ber that around that time I once rode up three cols. It was a challenge open to all categories and I came third. It was around 1975-76 when I started to pay more attention to cycling. I remember Bernard Thevenet being the hero at the time. I was a fan of the Peugeot team for whom he rode. So fanatical about them was I, and so determined to ride around wearing a Peugeot team jersey, that I went so far as making one myself, as I didn't have one. I had a white T-shirt and I drew those famous black Peugeot squares on it. I drew my own jerseys. They were happy times."

Spirit

Those who know Mottet admit that while the little Frenchman has natural talent, what he has most is fight and spirit.

"I've always been a hard person - I had to be. First of all, I was a student. I followed a technical drawing course. I went to the same grammar school as Eric Comas, the Formula One driver, and Saint-André, the rugby player. We weren't in the same class, but we knew each other. When I was 19 I got my diploma, and later I could have gone to work at a building consultant's office, but nothing ever came of it. At that time I could make more as an amateur than I could earn in a proper job.

I just want to say that my studies demanded a great deal of attention. In fact, at that time I only trained on Wednesday afternoons, and if I got the chance, Saturday mornings, yet I still won my races. And that's the way it stayed until the end of my period in the junior categories. I hardly trained at all. I reckon that in the long term that turned out in my favour. In those early days I was also a track cyclist. I even rode the World Championship Team Pursuit. It was only later that I started giving it my all. And when I eventually turned professional, I still had plenty of energy in reserve. I still had a lot to learn too. Everything was new, I had never ridden a stage race in my life, for example."

Cyrille Guimard

Charly Mottet made the step up to the professional ranks in 1983. He was 20 years old, had just two years as an amateur behind him, and already had a provisional contract with Cyrille Guimard.

"It was good fortune to have ended up under the wing of Cyrille. Primarily because it has meant that I have always ridden for a big team. Just imagine how it feels, signing your first professional contract and becoming a teammate of Bernard Hinault, Greg LeMond, Laurent Fignon, Marc Madiot and Maurice Le Guilloux. Incredible, obviously. I was going to make sure I did my very best. By March that year, I had won my first race: my 31st of the month. It was in the Tour du Midi Pyrenees, on the penultimate stage to Saint-Gaudens. There were 7 of us up front: 4 Peugeots, including Duclos-Lassalle. Stephen Roche was there too, and I was there with Bernard Hinault. "Don't ride," Hinault said to me. "I'll take care of everything." I listened to him. Then, with one kilometre to go, I attacked. I really rode out of my skin and I won, climbing, as a result, to second overall."

Wear and Tear

Mottet says that he was always happy riding for Guimard, but the fact is, even that relationship finally came to an end through all the wear and tear. At the end of 1989, Mottet signed for RMO, a team sponsored by a company which operated a chain of temporary employment agencies. "I don't want to say anything about why I split with Guimard. He was, and still is, a marvellous directeur sportif; for young riders especially. I became a top rider with him. I learned my job under him, but I was a good student too. For professionals making their debuts, he is the best master you could wish for. The strange thing is, though, that it is right that all those who become famous with him, move away at some point - me included. With me it was primarily for financial reasons. I know Laurent Fignon stuck it out longer, but that's because he and Guimard had common business interests. I never did."

The young Mottet wins the 7th stage in the Tour de l'Avenir 1984.

Too Long
Those in the know say that Mottet stayed with Guimard for one season too long, and he agrees. "I think I wasted a little too much time while there. In any event, I should not have stayed with Fignon for so long. Fignon had a reputation, and my personality wasn't forceful enough to push him to one side when he had his achilles tendon trouble. Guimard kept playing his Fignon card, and instead of demanding a better deal for myself, I swallowed it all. I realised I ought to do something about it during the Grand Prix des Nations in 1987. I won that event, catching Fignon and leaving him behind on the way. From that moment on, I wanted to be the team leader myself. I had had enough of melting away in the shadow of Fignon, but Guimard persuaded me to stay with him for one more year. I should never have taken him up on it. During that entire year I was never really happy. Fignon and I were too preoccupied with our own personal goals to complement each other. We are also completely different types of people. He is an urbanite, whereas I'm from the provinces. Not once did Fignon ever talk to me about his private life. That says something about our relationship."

Expectations
Charly Mottet once said, while still in his early years as a professional: "If I never manage to win the Tour de France, it will mean that I have chosen the wrong profession." His expectations during those early days were set extremely high, then. Yet Mottet was no exceptional rider as an amateur, but as a first year professional he made an enormous impression. On his debut in 1983, he won the 2nd stage of the Tour du Midi Pyrenees, and he won a stage in the Tour of Luxembourg. In his second year his victories included a stage in the Colombian tour, the Clasico RCN, and a stage and overall victory in the Tour de l'Avenir. Those in the know, however, did not agree with Mottet's high Tour expectations. Both Eddy Merckx and Bernard Hinault claimed Mottet was "too lightweight to win the Tour."
At the time, Cyrille Guimard made the following comparison: "Take Mottet and Fignon; the latter is a Ferrari and the former is a GTI. They can both go very fast, but for the Tour, Mottet's cylinder is too small."
They turned out to be right. Mottet did not perform badly in the premier tours. In the Tour de France he finished 4th in 1987, 6th in 1989 and 4th in 1991. In 1990, after winning a stage, he even finished second in the Giro, behind Gianni Bugno. There were no victories, however.
Mottet is intelligent enough to be able to draw his own conclusions. On Monday 16th July 1990, Mottet won his first ever stage in the Tour. At the press

conference held afterwards, Charly announced: "I've got to be honest with myself, it is fantasy to think I might still win the Tour. I always believed I could, but not any more. I knew it after the time trial. I had a short-lived glimmer of hope again, but in the Alps I was completely wiped out. On that day I forced myself to change my tactics. The classification was no longer going to be of any interest to me. I was only going to try to win stages. I immediately put a cross against one or two stages where I was determined to give it a good go. From today onwards I will be mainly looking out for victory in one day races and the shorter stage races."

Tactics

Mottet, however, has little to grumble about. In spite of the fact that his engine is thought to be too lightweight for him to win the Tour, he has chalked up an impressive collection of honours. Here is an account of his most prominent achievements. 1986 was a very good year, he won the G.P. Eddy Merckx, took two stages in the Vuelta and was desperately close to winning the World Championship at Colorado Springs; only Argentin was better on the day. A few weeks later he also finished 3rd in Créteil-Chaville. In 1987 he won the Dauphiné, the G.P. des Nations, the Criterium des As, and for the first time in his career he wore the yellow jersey in the Tour. In 1988 he took the Tour of Lombardy. In 1989 he won overall victory, including a stage, in both the Dauphiné and the Dunkirk Four Days, as well as the prologue in the Midi Libre, and the Tour of Latium. 1990 brought the Championship of Zurich, 1991 saw him take two stages in the Tour, and in 1992 he won the Dauphiné once again.

Peter Post

From 1989, Mottet rode for the French RMO team. During the 1992 Tour de France the company went bust, wages stopped being paid, and the sponsor himself landed up in prison.

"Sometimes things don't go the way you expect them to. Take 1991, the best season of my career. I won two stages in the Tour and I was in 4th place in the FICP rankings. I wanted to leave RMO even then, but no one else was interested. In 1992 I won the Dauphiné, but for the rest of the season I was struggling with health problems, I didn't perform well, and I abandoned in the Tour. By the end of the season I had raced for fewer days than I had in my first year as a pro. Yet, strangely enough, I received four offers at the end of it. I could have gone to Gatorade, but I wasn't interested. Mercatone Uno wanted me, but I didn't fancy that. I also had a good chat with Jan Raas.

I could have earned more money with him than elsewhere, but there were only two other Frenchmen in the team, and that was too few. Then along came Post. Peter was looking for a French rider who could win prestigious races, and I was looking for a fresh challenge. Everything I asked for has been given to me. I have six French team mates. I had personally pushed for Eric Caritoux to be signed as well. Peter Post had no objections and he got as far as sitting round the negotiating table with Eric, but they never reached an agreement."

Trust

As mentioned above, Mottet's first few years as a professional were spent riding under the wing of Cyrille Guimard. Charly makes a comparison between Post and Guimard: "It's a paradox: there is more freedom with Post than with Guimard, and yet there is discipline. There is more pleasure, the atmosphere is more loose, but you work very hard. The balance seems to be just perfect. You get the feeling that they have 100 % trust in you. I have not even been asked yet how much and what type of training I put in last winter. And you don't have to discuss it. Drawing up a training programme for me, for example, took a grand total of three minutes. If you ask for something, you get it. Everything is done to make things the way the riders want them. In my time, I have known things to be done differently.

I have always been in awe of Post. I've never had any dealings with him, but I have always bid him a good morning. He's not the sort of man you can ever really become a friend of, but you can count on him."

Nature

Charly Mottet is an unusual chap: he has a very wide range of hobbies. His favourite one is going with his wife, Françoise - a teacher - into the hills camping, with a rucksack on his back, carrying a tent and wearing hiking boots!

"We don't go as much as we used to, because we now have a young daughter," he explains. "Let me say, though, that I am a country lover. I come from Saint-Jean-en-Royons, a lovely little town at the foot of a mountain stream. There is a huge chalk rock, and at the foot of it the small houses are grouped. Life there is wonderful. The villagers drink Clairette de Dieu, a tasty white wine, and the countryside around is marvellous. I was in Japan in 1989, when the World Championship was held at Utsonomiya and I went to visit Tokyo. I could never live there, though, concrete everywhere. Where are the trees? The birds? Fields? Countryside? No sign of them. It was there that I realised how wonderful nature is. Had I not taken up racing, I might even have become a nature guide."

Hobbies

So although Mottet is primarily a country lover, he does have other hobbies. "I do a great many things. Flying fascinates me especially. I have a friend who does parascending and he has taught me. I only do it during the winter, though, and I don't know whether Post would approve of it. I am also taking flying lessons. I fly small aircraft, a Cessna and a Piper. The airfield is only 1.5 kilometres from where I live. I now live near Sallanches, the place where I once saw Hinault become world champion. I even go circling above the cycle track in the plane. If I may recommend something to you, take a trip above Mont Blanc if you get the chance, it is the ultimate experience."

Winning

Charly Mottet still has certain objectives and races he would like to win before he retires at the end of the 1995 season.

"I want to get back into the top ten in the FICP rankings as quickly as possible. Before I retire there are three things I hope to win: above all else a Tour stage, because there is nothing more pure or popular than the Tour de France. I have no ambitions as far as overall victory is concerned, though. I'm not ruling it out completely, it's just that it would be difficult. Unless

Indurain goes down with something before it starts, or unless I can pull off a coup such as finding myself in a break that gets away unchecked. Otherwise not.

"I would also like to win Milan-San Remo. To my mind that is the most magical of races. Everything about it is an extreme: the number of kilometres, the speed, the prestige, the age of the race itself. I would also like a world championship victory, but then, so would everyone else!"

Johan Museeuw

NORTH SEA AND DUNES

Johan Museeuw, brilliant winner of the 1993 Tour of Flanders, and the best Belgian rider at this moment, is a West Fleming through and through; a child of the North Sea, a son of the coast. His parents still live in Gistel, a village about 10 kilometres from Ostend and it is also where Johan lives with his wife Veronique and their young child Gianni, in a brand new house. He loves the sea, the sea air, the dunes. He knows the polders and the fish markets in the area. "I have an uncle who is in the fish trade. He buys fish and sells it in the Ardennes. I love the sea. I'd love to walk along the shore every day, but cycling takes up so much of my time that it's simply impossible. In the winter I have more time, fortunately, and then you can't keep me away. I drive to Ostend in the car and the always follow the same route: I head straight into the dunes and bike along the waterside up to De Panne, a trip which takes me an hour and a half. That's the way I became a cyclist, and it's the way I will remain a cyclist."

Football

"I simply can't sit still. I've been the same since I was a lad. I wasn't allowed to race bikes, but I played football for a while for Gistel, the village team. I played on the left side of the attack and it went very well. I'm left footed and that has its advantages. For two years in succession I was top scorer. Yet my heart was never really totally in it. All I thought about was cycling. I told the club that I was going to quit a year in advance of doing it, but they didn't believe me. A week before my 15th birthday, in October, I handed in my kit. The club directors and trainer stood there looking perplexed. The reason for that is that they were planning to transfer me to a bigger club, KV Ostend. I told them that they had seen the last of me and that I was going to become a cyclo-cross rider. It wasn't a difficult transition to make because I had already been doing a lot of training in the fields. My father raced in his spare time with the W.A.O.D., a small cycling organisation, and I used to go with him. In my very first race I finished fourth."

Johan Museeuw in the kichen with Jean-Luc Vandenbroucke

Cyclo-Cross Rider

"I was a cyclo-cross rider for two years. That's what Dad wanted me to do. He had been a road racer himself for years, and even spent several seasons as a pro, but he found it such a terrible experience that he wanted to keep me away from it. I didn't take part in a single road race when I was in the newcomers category, although I obviously did a lot of training on the roads. As a first-year junior I rode in ten road races and I won three of them. In my very first race I finished second behind a Canadian lad. It was a criterium and five of us rode in a group at the front. In the second year of the juniors I again rode ten races and I won eight times, in any way you could imagine: both in sprints and escapes. I mainly rode criteriums at that time. It was the ideal preparation for the cyclo-cross season. It suited me perfectly, too, the exertion was similar: short and sharp. Cyclo-cross was my favourite, and I was good at it. In my first Belgian Championship I came second to the man from Limburg, Dirk Maertens. A week earlier I had beaten him, and I even went into the race as the firm favourite, but I couldn't live up to the expectations. On the day, Dirk was stronger."

Negative

"I have no recollection of my father racing because I was too young at the time. He doesn't have any scrap books, either, he just has a few photographs. Recently I have been having a good look at them; more than I ever used to. It's only since my own son was born that I realise what a father and mother mean. Whenever my father used to tell me anything about cycling, it was always negative. Actually he wasn't very happy that I too became a road racer. But although I always kept putting off going in to it, in the end it was no longer possible to. My father rode for Whisky Okay for a while, Frans Verbeeck's team, but he never received pay that was due to him. Life at home, then, was hard and depressing. He was forced to retire because there was not enough money coming in to feed the family, and he set up his own garage business. Yet he was a very good rider. While he was a professional, he once came second in the race out of which the Amstel Gold Race grew. In the enthusiasts category he won 42 races. He was certainly a different type of rider to me: quicker in the sprint but less versatile. He had more talent but less determination. Yet determination is a thing I have in abundance: I assume I must have got it from my mother.

Going Out

"Cycling was in the blood in my family. Dad was one of eleven children: he had nine brothers and one sister. All ten of the sons tried their hand at cycling, but my dad was the best of them. I myself am an only child and they say that only children tend to be spoilt. Well I certainly wasn't. My father was a firm but also an understanding figure. He laid down clear ground rules. If I was supposed to be home by twelve o'clock, I had to be back by twelve or I would not be allowed to go out again for a month. I tried it once and found out the hard way.

When I was in the newcomers, juniors and enthusiasts categories, I regularly went out enjoying myself. I was above all a cyclo-cross rider in those days, and in the summer I didn't have a lot on. And I had a great time as a young man. I would recommend any young rider to do the same, because once you're a professional rider, it's like being a recluse. Life suddenly gets hard, very hard. You can't go out any more. To a young rider, any sport should be fun. That's the way my father told me to approach it. And later on, if my son wants to become a rider, I shall tell him the same."

Inside

"I'm fairly sensitive by nature. For instance, I've always been an animal lover. When I was young I had a pony and a dog. They both died shortly after one another and that was a real catastrophe time in my life.

My worst subject at school was Dutch dictation: my attempts at it were always riddled with mistakes. I was good at modern mathematics, though.

I spent my time conscripted into the army as a driver with the land forces in Lombardsijde. I even drove those big old army trucks.

I like America, while my favourite holiday destination is Gran Canaria. I like anywhere as long as there is sun and water, and plenty of fish! I love eating fish and any seafood, except for scampi. Other things: I drive a Peugeot 605. Dad is a Peugeot dealer, you see."

Education

"I went to school until I was 17. I followed the electronics course at secondary school, but I never finished it. At that time my father had someone working for him in his garage. One day, however, he suddenly left to set up his own business, and as my dad was suddenly short of manpower, I was immediately drafted in as an apprentice. That is the way in which I received training for self-employment, so that I would have something to fall back on later. Maybe I'll go back to it in a few years time, but that depends.

Cycling is a job like any other, but it does have certain clear advantages. People in ordinary jobs tend to work from eight till five. Often I start training at nine and I'm back home by two. On the other hand, racing is hard work

too, but, of course, it's the job you have chosen to do. The thing I find worst about it is the always being away from home.
I will keep racing until the end of 1996 and no longer. But if I find during the next year that it is not going well any more, I'll pack it in. I will definitely not become a directeur sportif or remain involved in cycling. Really, though, I still don't know what I will do."

Cautious

"According to José De Cauwer, my father has always been careful in the way he has brought me along, and I'm glad about that. In the days when I exclusively rode cyclo-cross, he wouldn't let me take part in more than one race a week. I am now reaping the rewards of that policy, because I still have reserves of energy left. As well as that, the type of medical supervision I received was one in a thousand. I knew nothing about the subject when I was an amateur, for example, I never used vitamins. Few people believe that, especially when you hear what amateurs take nowadays, but it's the truth. I was regularly examined by a doctor because that's the way it had to be done: my medical book had to be in order. I have only recently become serious about nutrition. And my father didn't make me do a lot of training. Extra training was unheard of. The fact is, I never really needed to do much training to ride well. Racing was for fun, it really was."

Flop

"When I was 19 and in my first year as an amateur, I consciously set my career on a new course. It was then that I began intensive road racing. Ghent-Staden was my first important race and I came fifth in it. Dirk Baert, who was then still coach of the national amateur squad, spotted me. "I'm taking you to France with the team," he said, and I was selected for two races, including Paris-Dijon. What an experience that was! I was totally blown away, I couldn't keep up with them; it was a disaster. I had done enough to earn my place in the national team, however, and that meant that I rode the Giro dello Regioni, the Tour of Austria and the Tour de l'Avenir two years in a row. The first year wasn't a resounding success, but the second year went a good deal better. I didn't win a stage, but I came second on several occasions. Zanoli and Konyshev were the men to beat then. My position on the final classification was, frankly, poor. I couldn't do anything on the climbs. It even went so abysmally that I was only able to get over the mountains in the very last stragglers' bus. Since then I have improved my climbing greatly. So much so that I even thought I was the best climber among the sprinters. The truth, however, was hammered home to me in the 1992 Tour. Laurent Jalabert is better, much better than me. That's why I failed in my bid for the green jersey."

Quiet

"I turned professional in 1988. If I had wanted to, I could have made the step-up a year earlier. I received offers and could have earned the minimum salary, but that was not the way I wanted it. I knew how much I could earn at my father's garage, and I wasn't going to turn pro for less than that. At the end of 1987 José De Cauwer made me a good offer and I took him up on it. I was now a pro, but I had no experience. My father knew a great deal about racing, he helped me a lot, yet I still had the impression that I was quite simply overwhelmed during that first year. I was a quiet lad, but I was always a good listener. Other riders would tell me they had gone out on 250 kilometres training rides, while I never went out for more than 120 kilometres. Even in my first year as a professional I didn't train that much. Twice a week I followed the group training sessions, but I didn't think there was much point in doing more than that."

Johan Museeuw was voted Belgian Professional Cyclist of the Year in 1991.

Room

"The first professional race of any consequence in which I contested victory was the Tour of the Americas, which was partly ridden in Venezuela and partly in Florida. It went really well. In that first year I spent a lot of time sitting in my room with José De Cauwer. We got on very well with each other; it clicked between us. He opened my eyes. He worked out training schedules which I then followed, and I started to blossom. I am now passing on the same advice to Marc Wauters. I've recommended to him that he should ride the Tour this year. At one time I was in a similar position to the one he is in now. I had also raced a lot during he months leading up to it, and because I had ridden a good Tour of Luxembourg, José asked me if I wanted to ride the Tour. Dad was frightened by the prospect, however, and so was I. Adri Van Der Poel was sitting nearby when I was asked. "Do it," he said. "You will be a better rider for it when you come back, and you'll be able to push yourself further. You need to have that ability." Adri was right. Three days before the end of the Tour I had to abandon. I was completely drained, but I was stronger. I could clearly feel that the following year."

Allergy

"Did you know that it is only since 1992 that I have been careful about what I eat? I have quite a bit of trouble with hay fever. Some years it isn't too bad, other years it's bad all the time. Dr De Wit is a specialist in detecting all kinds of viruses. He follows a German method which works very accurately. I was examined for ten weeks and the results showed that I am allergic to pork. Now I eat a lot more fish and less and less meat, and I feel a lot better for it. And I no longer have coffee, milk products, pineapples and tomatoes. It isn't always possible to give them all up all the time: when we eat muesli, for example, it contains soya milk, and normally I shouldn't have that. But I don't want the soigneurs to have to make something different just for me, as I'd rather not be the odd one out."

Disappointments

"Like any other rider, I have obviously had to learn to live with disappointments. It isn't always plain sailing. After I abandoned the Tour in 1991, I wanted to quit cycling. I had pulled out of the race because I was sick. For three days I was really at a low ebb. My parents and my girlfriend were at the Tour. We took our mobile home to a campsite somewhere and just stayed at that spot for five days. For three days I didn't go near a bike. I was so disillusioned that I didn't even watch the television. The only stage I saw was the last one on the Champs Elysées. It took my father to persuade me to give it another go. After that I also received a lot of letters from people telling me not to give up and urging me to carry on.
I was also hurt by what was written in the press after the Belgian Championship in Peer. I still don't think it was fair. If ever a rider deserved to win a championship, it was me. I don't know entirely what was going on behind my back, and I simply don't want to know. I have the finishing sprint on

videotape, but I still haven't watched it, and I won't. I'm afraid to see it, I must admit."

Belt Tightening

"Another disappointment was my fall two days before the World Championship in Benidorm. The socket in which the thigh bone fits into the pelvis, broke, and because the inside of it wasn't displaced, the healing process took a long time. My world, however, did not collapse around me. Anyone competing in top-class sport knows what risks are entailed. I wouldn't let it stop me.

And I wouldn't take it for granted that without the injury I might have become world champion. I watched the race on television in the hospital. I was certain Jalabert was going to win. He shot through perfectly, taking Chiappucci and Indurain with him. The French team had done a great job helping him. Jalabert is pure class, but Bugno was stronger. I don't know whether I would have been able to beat him.

Something that really annoyed me was the way my sponsor, the national lottery in Belgium, responded to my inactivity. One day my wages were suddenly cut right back to the minimum; £500 was all that was transferred to my account. I was aware that this could happen, having read the small print on my contract, but I never thought Lotto would implement it. I was disappointed with the way the team leadership let me down so much. I helped Lotto to a guaranteed Tour ticket for three years on the trot; I won stages for them and I was the national champion. I couldn't help falling while out on a training ride. Anyway, I regard it as an ordinary accident at work. Not that I've had to really tighten my belt, but honestly! I have to make repayments on a loan and I have other expenses; I'm a married man, after all. My vitamins and food alone cost me £500. It wasn't fair treatment. It was a harsh punishment for the fact that I'm riding for the GB team in 1993."

Aims

"I see myself as a perfectionist. I'm always looking to improve. I am interested in all aspects of the sport and can accept other's opinions. Besides that, I feel I am ambitious too. In everything I do, I try to keep my aims clearly set out before me. First of all I wanted to win a stage in the Tour de France and in 1990 I achieved that, winning two, even. Next I wanted to win the Belgian Championship, and I did that too. In spring of this year I won the Tour of Flanders, going one better than my previous best; second place in 1991. That leaves Paris-Roubaix, which I want to win as soon as I can. In 1991 I finished seventh in Roubaix, but I know I can do better. I am also keen to win the world title, the question is: when will I get a course that suits me? In recent years it has always been designed to suit the top Tour riders. That is not sour grapes, it's a fact."

Koksijde

"Nevertheless, my ultimate aim is to put everything into cyclo-cross again at some point in the future. Eric De Vlaeminck has been trying to persuade me for years now. One day I'd like to, but at present it's impossible. My road racing schedule is so busy that it would mean riding through the whole winter, and that's something I simply can't do. When the Belgian Cyclo-Cross Championship is organised for immediately after the Tour, they won't be able to ride me out of it the way they did in January. If it should go less well on the road - as it is for Adri Van Der Poel at the moment - I'll give it a go. I have a sneaking feeling about the world championship in two years' time that's being held in Koksijde. We shall see. Whatever happens, at least I know the circuit."

Pay

"For the 1993 season I moved to the GB team; purely for financial reasons. Until my wages were drastically reduced after my heavy training fall, I was always very happy at Lotto. After that, however, I could no longer stay. I've heard it said that I had to leave for the sake of my career, and that the team wasn't strong enough to help me. That's not how I see it, though. My teammates always did their very best. It was obviously no Peter Post team, but no one ever expected them to be. Few of Post's riders earn less than £80,000 a year; whereas Lotto don't have many riders on more than £20,000. I always felt at home with Lotto. Over the last few seasons, my market value has increased, of course. Four teams were seriously interested: GB, Lotus-Festina, Carrera and Gatorade. From the financial point of view, the offers were fairly similar. I never considered joining Lotus, Sean Kelly's current sponsor, and Carrera and Gatorade are too Italian and that put me off them slightly. I'm no Dirk De Wolf - he's happy anywhere. The fact that GB are partly a Belgian team, was the deciding factor for me. The directeur sportif and his assistants are Belgian, and that's how I prefer it."

STEPHEN ROCHE

BABY FACE

Write off riders of proven class at your peril because the day tends to come when they strike back unexpectedly. In recent years it has often been said of Stephen Roche that he was finished. In the 1992 Tour de France, however, he was suddenly back. The 32-year-old Irishman even won a stage.

In 1990, Roche was riding for Willy Teirlinck's Histor team. Patrick Valcke - at the time a close friend and source of support for Roche - had also made the move to the Belgian team and, as assistant directeur sportif, he turned the whole team upside down. Roche was still in contract for the 1991 season, but he had to go: he was no longer producing the goods and the Flemish riders were fed up of the foreigners. Yet it was Valcke who was the rotten apple.

Roche went to Roger De Vlaeminck's Tonton Tapis team, but he never lived up to his name. His career reached an absolute nadir when he missed the start of the team time trial in the Tour and arrived outside the time limit. The curses rained down on him: Roche was a weakling; he didn't take his profession seriously, once again he had to go.

La Bourboule

But Roche is nothing if not a grafter and a battler. He went on his way and it took him to Carrera, the team with which he had enjoyed his greatest successes, winning the Tour, the Giro and the world title in 1987. He teamed up with Claudio Chiappucci again, and found the ambition and the will to set the record straight. Roche came back. For months on end he complained about the pain in his back but, nevertheless, rode a decent Tour of Spain and finished 15th. He then rode the Tour de France, eventually finishing 9th, and winning the stage finishing in the fog at La Bourboule. Roche acted as sidekick to fellow team leader Chiappucci, who had made clear his intentions of hotting it up for Miguel Indurain. When Chiappucci eased up a little, Roche attacked. Stephen Roche rode a superb Tour.

Green

Sagy-Sailloncourt is a small, leafy village 30 kilometres from Paris. The place has at most two streets. It has no shops, no bars and one telephone box. Halfway along the main road to Sagy is where Roche lives. As befits a star, his house is surrounded by a high wall. There are two automatic gates and an intercom with a security camera. The Irishman can afford it: he is the happy holder of a sizeable bank account and an impressive honours list. In 1987 he won the Tours of Italy and France and the World Championship, a feat only ever previously achieved by Merckx.

Roche was born in 1960. He is married to Lydia and they have two children: Nicholas, 8 and Christelle, 6. Lydia is a woman with a lot of get-up-and-go. She has taken a secretarial course and studied languages and marketing. "I was 18 when we got married. I met her at a race. Her brother was a cyclist too, and one thing led to another. When I was a young professional, her family helped keep my head above water. They had a shop and there were several spare rooms on the floors above it. I was allowed to live there rent-free. At that time I was earning about £300 a month net and I had to make that go a long way. I can tell you now, they were hard times.

I have stayed in France because my wife is French. I still feel a great affinity to Ireland, though. I grew up in Dublin. The climate and training opportunities are ideal and I miss the country a lot. I love hearing my children speaking English. I have had a satellite dish installed on my roof so that they can learn to speak it like natives."

Stephen Roche with the cheese he received as a gift for his Tour stage win in 1992.

Newspaper

At one time, becoming a cyclist was not the sort of thing an Irish youngster would do. "I started riding because it's something my parents enjoyed doing. My mother and father even met each other on a cycling trip. I also had an uncle who raced. When I was 13 I got a racing bike those thick tyres. Mum and dad didn't know that I was already entering races until they saw the result of my sixth race in the newspaper. At the time, though, I was really riding for pleasure. Sean Kelly was always on a bike, but I wasn't. I marvel at how Sean has kept going, but it's my only explanation for why I still have reserves of strength. Without my them I would not have been able to come back the way I did. I'm hard on myself and so is Kelly. We're typically Irish and we're close friends. His wife, Linda, is the godmother of our son Nicholas, for that matter. For years we prepared for the season together. All we ever thought about was racing and training. We would be away from home for two months at a time. We didn't have it easy."

God

Although Kelly and Roche are big friends, they are also opposites.
"I've never done anything that would hold Sean back, and he hasn't to me. Sean began racing four years before me and to me he was an unreachable God. Some people said that riders of his calibre only come along every 25 years, and as I wanted to match him, I thought that was a shame.
Our backgrounds are completely different. I could never live like Sean. For years he lived with his brother, but I wanted to have my own house as soon as I could. He is a country boy and I'm a city slicker. I was often reminded of that fact. Many people had made their minds up. "Roche from Dublin? He'll never make it." "Roche going to France? He'll do a lap round the Eiffel Tower, then he'll be back on the first boat home." And so on."

Boat

As it turned out, it didn't all end with that boat trip. "That's not the sort of thing I had been brought up to do. I didn't have an easy life at home. My father was a milkman with a round in Dublin. If I wanted some pocket money, he let me go with him. We were doing our rounds of the streets at half-past five in the morning. My father sat in the float, while I ran alongside and delivered the bottles onto the doorsteps. After that I then had to go to school. That wasn't without its problems either, but I did get a certificate in plumbing and that helped me get a job in an engineering works. It was a awful job for a cyclist: the hours of work were terrible and there was a lot of

Stephen Roche sprints to the World Championship in 1987.

overtime. I was forced to cycle to work, and in the evening I had to make a massive detour to get in my required training mileage. I worked a lot of overtime and with the money I earned from the job, I could afford the boat to France to go racing. I set off back on the Sunday night, arriving back on a Monday morning."

Contract

Like so many young English-speaking cyclists, Stephen Roche joined Lucien Bailly's ACBB club in Paris.

"We met in Ireland and he told me that I would have to live a normal and regimented life if I wanted to become a rider. I took six months unpaid leave, but at the end of that time I was absolutely no further on. I wanted to go back home; my dream had turned sour since no professional teams had shown an interest in me. "It's because you haven't won a big race," said Bailly. The very next day I won Paris-Roubaix for amateurs, and with that my contract with Peugeot was in the bag. Things can soon change."

Baby Face

Stephen Roche is, without any doubt, one of the most popular riders in the peloton. The French idolise him. Having once again ridden a good Tour, he was now appearing for the cameras on an almost daily basis. He puts his fame not just down to his racing feats, but also to his baby face; his boyish, laughing, endearing countenance. Yet it is also said of this self-same Roche that he can be difficult. At all the teams he has ridden for, problems have arisen sooner or later: Carrera, Fagor, Histor and Tonton Tapis. "I still say it had nothing to do with me. I now know that Valcke was a bad influence. I took it on myself to protect him and I shouldn't have done. The reason I did it was that I was the captain and carried the responsibilities. Afterwards, it was me who took the blame for everything. Why is that, do you think? Valcke was a good friend and I had much to be thankful to him for. It clicked between us. Even in our rare periods of free time, we knocked about together. For a time I drove car rallies with Patrick as my companion. When I put an end to our working relationship, I soon discovered the true Valcke. He launched a real smear campaign against me in the newspapers.

I don't want to lay it all at his door, though. When I was with Tonton Tapis, I never rode well. The main reason was that I just couldn't get on with Roger De Vlaeminck. He would tell all and sundry how poor I was, but he wouldn't say a word to me. That was his biggest problem: he could never have a reasonable conversation with his riders. Yet for a directeur sportif that is essential. I wanted to save myself and I suggested bringing in Jean-René Bernaudeau as assistant directeur sportif, but he wouldn't have it."

Actor

To find the absolute low-point of Roche's career, we have to go back to the 1991 Tour when Roche arrived too late at the start of the team time trial. Roger De Vlaeminck had really laid into Roche again just before the start of the Tour: "He is an idle so-and-so and he doesn't put anything into the sport." It looked suspiciously as though Roche had pulled out of the Tour deliberately. The Irishman, however, dismissed that rumour straightaway. "Why would I want to do that? For the first time in my career, my wife had been able to get three weeks off work so that she could follow the Tour. My parents had came over from Ireland and I had hired a caravanette for them so that they could follow the stages in Normandy and Brittany. Do you think that I would have chosen that moment to boycott the race? If that's what I wanted to do, I could have thought of a thousand and one other ways. I could have just reported sick and I would have been seen as a martyr. No, Roger De Vlaeminck had simply given me the wrong start time. The other lads in the team knew to always check the information De Vlaeminck gave them, but I didn't. Because I was sacked there and then, I demanded a hearing. Mr Demeulenaere, the sponsor, made it seem as though he had called me in to carpet me, but that wasn't true at all. I'm annoyed by that as well. In the meantime, all of this was getting me a terrible reputation. I know they have complained about me in other teams, but people who know me well, see things differently. I've been a professional for 11 years now and anyone who can keep up a comedy act for that long must be a bloody good actor."

Knees

1987 was the absolute pinnacle of Roche's career. He won the Tour de France, the Giro and the world title. It seems a little strange, then, that he doesn't like looking back on those times. A reason for that is because he never got the chance to confirm his supremacy at a later date. His knees began to cause him problems. In 1984 he had fallen during the Paris Six Day track meeting. They operated on him, and then had to repeat the operation, but he was soon back in the saddle. In 1987 it did not look any rosier, and in November they operated on him again, but the pain kept returning.

"I had resigned myself to never getting back to fitness again. Just one more operation and my career would have been finished for good. My whole dream world was shattered. During the previous winter, after my three big victories, I had said to Lydia: "I've been riding all these years for so much a season, and now we're finally sitting pretty." It was a great feeling. We immediately bought a house in Ireland and Lydia opened a boutique in Dublin city centre. By the beginning of 1988 we had sold it all again and I felt very despondent. Then, along came Dr Wolfarth-Müller. He was also to treat me for my back pain during the 1992 Tour. At first I didn't want to know the man. To me, he was just the umpteenth doctor to whom I had to explain over again the hell I was going through with it. "Yes, but he's the team doctor for the Bayern Munich football team. The man has a golden touch," I was told. To cut a long story short, I let him talk me round. The Bayern and Belgian international goalkeeper Jean-Marie Pfaff was puffing away and sweating it out in his gym, and I recognised Boris Becker, Daly Thompson and Sören Lerby in his waiting room. It was clear to me right away: he couldn't have been such a bad doctor. He had a very different, unique approach. Other doctors always immediately asked me where the pain in my knee actually was. But it was Dr Wolfarth-Müller himself who told me what the matter was, where the pain was concentrated, and how he would treat it. I called in at the first supermarket on my way home and bought a pair of pyjamas and a new set of clothes and underclothes. The next day, I was in for treatment."

FICP

It took another three years before Roche was back riding at his old level. In 1991 he won the Catalan Week and the Criterium International. In 1992 we had to wait until the Tour of Spain before we saw him ride one of his better races. Roche, however, was still struggling with a back injury. Then he won a stage in the Tour de France and, along with Chiappucci, was the most persistent attacker.

"The foundations for my good season were laid in the winter. I had sold all my vintage cars - even my rally car - because I wanted to put everything I had into cycling again for one last time. Another important factor was that at Carrera I was not going to be the only team leader. At the end of 1991, I was also considering offers from Amaya, from Lotus - Kelly had not yet been signed - and from the Italian Jolly team. I could have earned more with any of these teams than I could with Carrera, but in each of them I would have had to carry full responsibility of team-leadership. They all needed me in their team to score FICP points so that they could get a place in the Tour de France. That was precisely the sort of pressure that I no longer wanted. At Carrera, responsibility is shared between Chiappucci, Abdujaparov and me.

I have always got on very well with Chiappucci. When I won the Giro in 1987 and there was a row within the team because Visentini kept demanding

Roche's wife Lydia is French. They live in France.

the role of leader, Chiappucci sided with me. It's possible that he thought that as a long-term decision, it would be more opportune and safe, but even if that was the case, he was right. His attitude back then forged a bond and we have both profited from it since."

Carrots

You would expect that in the case of Roche, an employer would play a cautious game and pay him a fixed monthly wage to be supplemented by attractive win bonuses. "That's how it was done at Histor and Tonton Tapis, but I wouldn't sign contracts with those sort of conditions again. I don't want to be always chasing a carrot in front of my nose. Carrera pay me well and that has helped give me peace of mind. When the season began I didn't know how it would turn out. The business with Roger De Vlaeminck in the previous year's Tour had broken something within me. At first I wanted to retire, but then a voice inside told me that I shouldn't finish my career in such a way. I felt that something was still smouldering, the flame just needed to be fanned. A decent Tour of Spain, the enthusiasm within the team and Chiappucci's presence were what did it."

Future

Stephen Roche will be 34 years old in November 1993, so he doesn't have a great deal of time left as a rider. Just like Sean Kelly, he is very concerned about the future of cycling in Ireland. "I'm afraid that the sport will slowly bleed to death in our country when Sean and I retire. Many people don't realise that. At the moment many young riders are trying out cycling, the sport is still very popular. All they know about, though, are the wonderful stories about the heroes, Kelly and Roche. There is always the other side of the coin. Many riders retire from the sport disenchanted and stay away from it forever. You rarely read their stories in the newspapers. Many of my young countrymen will experience this disillusionment for themselves.

As far as my own future is concerned, I won't be riding for much longer; probably for one more season. Whatever happens, I won't keep going until it starts to go downhill again, because by then it will be too late. Your final impressions always stay with you. I want to round off my career in style. I am also getting more and more homesick. I would like to make more time free to spend with my children. What I'm going to do, though, I don't yet know. A PR job would suit me fine. Perhaps I'll become a television commentator or a journalist. During recent Tours, I have written pieces for an Irish newspaper, and last year I did some for Le Parisien, too. They polish up the texts a little, but the editor thought that they were more than reasonable. At the same time, though, I have rediscovered that writing is actually more stressful than cycling!"

TONY ROMINGER

CONDUCTOR

The Swiss rider, Tony Rominger, winner of the Tour of Spain and the Tour of Lombardy in 1992, is a case apart in the peloton. He arrives every morning at the start of a race, unshaven. His chin is usually covered in thick stubble, but he is unconcerned about it.

Rominger is a polyglot. His mother and grandmother live in Denmark, his father in Switzerland. He comes out with a sort of German that a native speaker couldn't help having a chuckle at, and he gets by in more than passable French, English, Italian and Danish. The peloton has two things to say about him. "Tony is like a computer, so clever that he can programme himself." The second thing is that wherever you see Rominger, his wife is bound to be not far away. Wherever he goes, she goes.

Birgitte

It is true. The pretty Birgitte is small and charming. She is there at the start, she stands on the podium, she roams around the hotel, and Tony beams his approval. That was the case in the Tour of Spain, Rominger's biggest triumph in 1992. And it was just the same in the Tour of the Mediterranean, Tony's first venture of the 1993 season. Juan Fernandez, Rominger's directeur sportif in the Spanish Clas team, knows that by being around, she helps keep his team leader's morale high. So he keeps inviting her along. "I need her to be there," declares Rominger. "Her being there doesn't determine whether I'm going to finish 10th or 100th in a race. I don't ride any better, but she helps keep my spirits fresh, and after a race I have someone I can talk to. I tell you, I would like to keep racing until I win the world championship, up to the age of 35 if that's necessary, but Birgitte will tell me to keep going after that. I am pretty much a family man, my family life is sacred to me."

At Home

Ask Tony Rominger what has been the best moment of his life and this is what he will tell you: "I have a little daughter. One morning I rang home and my wife put the receiver to her mouth. "Papa," she said for the first time, and I thought that was brilliant. Even though it happened over the telephone, it

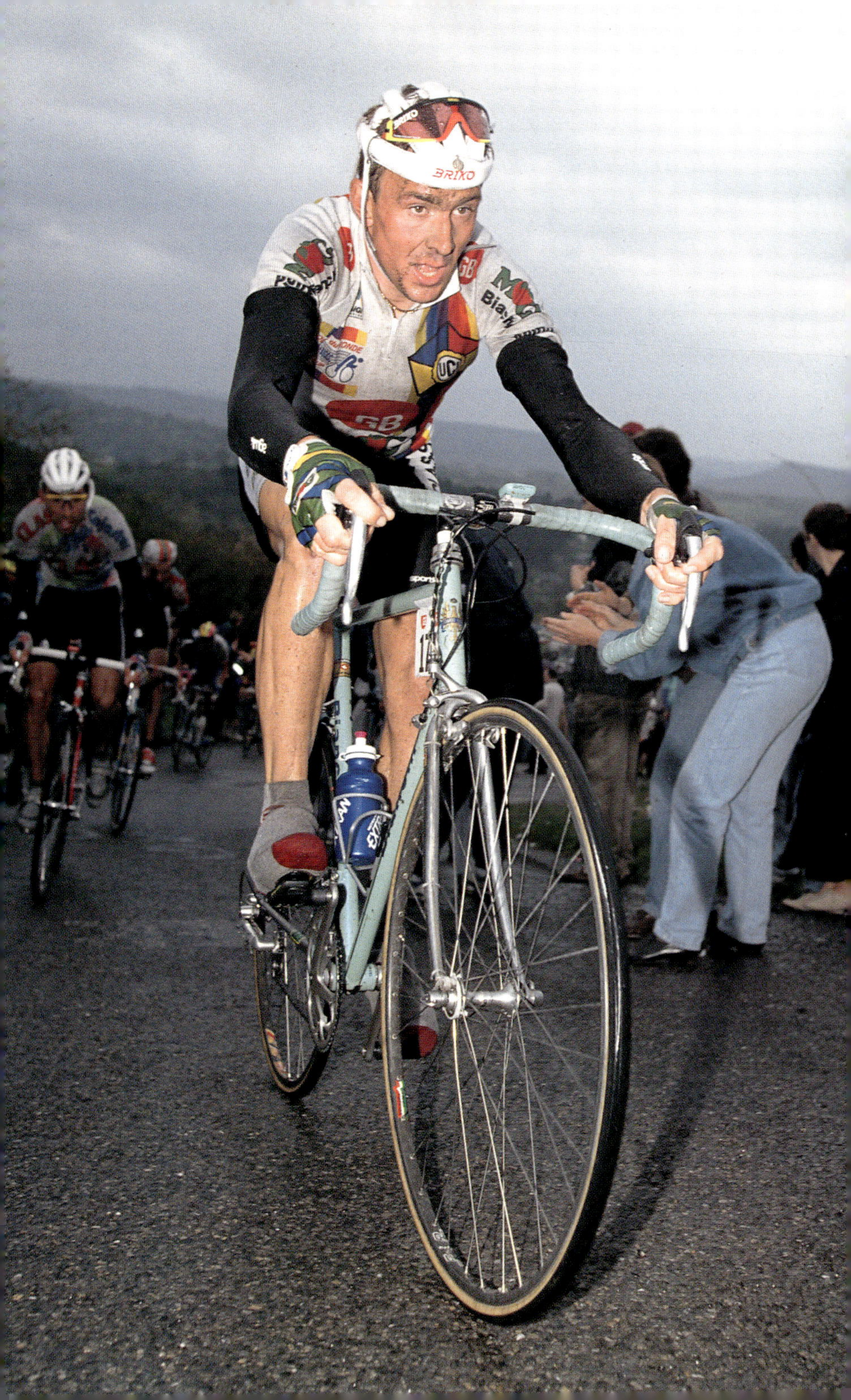
BRIKO
GB
UCI

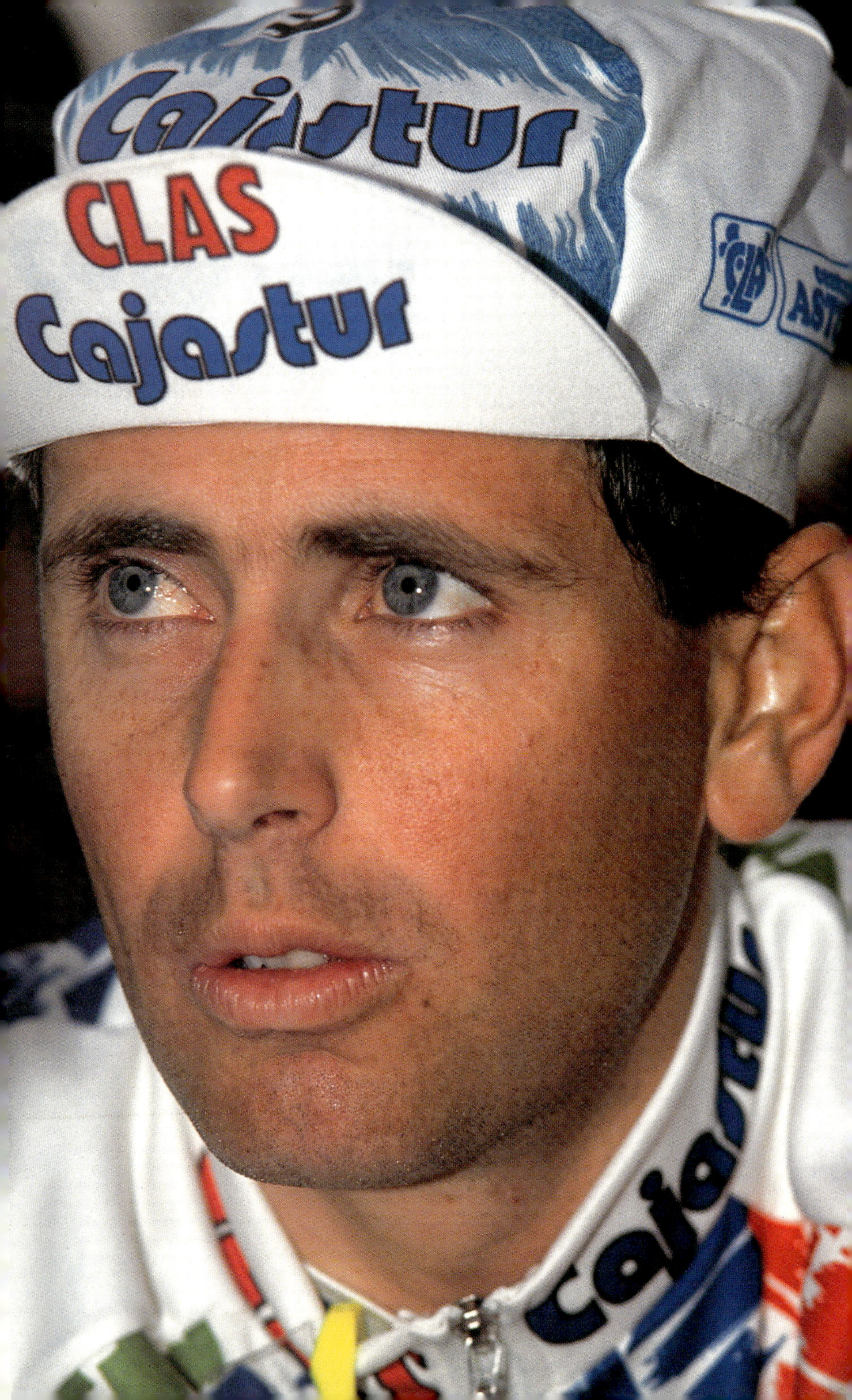
Cajastur
CLAS
Cajastur

was a really fantastic moment. You know, really I prefer being at home more than anything else. I'm away more often than many others. I miss the being at home because I didn't grow up in that typical cycling atmosphere. I only began racing when I was 21. Before that, I had never taken part in any sport."

Computer

His wife is always with him and so is his self-confidence. Rominger says that to some extent he evaluates himself and conducts himself accordingly, and that he races the way he has planned it, the way he has sketched it out beforehand.

"Take the world championship," Rominger says, by way of an illustration. "Up until September 1992 I had never performed well in it. At Benidorm it was time all that changed, and it did. I didn't win, but the condition was there. That was the basis for my victory in the Tour of Lombardy later - my second in that classic. It really suits me perfectly. Prior to that I also wanted to win the Vuelta, and I did. I don't like things to go wrong.

In 1993 I have three goals: win Liège-Bastogne-Liège, the Vuelta and the Tour de France. I have the chance of riding a good Tour. I'm not saying I'm going to beat Indurain, but I have a chance of getting on to the podium. I'm 30 now, I won't be getting any stronger, but up to now I've surprised myself every year. I don't like it if things don't go according to plan."

Anger

Rominger is very ambitious and it is that which drives him. "Do you know what, I started racing out of a sense of anger. I was 20 and my brother 15. At the time he was much better at sports than I was. When he went riding his bike, I went with him, but on climbs I had to let go of his wheel. Back at home later on, he would throw it in my face. "You can't keep up with me," he would say, laughing squarely at me. In the end I got sick of it: "Just you wait. You're in for it now. I'm going to train so hard that you'll be seeing stars before your eyes." And so I did, and I just kept going with it.

The next target after that was to become an elite amateur rider. Then at least I would have had something to tell my grandchildren. And so I did. Then I wanted to become a professional, then win the Tour of Lombardy, then the Vuelta too, and for 1993 I am aiming for a place near the top in the Tour de France. It is the sense of challenge which keeps me going."

Boring

Rominger has a lot of nerve. An example of it was when he was an amateur and he wanted to ride the Grand Prix des Nations. As no one had contacted him about it, he offered his services himself. "I wanted to ride it and as luck would have it, not many professionals did. "O.K.," they said, "even though you're still an amateur, you can take part. Make the most of it." I wasn't far off winning it either, and afterwards the manager of the Swiss Cilo team asked if I wanted to turn professional. That lasted a year, then the team folded and I had to look elsewhere for employment.

The nerve I have is one-dimensional. During races I am the captain, but outside I'm not. I don't go around complaining about things. That is the team manager's job. That's what he's paid for. There is only one thing I protest about: I don't want soup every day. Riders need spaghetti and carbohydrates,

The Tour of Spain 1992 top-three:
Jesus Montoya, the winner Tony Rominger and Pedro Delgado

that's what I want on my plate. We are sportsmen at the top of our profession, and we should be treated as such. I am not someone who goes round telling jokes. I'd much rather listen. Really I'm a boring old sod. They write that I play a lot of tennis and go skiing, but it's not true. It's my wife that does all of that, I prefer lazing about in my armchair."

Monaco

Tony Rominger is Swiss, but he lives in Monaco because of its great tax privileges. "When I retire in a few years time, I will go back to Switzerland, but not yet. In Monaco life is very good. From my home I can see Boris Becker's house, we can also see the Royal Palace. I have never bumped into Princess Caroline, but my wife Birgitte has. Moreno Argentin also lives nearby and he has become a very good friend of mine. We often go out training together. It has become a regular thing for him to bring his wife and children round for coffee on the day before he goes back to Italy."

Allergy

A problem that often made life miserable for Tony Rominger during his early days as a professional was that he suffered with a bad allergy, and for a long time it stopped him performing well during the summer. "In spring and autumn nothing stops me, but in the summer I spent years getting nowhere. I would be sick every year at the same time, I felt listless, there was no strength in my legs and my breathing was affected. After a couple of days the suffering would get worse. Then I went to a Swiss doctor for treatment. He carried out an extensive series of tests to try to pin-point my allergy. He promised me that he would finally cure me with new medicines. I pinned all my hopes on that. In 1989 I finished second in the World Cup, I won the Tour of Lombardy, but I will only call myself a real rider if I have won the Tour de France. That is my biggest dream. A stage race means much more to me than any of the one-day races."

Spanish

Tony Rominger is no fool. He speaks fluent Danish, German, French, English and Italian. The strange thing is that he knows at most five words of Spanish. And yet he rides for Clas - a dairy products collective in northern Spain - and most of his team-mates are Spaniards. "Last year I wasn't in the right frame of mind to learn any, but this year, hopefully, I will. I'm going to make a start on it," he promises.

Money

Rominger is quite prepared to admit that he rides for the money. But he still has his principles. "I'm not a cycling fanatic, I can live without it. Racing is becoming harder and faster, it's a hard life, so it has to have its financial rewards. Don't get me wrong, I am no more expensive than any of the other riders in the FICP top-ten, it's just that I want security. I always insist that I receive a fixed wage, because I like to know in advance what money is coming in. I am not interested in bonuses and prize money. If my teammates have done a good job helping me, they get all of it. That's the way I like working best. I'm professional enough to win the required number of races to warrant my salary."

Contract

At the end of 1992, Tony Rominger won both the Rider of the Year and Sportsman of the Year awards in Switzerland. His cycling award, however, will be coming under threat from Zülle, Zberg and Jeker, the up-and-coming new Swiss talent. But Rominger has one single motivation to keep him at the top of the pile: his contract at Clas is coming up for renewal. "Zülle, Zberg and Jeker are all classy young riders, but we'll see how far they have come on in the major stage races. It will take them at least three years to reach the top, and by then my reign will be over.

As far as my contract is concerned, maybe I will stay with Clas. At least if they play by the rules: because if that is the case I will earn more money than I do now. I have to take into account who I want for team manager. Juan Fernandez, our current directeur sportif, is the ideal man for the job. I wouldn't fancy working with someone like Paul Koechli. He creates problems. His methods are all based around tactics. "You attack there, you there. You do this, you do that." Well that's not my cup of tea. I'm rather old-fashioned: I am the leader, the rest of the team work for me, and I come up with the results."

Hour Record

If you are one of the world's top riders, you are expected to say that you are going to have a crack at Moser's world hour record. As Rominger is an outstanding time triallist - in 1991 he won the final time trial in the World Cup - he is no exception. "I am interested. The only thing against it is that the whole undertaking is so expensive. What company is likely to be prepared to put so much money into it? I am waiting to see what Miguel Indurain is planning to do. If Indurain makes a successful attempt, then I'll have a go at it too."

Italy

Tony Rominger has mainly ridden for foreign teams since he turned professional in 1986. For two years he was a member of the powerful Chateau d'Ax squad assembled around Gianni Bugno. While riding for the Italian team, he won Tirreno-Adriatico and his first Tour of Lombardy in 1989. In 1990 he won Tirreno again, but then he upped and left Bugno.

"Because I didn't want to ride in his service for yet another season. Then I moved to Toshiba, the team which, at the time, were about to embark on what was to be their final year. As a result of that, there was quite a bit of squabbling, but it was with them that I really developed fully as a rider. I won Paris-Nice, I won the Tour of Romandy, I won the final event in the World Cup, and I came second in the competition overall. All of those results made me feel as though I had made the next step forward.

Don't get me wrong, I have happy memories of Italy. It's just that I have the impression that in recent years it is stagnating there a little. There is no longer any progression. At the moment the Netherlands seems to be the most advanced country. There are many reasons why I quit Italy when I did. It was at precisely the time that the football World Cup was being organised and there was no spare money for cycling. For two years companies had

Tony with his wife and daughter

been setting aside money from their budgets for it. Everyone felt morally and promotionally obliged to join in the circus. Money which would otherwise have gone into cycling was diverted, as a result. That policy proved to be financially disastrous for me personally. I had just enjoyed my best season so far. I had finished second in the World Cup, I had won the Tour of Lombardy, and I had won Tirreno-Adriatico. Yet my team sponsors refused to give me a raise. "You've got a two-year contract," they said, "and you will see it out." I got out of it. Riders who had won a World Cup race, however, were earning three times what I was. And I was aware of that. At the end of 1993 my contract with Clas is up. I can assure you now that anyone who wants to sign me for next year will have to offer big money."

Eric Vanderaerden

BLACK AND WHITE

From the point of view of the publicity he generated, it was clear from that very first day of his professional career that Eric Vanderaerden was going to be an interesting rider. He was one of the very top amateur riders, and everyone expected him to make it big as a pro. In 1983 he turned professional with Aernoudt, and he made an instant impression. In his first Milan-San Remo, he went with the attacks. World champion Beppe Saronni won that day and Vanderaerden came in with the leading group from which the Italian had escaped. Vanderaerden 'only' came fourth and wasted no time in showing that he was not short of 'bottle' by saying: "If top riders like Moser and Raas are forming combines, it's not difficult."

Villard-de-Lans

Eric had not let his entry into the pro ranks go unnoticed. A little later in that 1983 season, he triumphed in his very first prologue in his very first Tour de France. He even wore the yellow jersey for two stages. In 1985 he won the Tour of Flanders, and in 1987 Paris-Roubaix. He won the Belgian Championship at Hoeselt in 1984, won Paris-Brussels the same year and Ghent-Wevelgem the following year. His most gallant victory was his win in the time trial at Villard-de-Lans during the Tour in 1985, beating Bernard Hinault and Thierry Marie in the process. "As far as I'm concerned, that was my best performance ever," says Vanderaerden. "Before the start I had a feeling there was something in the air. That morning I had eaten breakfast and gone out to familiarise myself with the course. When I returned I asked the mechanic to fit a 56 at the front. "Have you gone mad?" he replied. "How are you going to get round with that?" "Just do it!" I said. Ruud Bakker, my physio, pinned my number on. I took a piece of paper and wrote my prediction on it: 1st Vanderaerden, 2nd Hinault at 1 minute, 3rd Ruud Bakker. I beat Hinault by 1'05". By the time it was slowly becoming clear that I might have won the stage, I was back at the hotel. I therefore had to make my way back to the finish, but there was no car to take me. A Dutch radio commentator gave me his helmet, started up his motorbike, and took me - still in my shorts - over the course to the finish. All of a sudden who was riding in front of us? None other than Bernard Hinault, who was just entering his final kilometre. We stayed on his wheel, all the way to the finishing line. It gave me an incredible feeling. I myself gave a live commentary on the Frenchman's last kilometre. It really annoyed me when, soon after the finish, I was made to put my racing clothes back on again. Antenne 2, the French television station, had no shots of me, but they were determined to feature me in their evening programme. Post even got me to ride a section of the time trial course again. I wouldn't do it nowadays."

Green

In that same 1985 Tour, Eric Vanderaerden also won the stage to Bordeaux and for seven days wore the green jersey. In 1986 he didn't win a stage, but this time he did take the green jersey back home with him to his home village of Lummen, near Hasselt in Belgium. Eric won the coveted jersey on the first stage and never lost it again.

Up to the present date, Eric has won five stages in the Tour and three in the Vuelta. He has won stages in nearly all of the minor stage races in which he has taken part, yet many people think he could have done even better. "That depends on how you look at it," says Vanderaerden. "I'm happy, anyway. Too much was always expected of me, not by myself, but by others. I was a star before I'd even turned professional; I had already given interviews on the radio. At that point in time, Eddy Merckx had been off the scene for a number of years, Freddy Maertens had fallen away and Roger De Vlaeminck had retired, and I was expected to succeed them. I had a different set of priorities, though. As a young boy I had dreamed of life as a professional rider. The stars were idols and I wanted to ride with them in the peloton. I was among the better amateurs and wanted to turn professional as soon as I could. I wanted to win classics. At the time the Tour didn't really appeal to me, but I wanted to make a name for myself in the Tour of Flanders, Paris-Roubaix and Milan-San Remo and I wanted to win the Belgian championship. I didn't really give much thought to Liège-Bastogne-Liège or the Tour of Lombardy. Apart from Milan-San Remo, I have won all the races I set out to win."

Eric Vanderaerden and his wife, Patricia, on their wedding day

Prankster

On the one hand Eric Vanderaerden is a shy and timid man, on the other he is, and will always be, an incorrigible prankster and a clown. His pranks certainly liven up the peloton. Vanderaerden and Eddy Planckaert once took a hotel room door down in a lift, before running into Peter Post. Vanderaerden also supplies the entire peloton with nicknames. Just before abandoning the Tour in 1992, he had a bet with Marc Wauters that the one of them that finished lower on the Tour classification would have to push the other one through Lummen in a wheelbarrow. "The Tour was a big disappointment. If I could ride it again, I would definitely go with the attackers on the first climb during the first stage to Sestriere. At the time I thought I would easily get back to them on the descent, but Chiappucci had gone on the attack."

Sometimes Vanderaerden takes it even further. At the World Championship held at Goodwood in 1982, he did his business in Nico Emonds's travel bag. "I took full blame for that, even though Dirk De Wolf and Marc Somers were involved just as much as me. At that time Nico was a real bastard. We were all in the national amateur squad and had arranged to go training together. Nico would also come with us, but the same thing happened every time: he would ride at the back then suddenly, without being noticed, he would veer off and go training on his own. He never stayed in our company. He would never speak openly and honestly to us, but remained very secretive. Whenever we wanted him, we always had to go looking for him. We just wanted to get him for it."

Jealous

Eric Vanderaerden is clearly the most controversial Belgian rider of the last decade. People are either for him or against him, there is no in-between. When he wins he is worshipped unconditionally, but when he loses he is almost regarded as public enemy number one. Vanderaerden has never really let it get to him, though. He was always valued for his commitment in Jan Raas's Buckler team, and it will be no different now that the team is sponsored by WordPerfect. There are not many races his team-mates win, in which he hasn't played his part. "People don't like riders who win too often. If you win they are jealous; if you lose they get on your back. It's always one or the other. Besides that, I find it hard to play up to people for the sake of it. To me things are black or white, there are no grey areas in-between. If I was able to do it all again, I would be stand up for myself even more."

Cradle

Even when he was still a baby in his cradle, there was little doubt that Eric Vanderaeden would be a cyclist when he got older. His father, Lucien, was Belgian champion in the veterans category, and his sons, Eric, Danny and Gert, inherited his love of the sport. They have one sister, Carine.
"I really don't know what I would have done otherwise. All I've ever wanted to do was be a bike racer. I was born into it. I could ride a bike without stabilisers by the time I was two and a half. My son Michael is now 5. He has four footballs, but he never plays with them. Yet when he starts tearing about on his little bike, the difference between him and other children of his age is enormous. He undoubtedly has talent, but whether he will ever become a rider is another question. We shall have to wait to find out."

The Netherlands

"I have never played football or any other sport. There was a time when I did go training once or twice, but after a short while I started staying at home again.
I was 11 when I rode my first cycle race. By that time my father was racing in the veterans category. He knew a Dutchman who arranged for them to think that I lived in Eindhoven, and that meant I had a right to a licence to race in the Netherlands. That year I won 10 out of the 15 or 16 races. Someone grassed on me during the second year, and just before a race in Tilburg I found out that I wasn't allowed to start. And that was the end of that."

Inside

"There is one sort of person that I cannot stand: the type who hogs the fast lane on motorways.

I don't have any real hobbies. I used to have a moto-cross bike, but in the last three years I hardly rode it, so I sold it. I like being at home. My favourite subject at school was truancy, and physical education. I didn't like going to school. I started following a course in sanitary engineering at the technical institute in Beringen, but I never completed it. I don't have any qualifications, then, besides a 100 metre swimming certificate. As far as my father was concerned, I didn't have to go to school. If I had a 'workshop' during the week before a championship, he let me come home, as he didn't want me standing the whole afternoon. I was conscripted into the army, first at Koksijde and then at Leopoldsburg. I worked in the stores and was a runner. I had to distribute the soap, toothpaste and sheets. I didn't like doing it, but I never had to spend time in the 'slammer.' I was lucky that that was the year the world championship for the military was being held in Belgium, and because I was a good rider, I was allowed to train as often as I wanted."

Sad

"The saddest moment in my life was, without doubt, the unexpected death of my mother in October 1990. My mother was a very important figure to me. She stayed in the background, but she was always there for me, any time, any place. She would get extremely annoyed when she heard criticism of me. Sometimes she would be tetchy all day long. When I won, she was proud of course. But I think I should really have got more of my father's character. He is a roofer, he used to go to work every day and then train afterwards. Yet he still won his races. I have a great deal of respect for his way of thinking. He never made me do anything other than racing."

Concentration

"I have my good side and my bad side. My wife, Patricia, says that I find it difficult to concentrate. We met at a race when we were only 15. Our mothers were cousins. On Sundays she usually went to girl guides, but on that day she was suspended and had to go with her father to the race.

I really like travelling. I would love to go to Thailand or Japan, yet at the same time I'm reluctant to go on such a long journey. I'm away so much anyhow.

I don't know what I'm going to do when my career is over. As long as I can earn more by riding in the peloton than in normal life, I will keep racing. I realise I will have to work at some point in the future, but I still don't know how or at what. I have connections with a leather business near where I live. We are trying to set up a second sales outlet in Antwerp. Maybe I will eventually devote more time to that. For the time being, my only involvement is that it carries my name.

I would like to become a directeur sportif if I got the chance, especially when I think how little time they devote to their riders. When I look back on the way I was supervised in my early days, I realise that I must have been mollycoddled from far too early on and I would like to make a better job of it than they did. To put a team together requires a lot of money and where do you get it from?"

Burnt Out?

"They've been saying that I'm burnt out since I was 15. In my first season in the newcomers category, I won 22 races. "You see," was the reaction then, "he's already burnt out. Compared to the ease and the authority with which he won races in Holland, there isn't much left." The year after that I won 52 races. Then they started saying I was taking things. I'm used to those sort of comments.

I have always been very careful. I have three children and I don't want them to see me become a pathetic wash-out in later life. I've won four classics and five stages in the Tour and that has given me great satisfaction. You won't catch me messing about medically just so that I can add a few more to that number. It wouldn't be necessary, anyway. I'm still strong enough. I'm certain I can still win a big race. Riders whose results are consistent do not use doping. You can look at my top three finishes for any season you like to see that. I question those young riders who fly for two weeks and then can do nothing else."

Theft

"If you want to win a big race, everything needs to be in your favour. You can't plan something like that. In my first Tour, in 1983, I won the prologue. In subsequent prologues I finished twice three times, fourth once and fifth once, but I couldn't win again. You need to have a super day, and that applies to everyone. Usually riders get to know the course a couple of hours before the start. An hour later they start warming up.

On the morning of the 1983 prologue, my bike was stolen. Two special wheels I had made for it, and which I had been very careful with, had disappeared too. I had paid for them myself, with all my spare cash. I went back to my hotel to sit and sulk, while my mechanics hastily put a new ordinary bike together for me. So I was very poorly prepared for the event. That victory and the yellow jersey obviously gave me a fantastic feeling.

I was a already a star when I was in the juniors and amateurs. I won many times, and everyone was watching to see how I did in that first Tour. "How's he going to do? Now we'll find out." When I won, it surprised many. "What? He really can do it, then." From that day on, I've been expected to win every race I compete in, if I don't I've failed."

One of Eric Vanderaerden's best victories: Paris-Roubaix in 1987

Automatic

"Not everything in my career has gone the way I planned it. Since 1989 - no, actually it goes back to my first year with Post - I have become a little too lazy. Post was my guardian angel, and he never wanted to hear a bad word about me. He turned me into a great rider too soon. He should have driven an attacking instinct into me, but I was immediately given the role of the team's sprinter. I was not allowed to ride at the front of a race. That was all very nice, but it was fatal for a young rider. It also went against my nature. In the youngsters' categories I fought and battled throughout races, but Post didn't want any of that. "Stay calm," he would say, "ride on other people's wheels." When he signed new riders, it was specifically for how they could best serve me. He provided me with team-mates capable of launching me towards the finishing line. If I failed, it was never a disaster. In his team's top years, there was always someone there who could retrieve dodgy situations. Post always had ready-made replacements available. I now realise that I stayed with him too long. In the end his tactics for me showed serious signs of wear and tear. I had also turned an incorrect approach to racing into something automatic: I only knew how to play a waiting game while racing."

Changing

"After six years with Post I moved on to Jan Raas's team. One of the things I wanted to get out of the move was to steer myself clear of those bad habits. And that was possible, because Raas's working methods are different. He wanted to see the Vanderaerden of old. I too also wanted to race in a more explosive style again; I missed getting stuck in during races. I did my very best, but I won a lot fewer races. My most successful season was 1989 when I won 22 races. "All minor ones," added the sceptics. Although I won fewer races between 1990 and the end of 1992, I can assure you that I rode at the front more in that time than during the rest of my career put together. I am not a domestique. There are no longer any domestiques. Domestiques fetch rain capes and drink bottles, and that's something I don't do. I play my part in the team, the way everyone else does."

Telephone

"It was good for my career to split with Post. I have always had a lot of respect for him. He is the ideal manager for a top company: as hard as nails and uncompromising. He is both a gentleman and a military commander. Everyone must stay in line with him. The youth of today have trouble with that. In recent years much of my respect for Post has eroded. When I finished outside the time limit on a stage of the 1990 Tour, he said some terrible things about me. According to him I was good for nothing and at the time he really hurt. He knows that he was wrong to say what he did, but he is too proud to take it back. I know him well enough to know that. I like a laugh and still give him a friendly nod, but he never acknowledges me. In the Tour of Switzerland in 1991, I had to step aside or he would have driven over my toes. He has his own peculiarities. If he phones a rider and the rider's daughter answers, he puts the receiver down!"

Teasing

Jan Raas is hard too. He knows how to deal with things. He also knows that he doesn't have to tell me how to ride a race. He radiates such authority that the team runs just as smoothly when he's not there. But when he is around, it doesn't cause panic in the team. Nor is there any stress. During my time with Post, whenever he showed up the atmosphere would change. No one felt at ease, the pressure increased. Now, I can be myself. Post often accused me of not being one hundred per cent committed to my profession. He couldn't handle me making jokes. But that's simply the way I am. When I'm at home with my children sitting around the dinner table, I tease them too."

News

"Jan Raas is firm but fair, never underhand. You know where you stand with him. I remember a race in which the team had completely missed an escape. Raas came driving up alongside the peloton, hammered angrily on the wing of the car and was cursing and swearing. That evening at the dinner table, he brought the subject up once more: "I have some good news and some bad news. The bad news is that you will all have to go to Nice tomorrow for a photo session; the good news is that you will all be flying from the start tomorrow and are going to win the stage." And that was the end of the matter. Everyone knew what was expected of him. It was typical of Raas: get things clearly straightened out first, then drop the matter. Post would have spent the whole evening harping on about it. He also knew how to hurt people and most riders were afraid of him. Fear is good for nothing."

Super Day

"I have probably put many defeats down to the fact that it was not one of my super days, and even if that sounds implausible, that's is how it is. In the past you could win races by reaching 90 per cent of your capability, but nowadays you have to reach 110 per cent. It is a feeling, a question of condition and confidence. At such times you are not afraid of anyone or anything, you don't let yourself be squeezed out, you go on the attack yourself. You feel that indefinable certainty that you are going to win. In the Tour of Flanders I punctured just before the Koppenberg. No problem: I jumped back on my bike and slalomed through the fallen riders to the top. If you let your head drop at times like that, you have had it. On the morning of a big race, you know what sort of a chance you'll have.

You must be able to cope with a certain amount of pressure. You must learn how to live with it. What Axel Merckx and my brother Gert are experiencing at the moment, will shape their character. From their first day of racing, the whole peloton has been riding on their wheel because they happen to be the son and brother of famous riders. It can be terrible to watch at times. If they can survive this stage of their careers, they will become good riders."

Nijdam

"If there was one thing I would blame myself for over the past few years, while I've been in Raas's team, it is that I have thought about myself too little. At first that never really bothered me. I was in a new team and I had to adjust. It was not up to me to thump the table and fly at everyone's throats at the slightest mistake. Where would that have got me a year later? So I kept my mouth shut.

In 1992, my third season with Raas, I had to stick up for myself a little more. Jelle Nijdam had promised that he would occasionally lead out a sprint for me, but up to now that has only happened once, at most, during the Tour of Spain. And I won the stage. In every other race I have had to do it myself. The tenth stage in the 1992 Tour de France was the absolute low-point. Nijdam flatly refused to help me. O.K., maybe my ultimate sprint is no longer there, but when I'm at the peak of my strength, I'm as good as ever. I don't force my way through, push and pull like I used to, I daren't. I'm not superquick any more, either, but that doesn't mean that I'm never going to win again, as long as I was given a proper lead out. Nijdam is the ideal man to do that, with his hard riding."

Money

"In financial terms, my last two years with Post - 1988 and 1989 - and my first two with Raas - 1990 and 1991 - were my best. I have never felt I was paid too much for what I achieved. My sponsor was always happy, and so was I. It is not my fault that sportsmen are so well-paid. In 1992 I cut back a little by not riding criteriums as my starting money for them has been lower for several

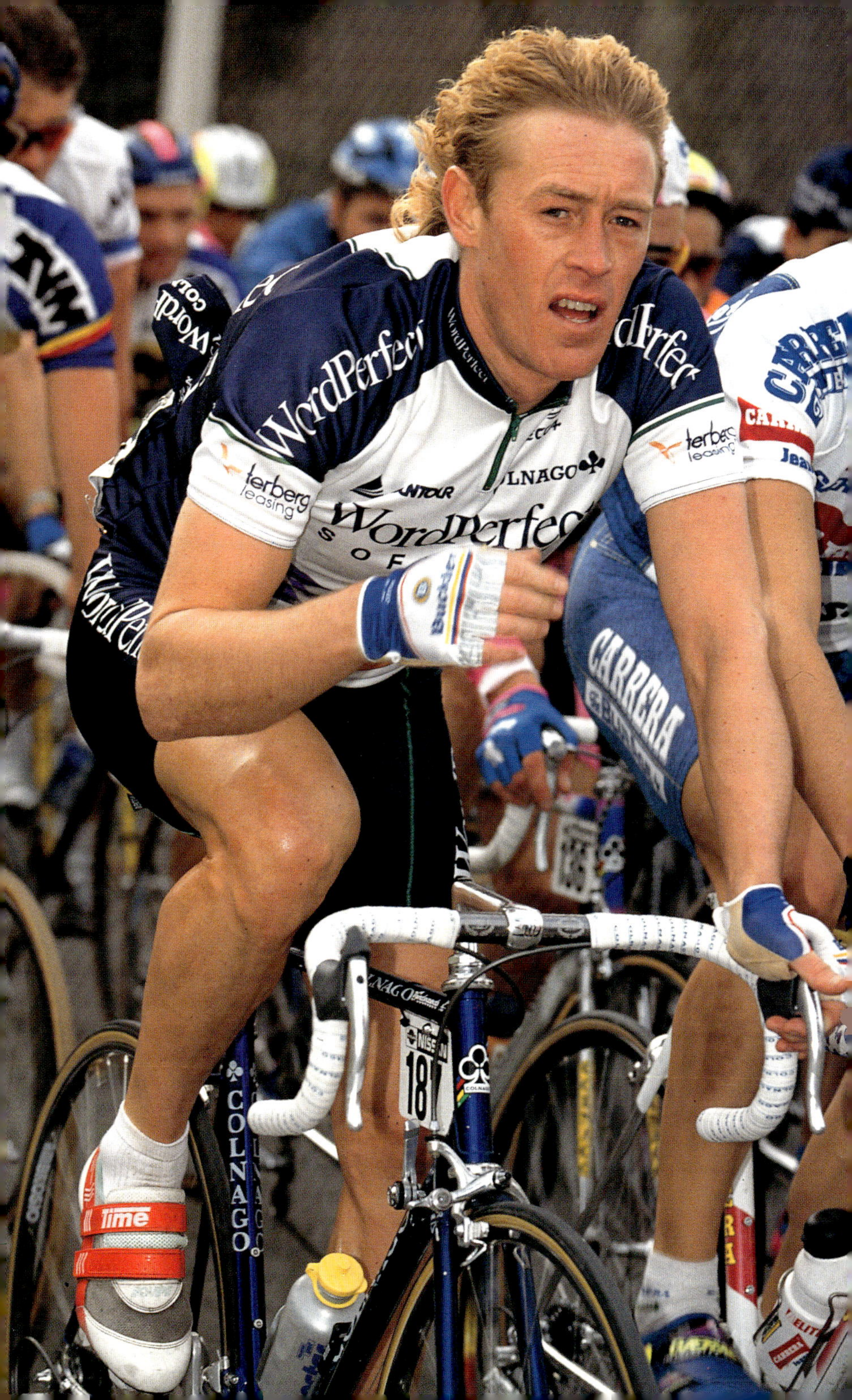

WordPerfect
terberg leasing
COLNAGO
CARRERA
Time

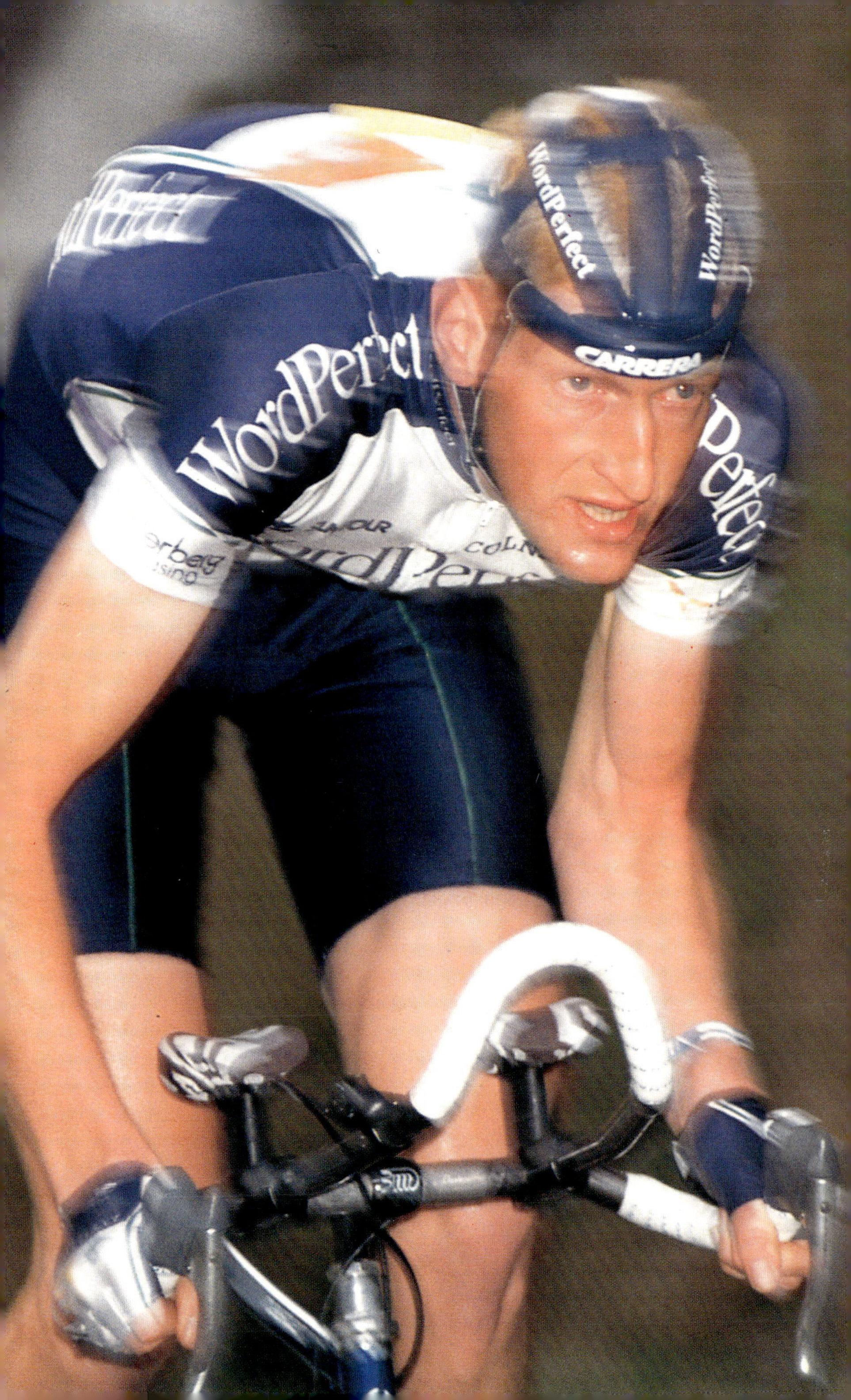
WordPerfect
CARRERA
WordPerfect
WordPerfect

years now, but it cuts both ways. Since 1990 I have had a quieter summer and it has done me good. I have been able to go to the coast with my two daughters, Melissa and Tattiana, and my son Michael.

Interest in Vanderaerden has decreased somewhat, but people still know who I am. Sometimes they ask if they can take a photo of me, or girls send me photos of themselves. Once, I even received a cassette with a recording on it. I don't really enjoy my popularity. What I prefer most is lounging around at home."

Slippers

"When I raced in the amateurs, I never imagined my bike would earn me enough to build a house. But I get the impression that the people round here begrudge me my wealth. Well, I'd just like to say that I have earned every cent through sheer hard work. I really can't understand their attitude. Many people have objections to us, to our way of life. We are accused of acting in a high-handed manner. Why should we? Comments like that hurt, because it is certainly not my intention. I didn't build this house to make other people jealous, but because I think it's nice and because I can afford it. If I were to have another house built it would be smaller, but only so that it wouldn't offend anyone. I just want to be treated like everyone else. Fortunately my children are not aware of any of this. It was once commented that they wore new slippers every month. So now my wife dare not buy them new ones."

Brother Gert

Vanderaerden is very committed to the youngsters in the peloton. In 1991 he towed Rudy Verdonck over L'Alpe d'Huez, and in 1992 he pepped up a desperately struggling Marc Wauters. Eric is also involved in his brother Gert's career. It is hardly surprising, then, that after his own active career is over, he would like to work with young riders.

"I'm pleased that my youngest brother Gert has also become a rider. He's doing well too. He is small but brave, and that is his trademark. If people watching the race ask me which one Gert is, I always say: "Don't bother looking at the numbers. The little one always gritting his teeth and riding at the front, that's him." People remark on how nice a lad he is. That was something that was never said of me; I was bigger and I won too often. I often hear it said that physically he is like me: he has my shape and my posture. His career, however, will follow a path of its own. He has the class, but it will be more difficult for him. He must make sure he continues to let his attacking instincts drive him. He is a fighter, you see, and probably that is what I should have stayed."

EDWIG VAN HOOYDONCK

NAPOLEON

When Edwig Van Hooydonck won the Tour of Flanders for the first time in April 1989, the Belgian cartoonist Nesten drew him in full regalia on the highest podium with the 'great' Napoleon Bonaparte as an insignificant little figure in his shadow. When Edwig won the same race in 1991 for the second time, he earned himself a nickname: 'Eddy Bosberg'. 'Eddy' referred to Merckx and 'Bosberg' to his incisive attack on the last climb of the race. "Hilaire Van Der Schueren, our assistant directeur sportif, has said that they will erect a statue of me on the Bosberg if I win for a third time," grins Van Hooydonck. "I don't mind them pinning their hopes on me in this race, but please, no statue. In that event they should erect them all over Flanders. A doctor friend of mine recently dug up one of the cobbles from the Bosberg, and has had a trophy made out of it. "Bosberg 1989, Bosberg 1991" it says on it, and that's enough. I wasn't brought up in that sort of fanatical atmosphere. I was seven when I began racing. I won too many races from the start, but was lucky that my parents didn't get carried away by it. Whether I won or lost, we always drove home from races in a happy mood. On the other hand, I don't think my father ever congratulated me, it was just something he didn't do."

Image
Edwig Van Hooydonck doesn't like idle chatter. He is a quiet, shy, serious rider. "I don't know whether I'm popular. I have the feeling I'm well-known, but that doesn't affect my ego. Really I prefer to be just left in peace and quiet. My wife says that at home I'm not the Van Hooydonck that you see on television. "When you are like that you're different, and I don't know you any more," she says. "On the television you're always so quiet and serious." I suppose I am, that's my character. "I don't know who you take after," my mother always says. I don't look like her, and I'm not like my father."

The Beginning

"I was very young, then, when I started, even though my father and uncles never raced. The lads who lived near me cycled a lot. Some of them had those marvellous little bikes and they must have helped get me interested in cycling. My brother Gino started first. He was eight, and old enough to race in Holland. I was only six, so I had to wait another year. I always went with him, though. I never missed a race.

In the winter I played football: I was a defender. The trainer always thought I was too slow to play anywhere else. I used to get substituted quite a lot. I certainly had the right build, and I really enjoyed it - more than cycling really - but I was better on a bike. What appeals to me most about cycling is the way you have to fight against yourself, the not giving up and the battling to the bitter end. Not a single other sport has such a personal involvement."

Cups

"I won the very first race I entered. Later races went really well too, they always followed the same pattern: I attacked very early in the race and then rode the rest of it on my own at the front. I never found it that difficult, even then I was that type of rider. During those early days, I was racing mainly to win cups, they made my eyes bulge. They weren't made of plastic like they are now. I still have them all, they're at my parents' house. At the end of 1991 I got married to Christel, and when we moved into our own house, I left everything behind. I didn't need them any more.

I was in the same youth category as Jac and Adri Van Der Poel. We still talk about it. The racing was hard, but it was great fun. I often say to my wife that

Champion of the Netherlands at eightyears old

it was the best time of my life. Cycling was fun, and to me that was the most important thing. With the professionals it is the complete opposite."

Learning

"For the first couple of years you're a professional, you should mainly use the time for learning. Take 1989 - the year I won my first Tour of Flanders. I still thought of myself as a stage racer, but my first Tour de France during that same year made me revise my opinions. The mountains were too difficult for me, and ever since I've devoted myself to the classics.

I have always thought learning was important. I liked going to school. Actually, that was the happiest time of my life. I had no worries, I didn't have to think about anything. It was 20 kilometres biking, 10 there and 10 back. In all the time I was at school I never got a lift, once. I got a secondary school diploma in woodwork and I'm glad about that. It wasn't a waste of time, because at least now I can knock up cupboards, tables and chairs. History and geography were my best subjects, I really looked forward to them. The only ones I had problems with were maths and one or two of the technical subjects. I passed my exams by the narrowest of margins, but I always got a ten for religion. I did my best in it, and the priest who taught the subject was one of my supporters. There was never any question of me going on to further education. A diploma when I left secondary school was really the absolute maximum, the best I could do."

Smooth Adjustment

"From my very first day as a professional it has gone smoothly. I didn't need a period of adjustment. Cycling is primarily about pedalling, and you already know how to do that in the amateurs. My first year as a pro was the easiest. ·When I attacked I was allowed to stay away, nobody was worried about me. I could ride as free as a bird. On top of that, as a first-year professional I was getting good publicity. Every performance was good. In that first year I came fifth in Paris-Roubaix and I got a lot more attention for it then, than when I came third in 1990.

The day you win a big race, everything changes, especially in Belgium, where they always see things in black and white. Either your season is a success or a failure: there's nothing in between. 1990 for example, wasn't a great season. But even though I was still only 24, I was already being written off. At least that's how it seemed in a newspaper interview with Louis De Laet, a member of the Antwerp section of the federation. "Van Hooydonck will never make it," he said. Well who on earth does this De Laet think he is to be saying that? He can hardly tell the difference between a front wheel and a back wheel."

Jan Raas
"I'm very glad Jan Raas offered me the chance of turning professional. The atmosphere is good and they look after you well. Yet I almost took up an offer with Walter Godefroot, for the same money, but he would not sign my brother, Gino. Raas did, however, and that's what clinched it for me. I sometimes look back on it. If I had signed for Godefroot's team, my career would have taken quite a different course, as Walter has had many problems with his teams.

Turning professional was a great feeling. I had expected that the top riders would shun me and never accept me, but that wasn't the case. In actual fact, I had more problems with the lesser riders in the peloton. Ronan Onghena, for

Tears of joy after his victory in the Tour of Flanders

example, was always stirring up trouble for younger riders. He ought to have been trying to show us what he could do. Unfortunately for him, he couldn't actually do anything. When all is said and done, all he ever really did was fetch Kelly from the airfield."

Atmosphere

"I get on well with everyone in the Raas team. The atmosphere is perfect. You couldn't wish for a better team. We are all friends. Because I'm Flemish, they think I'm far too mild-mannered. The Dutch are completely different. I recently read an article about the concerts by 'Kinderen-voor-Kinderen' (a Dutch group of children entertainers). The journalist thought the Flemish boys and girls they met were rather shy and withdrawn. Typical of the Dutch, of course. The Dutch children had no trouble standing on a stage in front of several thousand people. It's just the same in our team. The Dutch riders have a lot more self-confidence.

The only thing that upsets me is the feud with Peter Post. Up to the '92 Tour de France, that is. If I get up out of my saddle, one of Post's men is on my wheel immediately. That's not the sort of game Raas plays, though. He never gives those sort of instructions. Post's riders are brainwashed in that respect. Raas is like a red rag to a bull for them."

Mistakes

"Young professional riders always make mistakes, and I was no different. It still rankles with me that at Soumagne in 1990 I failed to take the Belgian title. My second place was the final straw. I made a mess of it and I was punished. I should never have let Claude Criquielion escape the way he did. I should have called his bluff. If I had won that race, everyone would have thought of me as a good rider. For three days afterwards, I was like a bear with a sore head.

1990 wasn't a good season, and it was my own fault. During the winter leading up to it, I was determined to lose weight, and that was a mistake. My climbing went to pieces and that upset me. I was a good climber as an amateur. Any amateur who can cause his rivals so much pain on the climbs of the Ardennes would think the same. I was convinced of how well I could climb when I was able to stay with the top climbers of the day during my first Dauphiné Libéré. Then, all of a sudden, my ability to do it disappeared, and I wondered why. The solution as I saw it was to lose weight, so that I would be carrying less around with me. I was three kilograms below my optimum weight when the season began. I have since realised that fat is synonymous with reserves, and I had left myself short and would have to pay dearly. After Paris-Roubaix I was on my knees.

Another problem at that time was that I always felt tired, physically and particularly mentally - and that had something to do with the serious accident my father had. Jan Raas felt I was training too much, so the following winter I trained much less intensively and I rode a lot better. I am also allergic to dust. I now have injections for it, and the carpet in my bedroom has been replaced."

Mad

"I'm telling you, when I climbed the Muur at Geraardsbergen in 1989, I had just one thought going through my mind: 'don't let them drop you here.' When I set off in that race now, it is in the hope of dropping everyone else on that climb. It's a question of confidence and attitude.

I'll always look back on my first victory in the Tour of Flanders as my favourite. If you had told me beforehand that I was going to win, I would have thought you were mad. My preparations had not gone well. I had been thrown out of the Tour of Valencia because I was supposed to have insulted a race commissioner, something, however, that had been blown up out of all proportion. A couple of weeks later, in Tirreno-Adriatico, I was dropped on numerous occasions. If Hilaire Van Der Schueren had had his way, I wouldn't even have been selected for the team.

In my first Tour of Flanders I came 18th. I had ridden very well and that had given me confidence: 'one day I'll win this race,' I said to myself. For years I have had the same feeling about Paris-Roubaix, too. My first experience of that race was when I was a still a junior. On that occasion I came seventh, not in my own category but in the amateurs! A year later I won it. When I rode it for the first time as a professional, I came fifth. It's a race made for me. I'd love to win it, but it hasn't happened yet. Being heavily built like I am is an advantage on the cobbles. I'm not a 'flyer' like Nijdam. My explosive bursts only come after 250 kilometres. My bike and I don't form a perfect entity, unlike the case with some of my rivals. I'm a worker, a battler, I always have been. I feel at home on the cobbles. I ride as often as I can in the middle of the road, and I never focus on the man in front, I decide for myself where I am going to ride."

Domestique

"Throughout my racing life, when I have won races it has always been by big margins. That has meant that I don't ride so well in a group, and that has been the lasting disadvantage of always setting the pace in the youth categories. I look on it as having been a handicap, as later in my career it has caused me to lose many races. Racing is not just a case of riding as hard as you can.

Take the Tour of Flanders. The climbs themselves have never been problem. What is a problem is the kilometres that lead up to them. I am, by nature, slightly afraid. It has improved a little, but it will never be completely cured. So I always need to have someone nearby. Fortunately, for a long time I had Ludo De Keulenaer to fulfil that role. It's a shame he was forced to retire, as he was very skilled in the way he could bring riders to the front. He was never a single metre too early, or too late; he would then drop back and we were away. I'm conscious of the effect that has on your rivals' morale. "Christ, we haven't seen him at all today, and yet he's suddenly here." That gives you a lift, but I don't try to play on it. I wish I had known Ludo five years earlier. He also taught me a few tactical points. He spent months hammering into me that the prizes are handed out only for what happens on the line. He also knew how to read how a race was developing. In the 1991 Tour of Flanders, I was too far back at the feeding-stage. I was hyper-nervous until he stepped in. "Stay calm," he said. "We're alright here." I don't believe Ludo intended to cheat at the dope control at Harelbeke when he was caught. I miss him."

Edwig Van Hooydonck and his wife, Christel

Knees

"It is always being said of me that I am big and strong. Big I am, yes: 6'4", in the peloton only Calcaterra is taller. There is nowhere for me to hide, then, but I have never had a complex about it. I am also supple. For a long time it was only the strength that was missing, and that left me lacking the punch to make all the difference on climbs during my early days as a pro. "I suggest you train on the climbs to improve it," said Dr Claes. And since I always do what he says, I went looking for a suitable climb. That turned out to be the Bosberg, because Hilaire Van Der Schueren lives at the foot of it, and because it is not far from the Muur of Geraardsbergen. I used to warm up on the flat section, then do five rapid climbs up the Bosberg, before moving on to the Muur and climbing that five times too. I did this three times a week, between December and the middle of February. I must have been up them a hundred times in all. I don't think I would still be able to make such an effort. At the time, though, it was no problem, nor was it for my brother Gino. It's not fair, really. We always train together and we put just as much into it, yet I have turned out to be a more talented rider than him. I thank my parents on bended knee that they have passed on that talent to me.

Dr Claes has been very influential throughout my career. He has always drummed into me that doping achieves nothing, and that it is training and medical care which are the most important things. In 1990 he had the frame of my bike made two centimetres longer. He felt that my riding position was too huddled."

Superstition

"When I won the Tour of Flanders for the first time in 1989, I had stayed the previous night in Beveren. The following year I slept in the same bed. 'It will bring me luck,' I thought, but it didn't work. Before the 1989 race, I had given away my racing cap to a girl of about 11 or 12 and one year later I gave it away again. Call it coincidence or not, but I had given it to the same girl, and though I wasn't aware of it myself, she, of course, was. None of this helped, however, as I didn't win it again. I had to wait until 1991 for that.

Traditionally the weather is bad for the Tour of Flanders. I have to tell you I don't like the rain, yet I ride well in it. During the week leading up to the Flemish classic, I never miss a weather forecast. I'm the same before Liège-Bastogne-Liège and Paris-Roubaix, too. You can never rely on forecasts, though. In 1990 it was supposed to be stormy, but on the day there was no sign of it.

The Tour of Flanders is a superb race. The starting place in the market at

Sint-Niklaas, with the town hall in the background, is lovely. But the crowd is allowed to get too close to the riders. Footballers aren't expected to mingle with the crowd half an hour before kick off, are they? Before the race I'm as nervous as hell, and I'm glad the team has a bus so that I can spend some time on my own, in privacy."

Nickname

"They call Eric Vanderaerden 'Terra' because his name means 'from the earth' and they used to call De Keulenaer 'Old Guard' because he was always comparing things with how they used to be. I'm 'Eddy Bosberg', and by now I'm so used to it that I don't even think of it as a nickname. The 'Bosberg' part was started by our team mechanics. Twice I have attacked and escaped at exactly the same spot. That is through a combination of planning and coincidence. It is quite simply the perfect spot; late enough to make sure you don't lose speed, and early enough to give you the chance to build up a big enough lead. The good thing about it is that afterwards you have a long downhill section. In 1989 I seemed to float over the remaining 13 kilometres, it felt as though I was no longer touching the ground. In 1991 I felt nothing. I had already been there."

Rage

"In the 1991 Tour of Flanders I wore a pair of shorts that went to just below my knees. The idea was actually Eric Vanderaerden's. While riding in the Tour of Valencia he had cut off part of his track-suit bottoms. I simply followed his example, but because I won the Tour of Flanders wearing them, it was me who was noticed. The following day, our clothing manufacturers Decca were driven mad by touring cyclists ringing up, trying to order a pair. I don't understand why the sponsors didn't start producing them. At least, after I retire, I will be able to look back on something I brought to the peloton. The ox-head handlebar was introduced by LeMond, the special time-trial bike by Moser, and the full-length shorts by me!

You would think that more youngsters would have taken up cycling in our village, but it is not the case. Wuustwezel is just not that sort of place. We have one amateur and one hopeful. My presence has obviously not inspired them. But at least the man in the paper shop is always happy to see me. He has done so well financially that he has been able to sell his business, move to Calpe in Spain and live a life of luxury off his earnings. When anything was written about me in the papers, he would hang it outside in a special display case. On that day, that particular newspaper would soon sell out. I reckon he must have made a bit out of me, you know!"

Money

"The Tour of Flanders has not brought me any financial windfalls, although when I won it the first time, my earnings suddenly went up four-fold. Before that I was paid very little, though, too little. In 1992 I wanted to win again, but the breakaway featuring Durand and Wegmüller messed everything up. Later on in the season, I won a stage in the Tour of Spain, but it was not the same.

I regard myself as a good rider, but not a great one. In order to be great, I would have to win Paris-Roubaix and some of the other classics. And with the exception of the Tour of Lombardy - I know that I can. A drawback is that I can only win when I'm on tip-top form, when I really dominate the race. Some of my rivals can win races when they have not ridden well, but I can't. That's why I have never performed well in the Tour de France. Last year was no exception, either, although that time there was another reason. My father died and I returned home immediately. I still harbour hopes of performing well in it in the future. I am only 26 in August and I want to race until I'm 35: at least, for as long as I'm still enjoying it."

Eric Van Lancker

THE DIARIST

Throughout Eric Van Lancker's professional career, he has been one of the most underrated riders in the peloton. Many pros earn substantially more than the man from West Flanders, but up to this season nobody could point to more World Cup victories than him. Gianni Bugno, for example, the 1991 and '92 world champion, has won three World Cup races, whereas up to June 1992, Eric Van Lancker had won four: the Amstel Gold Race in 1989, Liège-Bastogne-Liège in 1990 and the Wincanton Classic and the Grand Prix des Amériques in Canada in 1991.

This is the Eric Van Lancker who is known to his rivals in the peloton as 'the Moroccan'. He puts his nickname down to the darkness of his skin. The short jet-black hair sticking out from under his cap strengthen the former Panasonic rider's exotic image. "Vanderaerden came up with the name when he was still riding for Post," says Van Lancker. "He gave everyone a nickname. Now that he is riding for Raas, it is slowly dying away. That dark skin colour remains, however. If I ever go skiing, I come back looking like a black man."

Eric Van Lancker never makes much fuss. He keeps himself in the background, and remains modest in all he says and does. He is a quiet type of person. Yet if you spend time with him on his own, he quite happily chatters on to you about himself, about his qualities as a rider, and about his favourite race, Liège-Bastogne-Liège.

Marbles

"When I was young I was always a fan of Roger De Vlaeminck. At that time I played marbles a lot, and I named one of them after him. I thought Roger was a great rider to watch, particularly the way he sat on his bike. I am the totally opposite type of personality. Roger is a blabbermouth and I'm not. Maybe I'm too quiet. I don't want to be a darling of the media. There are some riders you see in the papers every day, even though they never do anything, and I'm against that."

Uncle Marcel

"I began racing when I was 15. It was not entirely unexpected, as racing is something of a tradition in our family. An uncle of mine, Marcel Van Lancker, tried his luck as a cyclist. Roger Lagrange, who once won a stage in the Dunkirk Four Days, is also a relative. In those days I often went to watch races. Later on, my brother had a go in the newcomers category. Touring cyclists had got him into it, but his career never took off. For me, however, it did turn out alright, even though I was never a winner.

One of the first highlights in my career was my second place in the Flèche Ardennoise, a race for amateurs. I expected some of the bigger teams to show an interest in me, but it never happened. Only Guido Reybrouck came knocking at my door, he wanted me for his team, Fangio."

Telephonist

"At that time I was working as a telephonist with the railways, although the job had nothing to do with telephones. I drew up the work schedules for the engine drivers, and had to provide social support if anything went wrong. I had a colleague who had witnessed six suicides, all of them people who had thrown themselves under trains. You certainly encountered some rare things.

Then came the offer from Fangio. With the railways I was earning £500 a month after deductions, and Fangio offered £360. I had to take a £140 drop in wages, then, to turn professional. I had just got married, so that made it even more of a gamble. Nevertheless, I took some leave that I was owed and tried it. I have always tried to stay very level-headed, that's something I got from my family. My father always worked for the luggage makers Samsonite, he knows how things can suddenly change. After I won the Milk Race in Britain in my second year, I had a choice of six teams to join. I chose Panasonic because I was fascinated by that team. I studied them and could see that there was some sort of charisma which radiated from them. Post has something about him, he towers above everything. It is striking the way everyone addresses him as 'Mister', and only start calling him 'Peter' after half an hour. Raas is 'Jan' to everyone, straightaway.

Since winning the Amstel Gold Race, I have been well paid, but I'm not on an annual salary of £600,000 like some others are. Not that I'm worth that much, I'm not an out-and-out winner.

Racing for Peter Post's team used to be ideal. I think that the criticism you hear of him for not giving young riders the chance to develop, and throwing them straight to the lions is totally unfounded. I was certainly given the chance to learn the job. Eddy Bouwmans too. In 1991 he wanted to go to the Tour. "No chance," said Post, "you're still too young." One thing you could say about Post at one time, was that he found it hard to lose: he would get into a terrible state. Who knows, perhaps that just might be his strength. In 1993 I'm no longer riding for Post. He didn't want me any more. I'm riding for Lotus-Festina."

Wife

"A rider needs a good wife. She must be able to accept that her husband will not do much to help around the house. My wife, Corinne, has no trouble with that. During the season I do little more than train, eat, sit in my armchair and sleep. I want to be looked after as well as possible and I appreciate it if my meal is ready for me when I come home. I could imagine that some wives would find that difficult to cope with, but my wife doesn't. The whole family supports me, for that matter. My father-in-law mows my lawn. "It's bad for your legs," he says.

I met Corinne at a race. "If you finish in the first five, I'll go for a drink with you," she said. And in the first five was where I finished.

My wife actually trained to be a bookkeeper. She worked for a solicitor for years, until I started to make it as a rider. So that she would have another string to her bow, she also took a pedicure course. Corinne has now started her own business, working from home. We have two children; the eldest is our daughter, Isaura, and our youngest is our son, Massimo, who is three-and-a-half years younger."

Weapon

Every rider has a 'secret weapon' which he uses to put one over his rivals, and Eric is happy to reveal what his is. "I pedal more than most other riders. The longer you can keep turning an easy gear, the more energy you save.

237

Most riders know that to be true, but few are able to do it. You must work at it in training, and that's what I do. I am also able to time to perfection when to peak. In actual fact, that is my speciality, I can master it because I know myself so well. For eight years now, I have been checking my pulse rate every morning. I write down precisely what sort of training I am doing, which gears I am using that day, which vitamins I take and how I feel. The most important thing is that I can see a thread running through the eight diaries I have filled in that time. I know exactly how I should train and for how long to be ready on a particular day, I also know exactly which pills have an effect, and that gives me a very assured feeling."

Eric Van Lancker winning the Amstel Gold Race in 1989

Training

"I have set routines I stick to. One is that I never stop training until I have reached an average of 30 kilometres an hour. Otherwise I have the impression that I haven't trained and I feel guilty. So I constantly check my kilometre counter, and if it tells me I'm not averaging 30, I turn the remaining kilometres into a real sprint, even if it does mean riding extra kilometres to bring the average up. I live at the foot of the Tiegemberg climb and it is an ideal location. If I want to train for climbs, I do that hill first, and then take in a whole series of Tour of Flanders climbs in the neighbourhood; if I want to train on the flat, I head off in the other direction, towards West Flanders."

Omens

"I know myself. It is a very bad omen if the team physio has to wake me on the morning of a big race. When I'm fit I wake early and feel thoroughly rested. On big days my morning pulse rate is 32 to 34 maximum. Whenever my heart beat goes up to 40, I know I'm coming down with something. And I've never won a race with a heartbeat that high.

Another factor is that I have to have good legs at the start of a race. Some of my rivals prefer being blocked-in for the first part of a race, and then they ride a strong finish, but I don't. My legs are the same at the finish of a race as they are at the start."

Favourite Race

"I love Liège-Bastogne-Liège, I have always ridden well in it. Every time I've raced in it up to 1992, I have finished in the top ten. I'm more suited to it than I am for the Flèche Wallonne. It is the shorter climbs which make the difference, and the Mur de Huy is a bit too steep for me. I'm not one of those riders who takes climbs with a 23, I prefer using something bigger. My favourite gear for climbing is the 19.

Liège-Bastogne-Liège is a fair race. Those who ride at the front, must have good legs. My 1990 win ranks as my most treasured victory. Criquielion tried for ten years to win the race and never managed it, I did, though. My name will be there on the list of winners for all time. On top of that, it had been 12 years since a Belgian - Jos Bruyère - won it, and that adds to the sense of achievement. The only thing I don't understand is why my team-mate, Stephen Rooks, was critical after the race. He implied I had stolen the race from him, when in fact it was he who threw the race away, just prior to my attack. Rooks was riding well, and he had gone to ride at the front with a group including Gert-Jan Theunisse, but that break was caught. Then Luc

Roosen got away, but there wasn't a great deal of power in his attack. Then it was my turn, and the rest is history."

Climbs

"The climbs in Liège-Bastogne-Liège suit me. The Wanne, for instance, is not particularly tough, but you have to make sure you're near the front or else you have a job fighting your way through. The reason for that is that the Wanne is the start of a 30 kilometre stretch which includes the climbs of the Hezalles, Trois Points, Stockeu and the Haute Levée. That part of the race always sorts out the group. If you are still with the leaders there, you must be a good rider. It is crucial that you know what gear to use on these climbs. I have kept lists of them, and I go over them the evening before. It is a question of not making mistakes.

La Redoute may be the last-but-one climb, but it is also classified as the most difficult of the race. That's where things are usually settled. La Redoute is a real struggle. You keep thinking you are at the top, but you keep coming to a bit of false flat and then the climb starts again. In two editions of the race I had a terrible time there. That started to trouble my mind. For that reason, during Paris-Roubaix in 1992, I asked Post if I could stay in a hotel at Spa. "O.K.," said Post, and he paid for the cost of my reconnaissance mission. Fondriest, Bouwmans and the two Russians in our team also came and we got to know the course. I shot up La Redoute twice, once after another, telling myself: 'This time I'm going to beat it.' "What's the matter with you?" asked my team-mates. "The race isn't until Sunday." "This is important for me," I said. That was the truth: I wanted to regain my self-confidence, and it worked; I rode all four of them off my wheel! Yet it still went wrong the following week."

Tank

"The Côte de Saint-Roch is the first climb in Liège-Bastogne-Liège. It is not very hard, being at most a kilometre long, but that's where it all starts. As a rider you have to endure all the things a course like that can throw at you. You don't see much along the way. Believe it or not, but during a race I have never yet noticed the old army tank which stands at the turning point in Bastogne. During the race my concentration is total. I like the countryside and nature in general, but I don't really notice it during races. I have just finished reading a book about the Amazon jungle, and now I am reading one about Venezuelan Indians."

Boulevard

"Les Forges is the last real climb in Liège-Bastogne-Liège. Actually it is a boulevard. The first kilometre is steep, then comes the only bend, and after that the road follows a long, wide stretch of false flat. What makes this climb so difficult is the kilometres you already have in your legs. I ride this one with my biggest gear, outside ring at the front, 16 at the back.
I've never seen the statue of Stan Ockers just past the top during a race, either. Sorry, but I must admit I never knew that Stan had ever won the world championship, or that he once won Liège-Bastogne-Liège. All I knew is that he died in an accident on the track.
The year I won Liège-Bastogne-Liège, I made my break between La Redoute and Les Forges. I was cheered on by the crowd all the way up Les Forges. That gave me wings. People along the route were chanting my name, and that carried me into Liège. Thinking about it gives me a glowing feeling. I have a really beautiful trophy as a memento of my 1990 victory: a cog with a pedal and chain, gilded in 18 carat gold. Financially my win did no harm, either: my starting money was immediately doubled."

Nice

"They say that I'm too nice to be a team leader, but I disagree. If I really want to win, then I come out and tell them. It's just that I don't shout it from the roof tops. I hold the principle that you should never mess your domestiques about. Over the years, team leaders never showed me any mercy, and I

Eric wants to win Liège-Bastogne-Liège for a second time.

responded in a rather contrary fashion. I did my work, but no more than was necessary, and really that's not enough.

You must always stay calm, but young riders don't always see it that way. Wilfried Nelissen in my team last year, for instance, is too impetuous. During Ghent-Wevelgem, he told me after a few kilometres that he was going to win. He even started demonstrating how he was going to throw his arms into the air as he crossed the line. Until we reached the Kemmelberg that was. There, he was left stranded like a beached whale."

Friendship

"I have no enemies in the peloton, but I do have two close friends: Marc Sergeant and Guy Nulens. They call us the three musketeers. We are friends both inside and outside the sport. During the winter we go out together to eat. They always come to my supporters' party, too. We have already agreed that after we have all retired from racing, we will meet up three times a year. Our personalities and interests are well-matched. I'm not the sort of rider who goes straight to bed to sleep on the evening of a race. I like to have a stroll down to the bar to sit and have a nice chat, and they do too. We also share a common passion: motor bikes. Marc has a Harley-Davidson and Guy has a Kawasaki. I'm planning to get one myself so that we can go touring with them together.

I also like snooker. Rudy Dhaenens has his own table and although I don't have one yet, I enjoy a game. That is except at the time of the big races, and the reason I don't then is that I'm too nervous. To play snooker well you have to be very relaxed. I'm not particularly good, but I'm not bad either, and I once made a break of 35!"

Van Lancker beside the statue of Stan Ockers

Future

"I want to keep racing until I'm 35 and then go and work. At that age you ought to have something to keep you busy. Maybe I'll start my own business, a sports shop or something like that. Whatever happens, I want to be free. In the four years I will have left as a professional after the 1992 season, there are still certain things I want to achieve. I would like to be Belgian champion, and I'd like to take the world title. That was the goal I already had before 1992. Winning a stage in the Tour de France would also be nice. The strange thing is that I have never ridden a good Tour up to now. Good for the team, yes, but not for myself. I don't have any explanation for it. I just never come into my own. Quite simply, one day races suit me better.

One race I definitely would like to win is the Tour of Lombardy. In 1987 I came second, behind Moreno Argentin, but I am sure I can go one better. In 1991 I was in the right condition to finish there or thereabouts but then, after my win in the G.P. of Canada, I had a bad fall while out training. My shoulder was broken and it left my end of season in ruins. It was a shame because I like that part of the season. It is the time when riders who have some strength of character flourish. You need to be able to summon up the will to go on 200 kilometre training stints. "You're mad," say colleagues when I go out at the start of a seven-hour training session. No, I'm not mad.

Another dream I have is to finish somewhere thereabouts in Milan-San Remo. Believe it or not, but I have never ridden that race. They say that a real rider must have ridden the Tour de France: I would add that a rider must have finished Milan-San Remo, and that's why I want to do it as soon as possible."

ALEX ZÜLLE

CRATE OF BEER

They are saying in the peloton that Alex Zülle is going to be a great rider. When, in your first season as a pro, you climb up to 9th place in the FICP rankings, winning the Catalan Week and the prologue of the Tour and riding in the yellow jersey for a while, you must have something special. He won eleven races during that first season, other successes being the second stage in the Sicilian Cycling Week, stage 1B in the Tour of Asturias and overall victory in the event, the fifth stage in the Tour of Burgos and overall victory and the fourth stage in the Tour of Catalonia.

He has also begun 1993 in terrific style. When you win Paris-Nice like he did in March of this year at the age of 24, you know that you have a real talent. Soon afterwards he superceded even that by finishing second in the Tour of Spain. For two weeks he wore yellow, and only succumbed to defeat in the mountains to the eventual winner, Tony Rominger. All of this has given great hope for the future. And more important than that is that Zülle has the right attitude. When he rides he goes to the front, making the others sweat and grit their teeth to hang on.

Dutch

Alex Zülle is no boaster, he is a smashing chap. He has money, but the only luxury he has permitted himself is his Alfa Romeo and a holiday to the Dominican Republic with his sweetheart. The rest of his wages go straight into his savings account. In the hotel he lounges around in a dull grey, rather plain track suit. Zülle is modern, he has an earring in his left ear and he wears a pair of small blue and black framed glasses. He is a little shy, but he is friendly and amicable. His mother is Dutch by birth. She was a chambermaid in Steenbergen and fell in love with a plumber from Switzerland. Alex and his sister were brought up in Dutch, so he can speak it very fluently. He chatters in the same way as he races: holding something back, sure of what he says, but correct and courteous. "Thank you," he says when we conclude the interview.

Self Judgement

Within the ONCE team they are very enthusiastic about Zülle. "Alex knows how to keep battling on when he is suffering," says his directeur sportif Manolo Saiz. "Even when he is 'dead' he still rides in the first 20. We already know he is ready for six-day stage races, we are now hoping he makes the same progress and will be at his strongest in two-week races."

Zülle gives himself the following mark: "Five out of ten for sprinting. I am no good at it. Unless it is in a small group or I am at the peak of my strength, but I do recuperate very quickly. My strongest card is time trialling. Although I enjoy mountain stages the most, it is when I'm riding against the clock that I achieve my best results. It's always been the same, when I was an amateur too. I used to be part of the national 100 kilometre team. 20 kilometres is my best distance, I am able to go all-out from beginning to end. I am good at getting stuck in and hanging on, I don't give up. For longer time trials, though, you have to have a different approach. You have to ration out your energy and I still haven't learned to do that. I now ride with a pulse clock and it starts bleeping if I am pushing myself too far."

Ladder

Alex Zülle comes from Will in Switzerland, a village near Saint Gallen, half an hour's drive from Zurich. He has a sister aged 21 called Claudia, and she is a keen gymnast. His father is a plumber with his own small company employing eight men. His mother is a skiing instructress.

"There have never been any cyclists in the family," says Zülle. "My father used to ride a bike as a hobby, but no more than that. Actually, I belong to a family of painters: my grandfather was a house painter and so was I. I did the painting all over the house: inside, outside, on scaffolding and on ladders. I had no sense of fear, I've been up and down ladders thousands of times."

Siesta

Zülle has a reputation for enjoying a glass of beer, and for living it up during the winter. "But when it is time to take it seriously, I take it seriously," he says, putting the record straight. "There is nothing unusual about wanting to go out. I have a girlfriend, Andrea, and I have a wide circle of friends outside the sport who I would like to keep. Imagine if I suddenly turned my back on everyone now, what would happen when I retire? For the rest of the time I behave myself. I am happy that things are done in a more laid-back way in Spain. I don't like the Swiss penchant for punctuality, it's exaggerated, almost military, even. I love Spain, I love the siestas in the afternoon. I have now introduced them into my own domestic routine."

Gold

Switzerland can feel proud to have such a talent as Zülle. The strange thing is, however, that he didn't turn professional with a Swiss team but with a Spanish one. "ONCE's offer was the only one I received. Yet as an amateur I had won the William Tell Tour, the Tour of Luxembourg and the Tour of Eastern Switzerland. I had hoped that at least Paul Köchli - at the time the team manager with Helvetia and himself Swiss - would have noticed. "I'm not interested," he said, and with that I knew it. I was really angry.

I was also hoping a little that my Dutch blood might perhaps create some interest in me in Holland or Flanders. But it was in vain. When you are Swiss you almost have to win the world championship before teams start to show an interest in you. That's especially true now that we no longer have our own full-strength team. It is fairly understandable I suppose. Teams are bound to look for talent from their own backyard first of all, or sign up name riders. Think how much money is tied up in it - it's a massive amount.

I was a member of the Mavic amateur team. In my early days there, the Australian Stephen Hodge was also a member. It was through him that I started to look towards ONCE. That was in March 1991. In the meantime I was also in contact with Paul Köchli's Helvetia team. For months and months I didn't hear a word from ONCE until late August, just before the World Championship in Stuttgart.

They said they would take me if I made my mind up straight away. My stage victory and second place in the overall classification in the Tour of Biscay had convinced them. I phoned Köchli immediately. "Come round and see me," he said, suddenly enthusiastic. But I plumped for ONCE: a very international team with an excellent reputation. It was a lucky choice too, as one year later Helvetia had disappeared from the scene.

I'm really pleased now that I chose ONCE. The directeur sportif Manolo Saiz is the ideal boss: he is a psychologist, he knows how he should deal with me. He is also a trainer and tells me how I should prepare myself. He understands racing. He is also very wily."

Pressure

Alex rode many races in 1992. It was said that his Spanish team manager squeezed him like a lemon. "He did not. If that was the case, he wouldn't have pulled me out of the Tour just before the mountains. And Manolo has said that he would do it again this year if need be. We are waiting to see how it goes during the months leading up to the Tour. He won't make me blow up, I'm not afraid of that happening. I am so strong mentally that I can put up with making great exertions. After I abandoned last year I rested for a week, but straight after that I started winning races again. So I obviously hadn't been drained empty.

I had never expected to win the number of races I did in 1992. I had one objective for every race I entered: make a good impression. That's what I was trying to do in the Tour of Sicily and I won a stage. The same is true of the Catalan Week: I was just going to give it a go and I ended up as the overall winner. There has never been any pressure put on me. I know that it will come in time, but I'm not afraid of it. I will use the pressure to help me perform better.

I know people are saying I will win the Tour de France one day. I don't know. I do know that I have the will to win to become a major stage-race rider. But as far as winning it is concerned, I don't know myself well enough yet to say. If Tony Rominger says something like that, then you have to attach some credence to it. But I'm still young, remember. Maybe when I have more experience behind me. At the moment I'm just taking it one stage at a time. But I would like to be as good as Indurain and Bugno one day."

Soldier

Alex Zülle is pleased he rides for a Spanish team. He talks most enthusiastically about the supervision and atmosphere in the ONCE team. Not only that, but now that he is working abroad he has escaped his military service.

"In Switzerland there is a rule which says you can do three-week stretches as a soldier over three years," sighs Zülle. "Imagine what would happen if I was called up during the Vuelta! Although I am a member of the cycling unit, it would make no difference: I would have to put a rifle to my shoulder, take a black bike dating from the Second World War which weighs a ton, and start pedalling. On the back of it is your tent and you have to go and spend the night camping in it in a wood. It's a complete waste of time and belongs to another age."

Nil

Alex Zülle wears glasses so he has been given the nickname 'Professor' by the peloton, probably after Fignon. "Professor is fine by me," laughs Zülle. "But I'm certainly no professor of cycling history. I don't know a great deal about the sport actually: I only started racing when I was 18. Before then I never read anything about it, I wasn't interested. I was more keen on skiing. My parents were ski instructors. I spent many days in the mountains. Until one day when I found myself in a queue for the cable lift again. The upshot of that was that I now know that Coppi was one of the greats, that Koblet and Kübler were champions and that Merckx and Hinault achieved some great victories, but I know little more than that. Don't show me too many photos."

Earrings

If Alex Zülle carries on the way he is now for the next ten years, he will never have to work again. He is already rather sparing with his cash. "I don't invest anything and I don't work with agents. There is someone who looks after my contracts, but he is paid on the basis of my good performances and not on the number of races I ride, as is the case with some of my fellow riders."

He may well go into business at a later date, because he certainly knows the ropes in his particular field. Claudio Chiappucci may sell vests but Zülle sells earrings! In his left ear he wears a meticulously made little golden bike and it

249

is very much in demand among the riders. "As they are only available in Switzerland, they come to me asking me if I can get them some. It started with Mauri, he wanted a set of them for his young daughter."

Over Eager

Alex Zülle has, as far as the rest of his career is concerned, youth on his side. He still has much improving to do. "Above all physically. I also have little experience. I was a late starter to cycling, I was 18. Before that I used to do the long jump and the high jump. When I was 13 or 14 I could jump over 1.50 metres easily. The club trainer told me that was quite good. After that I used to ski and it was only later that I started cycling. As a result of that I clearly lack a little dexterity, tactical awareness and race insight. I have made many mistakes during my cycling career: starting sprinting too soon or too late, attacking too soon, attacking and then blowing up and so on, but I'm a quick learner. I will also have to learn to be more calm. I'm over eager, I fly straight into it every day, and I shouldn't do that any more.

I know that when a first-year pro starts getting the results that I did, rumours soon start doing the rounds that it is down to doping. Each rider is entitled to decide for himself what he does to his body. But I know that when I leave the sport I want to be in good health."

Hand

Although he has not been riding in the peloton for a very long time, it has not stopped Zülle from already having pleasant recollections.

"After my victory in the time trial during the Catalan Week, Miguel Indurain came and shook hands with me. I knew that Miguel had put everything he had into that time trial and really wanted to win it, but I prevented him doing so. "Well ridden," he said. It made me beam with pride, for a rider like Indurain to say that to me. The way he turns the pedals is the sign that he is a true stylist. He never turns the pedals a single time too often. I want to be like him.

I am also happy that I have ridden in yellow in the Tour de France. Great though it was, it was only during last winter that I started to appreciate the magnitude of it. At the time something like that just passes you by. I want to stay level-headed. I think that they have taken my performances well in Switzerland. In the Sportsman of the Year competition I finished fifth. Honours went to Tony Romriger, then there were two skiers and an ice hockey player followed by me. Rominger was, of course, also the cyclist of the year and I came second - the correct result as far as I'm concerned."

Future

What about Alex Zülle's future? Expectations are high. "Manolo Saiz, my directeur sportif, is trying to keep me as calm as possible. In 1992 I was in form very quickly and we didn't want that to happen this year. At the training camp it was clear that I was not training as much as my team-mates. I worked to a specific programme, I was used sparingly. My first race was the Tour of Majorca. The first important race was Paris-Nice, later came the Vuelta and, of course, the Tour is planned. But I'm not going to lie awake at night worrying about it. I will start concentrating on the Tour when it is underway and not before.

As far as the classics are concerned it was a case of wait and see. I don't like Paris-Roubaix, for example. It is a race for specialists. A while back I rode the Franco-Belgian race on a couple of occasions and I bounced along like an empty beer crate over the cobbles. Races in which I would one day like to do something are Liège-Bastogne-Liège and the Flèche Wallonne."

COLOUR PHOTOGRAPHS

Moreno Argentin   p. 47
Eric Breukink   p. 48
Gianni Bugno   p. 65
Claudio Chiappucci   p. 66
Mario Cipollini   p. 99
Dirk De Wolf   p. 100
Maurizio Fondriest   p. 117
Miguel Indurain   p. 118, 151
Laurent Jalabert   p. 152
Sean Kelly   p. 169
Charly Mottet   p. 170
Johan Museeuw   p. 203
Tony Rominger   p. 204
Eric Vanderaerden   p. 221
Edwig Van Hooydonck   p. 222